Bad Therapy

Bad Therapy

Why the Kids Aren't Growing Up

ABIGAIL SHRIER

SENTINEL

Sentinel
An imprint of Penguin Random House LLC
penguinrandomhouse.com

Most Sentinel books are available at a discount when purchased in quantity for sales promotions or corporate use. Special editions, which include personalized covers, excerpts, and corporate imprints, can be created when purchased in large quantities. For more information, please call (212) 572-2232 or e-mail specialmarkets@penguinrandomhouse.com. Your local bookstore can also assist with discounted bulk purchases using the Penguin Random House corporate Business-to-Business program. For assistance in locating a participating retailer, e-mail B2B@penguinrandomhouse.com.

Library of Congress Cataloging-in-Publication Data
Names: Shrier, Abigail, author.
Title: Bad therapy : why the kids aren't growing up / Abigail Shrier.
Description: [New York] : Sentinel, 2024. |
Includes bibliographical references and index.
Identifiers: LCCN 2023046210 (print) | LCCN 2023046211 (ebook) |
ISBN 9780593542927 (hardcover) | ISBN 9780593542934 (ebook)
Subjects: LCSH: Child psychotherapy—Social aspects—United States. |
Child mental health—United States. | Child rearing—United States.
Classification: LCC RJ504 .S538 2024 (print) | LCC RJ504 (ebook) |
DDC 618.92/8914—dc23/eng/20231107
LC record available at https://lccn.loc.gov/2023046210
LC ebook record available at https://lccn.loc.gov/2023046211

Printed in the United States of America
3rd Printing

BOOK DESIGN BY CHRIS WELCH

Some names and identifying characteristics have been changed to protect the privacy of the individuals involved.

To my mother and father

and

Zach. Always Zach.

Sometimes love is not enough

and the road gets tough

I don't know why

—*Lana Del Rey*

Contents

Part III

Maybe There's Nothing Wrong with Our Kids

Author's Note

Talk of a "youth mental health crisis" often conflates two distinct groups of young people. One suffers from profound mental illness. Disorders that, at their untreated worst, preclude productive work or stable relationships and exile the afflicted from the locus of normal life. Theirs is a crisis of neglect and undertreatment. These precious kids require medication and the care of psychiatrists. They are not the subject of this book.

This book is about a second, far larger cohort: the worriers; the fearful; the lonely, lost, and sad. College coeds who can't apply for a job without three or ten calls to Mom. We tend not to call their problem "mental illness," but nor would we say they are thriving. They go looking for diagnoses to explain the way they feel. They think they've found "it," but the "it" is always shifting.

We shower these kids with meds, therapy, mental health and "wellness" resources, even prophylactically. We rush to remedy a misdiagnosed condition with the wrong sort of cure.

Introduction:
We Just Wanted Happy Kids

My son returned home from sleepaway camp this summer with a stomachache. When it didn't quickly abate, I took him to a pediatric urgent care clinic, where a doctor ruled out appendicitis. "Probably just dehydration," came the verdict. But before the doctor cleared us to go home, he asked us to wait for the nurse, who had a few questions.

In bustled a large man in black scrubs wielding a clipboard. "Would you mind giving us some privacy so that I can do our mental health screening?" he said. After a beat, I realized that the privacy the man wanted with my son was from *me*.

I asked to see his questionnaire, which turned out to be issued by the National Institute of Mental Health, a federal government agency. Here is the complete, unedited list of questions the nurse had planned to put to my twelve-year-old in private:

1. In the past few weeks, have you wished you were dead?

2. In the past few weeks, have you felt that you or your family would be better off if you were dead?

3. In the past week, have you been having thoughts about killing yourself?

4. Have you ever tried to kill yourself? If yes, how? When?

5. Are you having thoughts of killing yourself right now? If yes, please describe.[1]

When the nurse asked me to leave the room, he wasn't going off script. He was following a literal one. The "Script for Nursing Staff" directs nurses to inform parents: "We ask these questions in private, so I am going to ask you to step out of the room for a few minutes. If we have any concerns about your child's safety, we will let you know."[2]

Driving my son home from the clinic, I was haunted by the following possibility: What if I had been just a little more trusting? Children often try to please adults by producing whatever answers the grown-ups seem to want. What if my son, alone in the room with that large man, had given him the "yes" the questions appeared to prompt? Would the staff have prevented me from taking my son home?

And a child who *was* entertaining dark thoughts? Was this really the best way to help him? Separate him from his parents and present him with a series of escalating questions about killing himself?

I hadn't signed my son up for therapy. I hadn't taken him for a neuropsychological evaluation. I had taken him to the pediatrician for a stomachache. There was no indication, no reason to even suspect, that my son had any mental illness. And the nurse didn't wait for one. He knew he didn't have to.

We parents have become so frantic, hypervigilant, and borderline obsessive about our kids' mental health that we routinely allow all manner of mental health expert to evict us from the room. (*"We will let you know."*) We've been relying on them for decades to tell us how to raise well-adjusted kids. Maybe we were overcompensating for the fact that our own parents had assumed the opposite: that psychologists were the last people you should consult on how to raise normal kids.

When we were little, my brother and I were spanked. Our feelings were seldom consulted when consequential decisions about our lives were made—where we would attend school, whether we would show up at synagogue for major holidays, what sort of clothes fit the place and occasion. If we didn't particularly relish the food set out for dinner, no alternate menu was forthcoming. If we lacked some critical right of self-expression—some essential exploration of a repressed identity—it never occurred to either of us. It would be years before anyone in my generation would regard these perfectly average markers of an eighties childhood as vectors of emotional injury.

But as millions of women and men my age entered adulthood, we commenced therapy.[3] We explored our childhoods and learned to see our parents as emotionally stunted.[4] Emotionally stunted parents expected too much, listened too little, and failed to discover their kids' hidden pain. Emotionally stunted parents inflicted emotional injury.

We never doubted that we wanted kids of our own. We vowed that our child-rearing would reflect a greater psychological awareness. We resolved to listen better, inquire more, monitor our kids' moods, accommodate their opinions when making a family decision, and, whenever possible, anticipate our kids' distress. We would cherish our *relationship* with our kids. Tear down the barrier of authority past generations had erected between parent and child and instead see our children as teammates, mentees, buddies.

More than anything, we wanted to raise "happy kids." We looked to the wellness experts for help. We devoured their bestselling parenting books, which established the methods by which we would educate, correct, and even speak to our own children.

Guided by these experts, we adopted a therapeutic approach to parenting. We learned to offer our kids the reasons behind every rule and request. We never, ever spanked. We perfected the "time-out" and provided thorough explanation for any punishment (which we then rebranded as a "consequence" to remove any associated shame and make us feel less authoritarian). Successful parenting became a function with a single coefficient: our kids' happiness at any given instant. An ideal childhood meant no pain, no discomfort, no fights, no failure—and absolutely no hint of "trauma."

But the more closely we tracked our kids' feelings, the more difficult it became for us to ride out their momentary displeasure. The more closely we examined our kids, the more glaring their deviations from an endless array of benchmarks—academic, speech, social and emotional. Each now felt like catastrophe.

We rushed our kids back to the mental health professionals who had guided our parenting, this time for testing, diagnosis, counseling, and medication. We needed our kids and everyone around them to know: our kids weren't shy, they had "social anxiety disorder" or "social phobia." They weren't poorly behaved, they had "oppositional defiant disorder." They weren't disruptive students, they had "ADHD." It wasn't our fault, and it wasn't theirs. We would attack and finally eliminate the stigma surrounding these diagnoses. Rates at which our children received them soared.

In the course of writing my last book, *Irreversible Damage*, and for years after its publication, I spoke to hundreds of American parents. And during that time, I became acutely aware of just how *much* therapy kids were getting from actual therapists and their proxies in schools. How completely parents were relying on therapists and therapeutic methods to fix their kids. And how expert diagnoses often altered kids' perceptions of themselves.

Schools, especially, jumped at the opportunity to adopt a therapeutic approach to education and announced themselves our "partners" in childrearing. School mental health staffs expanded: more psychologists, more counselors, more social workers. The new regime would diagnose and accommodate, not punish or reward. It directed kids in routinized habits of monitoring and sharing their bad feelings. It trained teachers to understand "trauma" as the root of student misbehavior and academic underperformance.

These efforts didn't aim to produce the highest-achieving young people. But millions of us bought in, believing they would cultivate the happiest, most well-adjusted kids. Instead, with unprecedented help from mental health experts, we have raised the loneliest, most anxious, depressed, pessimistic, helpless, and fearful generation on record. Why?

How did the first generation to raise kids without spanking produce the first generation to declare they never wanted kids of their own?[5] How did kids raised so gently come to believe that they had experienced debilitating childhood trauma? How did kids who received far more psychotherapy than any previous generation plunge into a bottomless well of despair?[6]

The source of their problem is not reducible to Instagram or Snapchat. Bosses and teachers report—and young people agree—that members of the rising generation are utterly underprepared to accomplish basic tasks we expect all adults to dispatch: ask for a raise; show up for work during a period of national political strife; show up for work at all;[7] fulfill obligations they undertake without requiring extensive breaks to attend to their "mental health."

It's not unheard of for boys of sixteen or seventeen to put off getting a driver's license on the grounds that driving is "scary."[8] Or for college juniors to invite Mom along to their twenty-first birthday celebrations.

They are leery of the risks and freedoms that are all but synonymous with growing up.

These kids are lonely. They settle into emotional pain for reasons that seem, even to their parents, a little mysterious. Parents seek answers from mental health experts, and when our kids inevitably receive a diagnosis, they grasp it with pride and relief: a whole life, reduced to a single point.

No industry refuses the prospect of exponential growth, and mental health experts are no exception. By feeding normal kids with normal problems into an unending pipeline, the mental health industry is minting patients faster than it can cure them.

These mental health interventions on behalf of our kids have largely backfired. Recasting personality variation as a chiaroscuro of dysfunction, the mental health experts trained kids to regard themselves as disordered. The experts operate from the assumption that everyone requires therapy and that everyone is at least a little "broken."

They speak of "resilience" but what they mean is "accepting your trauma." They dream of "destigmatizing mental illness" and sprinkle diagnostic labels like so much pixie dust. They talk of "wellness" while presiding over the downward spiral of the most unwell generation in recent history.

With the charisma of cult leaders, therapeutic experts convinced millions of parents to see their children as challenged. They infused parenting with self-consciousness and fevered insecurity. They conscripted teachers into a therapeutic order of education, which meant treating every child as emotionally damaged. They pushed pediatricians to ask kids as young as eight—who had presented with nothing more than a stomachache—whether they felt their parents might be better off without them.[9] In the face of experts' implacable self-assurance, schools were eager; pediatricians, willing; and parents, unresisting.

Maybe it's time we offered a little resistance.

Part I

Healers Can Harm

The best of doctors are destined for hell.

—The Mishnah

Chapter 1

•

Iatrogenesis

In 2006, I packed up everything I owned and moved from Washington, DC, to Los Angeles to be closer to my then boyfriend. I had only ever visited California once, a few months earlier, when I had flown out to meet his parents. Outside of my boyfriend and his family, every single person who could identify my body in the event of an untimely demise lived on the East Coast.

Then twenty-eight and having recently graduated from law school, I faced the unpleasantness of having become a lawyer. I was restless. My boyfriend had a business in Los Angeles. If I wanted things to work out with him, I needed to move.

But I also knew it was entirely possible that in this new life—*his* life— I would go crazy. My best friend, Vanessa, lived in DC. We'd both been hired by law firms, which meant long hours and an impossible time difference, as far as calls were concerned. I needed someone to listen to my worries and misgivings on my schedule. I needed a stand-in Vanessa, available every Thursday at six p.m. And for the first time in my life, I could afford one. I hired a therapist.

Every week, for a "fifty-minute hour," my therapist lent me her full attention. If I bored her with my repetition, she never complained. She was a pro. She never made me feel self-absorbed, even when I was. She let me vent. She let me cry. I often left her office feeling that some festering splinter of interpersonal interaction had been eased to the surface and plucked.

She helped me realize that I wasn't so bad. Most things were someone else's fault. Actually, many of the people around me were worse than I'd realized! Together, we diagnosed them freely. Who knew so many of my close relatives had narcissistic personality disorder? I found this solar plexus–level comforting. In quick order, my therapist became a really expensive friend, one who agreed with me about almost everything and liked to talk smack about people we (sort of) knew in common.

I had a great year. My boyfriend proposed marriage. I accepted. And then, a month before we were due to get married, my therapist dropped a bomb: "I'm not sure you two are ready to get married. We may need to do a little more work."

I felt the demoralizing shock of having walked into a plate-glass door.

My therapist was a formidable woman. She had at least fifteen years on me, a doctorate in psychology, and an apparently strong marriage of long duration. She dropped casual references to never missing Pilates. I once caught her at her spotless desk before our session, eating a protein bar she had carefully unwrapped, and marveled at her obvious self-mastery, the dignity she managed to bring to our silly modes of consumption. Maybe I should have been thrown into crisis by her pronouncement, but for whatever reason, I wasn't. For all her training, she was still human and fallible. I had already moved across the country by myself, set up a new life, and by then I knew: I didn't agree with her assessment, and I didn't need her permission, either. I left her a voicemail expressing my gratitude for her help. But, I said, I would be taking some time off.

A few years later, happily married, I resumed therapy with her. Then I tried therapy with a psychoanalyst for a year or so. Every experience I've had with therapy has fallen along a continuum from enlightening to unsettling. Occasionally, it rose to the level of "fun." Learning a little more about the workings of my own mind was at times helpful and often gratifying.

When I agreed with my therapist, I told her so. When I didn't, we talked about that. And when I felt I needed to move on, I did. Which is to say: *I was an adult in therapy.* I had swum life's choppy waters long enough to have gained some self-knowledge, some self-regard, and a sense of the accuracy of my own perceptions. I could pipe up with: "I think I gave you the wrong impression." Or, "Maybe we're placing a little too much blame on my mom?" Or even, "I've decided to terminate therapy."

Children and adolescents are not typically equipped to say these things. The power imbalance between child and therapist is too great. Children's and adolescents' sense of self is still developing. They cannot correct the interpretations or recommendations of a therapist. They cannot push back on a therapist's view of their families or of themselves because they have no Archimedean point; too little of life has gathered under their feet.

Nevertheless, parents my age have been signing up their kids and teens for therapy in astonishing numbers, even prophylactically. I talked to moms who hired therapists to help their kids adjust to preschool or to process the death of a beloved cat. One mom told me she put a therapist "on retainer" as soon as her two daughters reached middle school. "So they would have someone to talk to about all the things I never wanted to talk about with *my* mom."

A few moms told me, in roundabout verbiage, that they had hired a therapist to surveil their surly teen's thoughts and feelings. *The therapist doesn't tell me what my daughter says exactly,* the moms assured me, *but she sort of lets me know everything's okay.* And occasionally, I gathered, the therapist relayed to Mom specific information gleaned from the little prisoner of war.

If the notion of "therapy" here seems vague, that's largely to do with the experts. The American Academy of Child and Adolescent Psychiatry offers a tautology in place of a definition. What is "psychotherapy"? "A form of psychiatric treatment that involves therapeutic conversations and interactions between a therapist and a child or family."[1] The American Psychological Association offers a similarly circular definition of psychotherapy: "any psychological service provided by a trained professional."[2]

What's a "clock"? *A device for measuring time.* What's "time"? *Something measured by a clock.* Any conversation a therapist has with a patient counts as "therapy." But you get the idea: conversations about feelings and personal problems styled as medicine.

Parents often assume that therapy with a well-meaning professional can only help a child or adolescent's emotional development. Big mistake. Like any intervention with the potential to help, therapy can harm.

Iatrogenesis:
When the Healer Makes Things Worse

Any time a patient arrives at a doctor's office, she exposes herself to risk.[3] Some risks arise through physician incompetence. A patient goes in to have a kidney removed, and the doctor extracts the wrong one. ("Wrong-site surgery" happens more often than you might think.[4]) Or negligence: the surgeon loses track of a stray clamp or sponge in the patient's abdomen, then sews her up.

Or he "nicks" an organ. Or the operation proceeds swimmingly, but the patient develops an opportunistic infection at the surgical site. Or an allergic reaction to the anesthesia. Or bedsores, from lying in recovery too long. Or everything goes according to plan, but the entire treatment was based on a misapprehension of the problem.

"Iatrogenesis" is the word for all of it. From the Greek, iatrogenesis literally means "originating with the healer" and refers to the phenomenon of a healer harming a patient in the course of treatment. Most often, it is not malpractice, though it can be. Much of iatrogenesis occurs not because a doctor is malicious or incompetent but because treatment exposes a patient to exogenous risks.

Iatrogenesis is everywhere—because all interventions carry risk. When a sick patient submits to treatment, the risks are typically worth it. When a *well* patient does, the risks often outweigh the potential for further improvement.

And here, what I'm calling an "intervention" is any sort of advice or corrective you would typically give only to someone with a deficiency or incapacity. So, telling kids to "eat vegetables" or "get plenty of sleep" or "spend time with friends" may be advice, but it isn't an intervention. We all need to do those things.

With interventions, a good rule of thumb is: Don't go in for an X-ray if you don't need one. Don't expose yourself to the germs of an ER just to say hello to your doctor friend. And—just maybe—don't send your kid off to therapy unless she absolutely requires it. Everyone knows the first two; it's the last one that may surprise you.

Psychotherapy Needs a Warning Label

For decades, the standard therapy proffered to victims of disaster—terrorist attack, combat,[5] severe burn injury—was the "psychological debriefing."[6] A therapist would invite victims of a tragedy into a group session in which participants were encouraged to "process" their negative emotions, learned to recognize the symptoms of post-traumatic stress disorder (PTSD), and discouraged from discontinuing therapy. Study after study has shown that this bare-bones process is sufficient to make PTSD symptoms *worse*.[7]

Well-meaning therapists often act as though *talking through your problems with a professional is good for everyone*. That isn't so.[8] Nor is it the case that *as long as the therapist is following protocols, and has good intentions, the patient is bound to get better.*

Any intervention potent enough to cure is also powerful enough to hurt. Therapy is no benign folk remedy. It can provide relief. It can also deliver unintended harm and does so in up to 20 percent of patients.[9]

Therapy can lead a client to understand herself as sick and rearrange her self-understanding around a diagnosis.[10] Therapy can encourage family estrangement—coming to realize that it's all Mom's fault and you never want to see her again. Therapy can exacerbate marital stress, compromise a patient's resilience, render a patient more traumatized, more depressed, and undermine her self-efficacy so she's less able to turn her life around.[11] Therapy may lead a patient by degrees—sunk into a leather sofa, well-placed tissue box close at hand—to become overly dependent on her therapist.[12]

This is true even for adults, who in general are much less easily led by other adults. These iatrogenic effects pose at least as great a risk, and likely much more, to children.

Police officers who responded to a plane crash and then underwent debriefing sessions exhibited *more* disaster-related hyperarousal symptoms eighteen months later than those who did not receive the treatment.[13] Burn victims exhibited *more* anxiety after therapy than those left untreated.[14] Breast cancer patients have left peer support groups feeling *worse* about their condition than those who opted out.[15] And counseling sessions for normal bereavement often make it *harder*, not easier, for mourners to recover from loss.[16] Some people who say they "just don't want to talk about it" know better than the experts what will help them:

spending time with family; exercising; putting one foot in front of the other; gradually adjusting to the loss.[17]

When it comes to our psyches, we're a lot more bespoke than mental health professionals often acknowledge or allow. And Tuesdays at four p.m. may not be when we're ready to confront our woes with a hired expert. Reminiscing with a friend, cracking a joke with your spouse you wouldn't dare make with anyone else, helping your cousin box up her apartment—without talking about your problems—often aids recovery far more than sitting around in a room full of sad people. Therapy can hijack our normal processes of resilience, interrupting our psyche's ability to heal itself, in its own way, at its own time.

Think of it this way: group therapy for those who experienced loss or disaster forces the coping to hang out with the sad. This may make the relatively resilient sadder and prompt the sad to stew. The most dejected steer the ship to Planet Misery, with everyone else trapped inside.

Individual therapy can intensify bad feelings, too. Psychiatrist Samantha Boardman wrote candidly about a patient who quit therapy after a few weeks of treatment. "All we do is talk about the bad stuff in my life," the patient told Boardman. "I sit in your office and complain for 45 minutes straight. Even if I am having a good day, coming here makes me think about all the negative things."[18] Reading that, I remembered saving up emotional injuries to report to my therapist so that we would have something to talk about at our session—injuries I might have just let go.

Interestingly, even when patients' symptoms are made objectively *worse* by therapy, they tend to assume the therapy has helped.[19] We rely largely on how "purged" we feel when we leave a therapist's office to justify our sense that the therapy is working. We rarely track objective markers, for example, the state of our career or relationships, before reaching a conclusion. Sometimes when our lives do improve, it's not because the therapy worked but because the motivation that led us to start therapy also led us to make other positive changes: spend more time with friends and family, reconnect with people we haven't heard from in a while, volunteer, eat better, exercise.

An embarrassing number of psychological interventions have little proven efficacy.[20] They have nonetheless been applied with great élan to children and adolescents.

D.A.R.E. to Say "Yes" to Drugs

Picture it: 1992. Blue eyeliner, Doc Martens, and acid-washed jeans shot out at the knees. Into your high school assembly room tromps a uniformed officer in clodhoppers, keys jangling at the edge of a stiff black belt, armed with a jeremiad about the dangers of drugs.

This was the decades-long D.A.R.E. campaign, designed to raise awareness that drugs could ruin your life.[21] Utilizing therapeutic techniques designed by Carl Rogers, one of the most influential psychotherapists of the twentieth century, D.A.R.E. counselors led students in a kind of group therapy. They entered schools and prompted kids to talk about their personal problems, confess their drug use, and role-play refusing drugs from each other.[22]

Turns out, you can lead a teen to D.A.R.E., but it might make him wink. The program flopped like Vanilla Ice in his parachute pants, humiliating everyone involved. Not only was the campaign entirely ineffective, but follow-up studies revealed that D.A.R.E. may have actually *increased* substance and alcohol use among teens.[23] Kewpie-faced Kirk Cameron pleaded, "You don't have to try 'em to be cool," but we sniffed a traitor, shilling for the Man. Kirk promised there were other avenues to cool, but teens who heard this message apparently figured drugs were quicker and more straightforward than most.[24] Participating in group therapy to discuss a problem you didn't already have? That may be sufficient to introduce it.

Wanting to Help
Is Not the Same as Helping

Therapists almost always want to help, but sometimes they simply don't. And while some therapies have shown success in circumscribed areas— like cognitive behavioral therapy has in treating phobias—those who study the efficacy of therapies often point out that the results across treatment types are not terribly impressive.[25]

Mental health experts have a long, florid track record of plying patients with ghastly treatments, introducing novel problems into the patient pool they claim to heal. Fortunately, they've abandoned many of the grisliest purported treatments: insulin-induced comas, deliberate infliction of malaria, and of course frontal lobotomies—all employed, not in the Medieval Period, but in the last century.[26] Therapists induced an epidemic of the phony ailment neurasthenia at the start of the twentieth century. A century later, they were still ginning up ailments: recovered memory syndrome and multiple personality disorder.[27] Therapists fell for the fraud of widespread satanic ritual abuse, too.[28]

In the last decade, therapists promoted the gender dysphoria craze, which led to a 4,000 percent increase in diagnoses for teen girls.[29] A growing army of young women who regret their medical transitions, "detransitioners," tell strikingly similar stories. Very often, when they trace their lives back to the junction where things sped dramatically off course, there stood a shrink playing railway signalman, flipping the switch.[30]

This shouldn't surprise us. The human brain is perhaps the world's most complex and least understood organic structure. Fixing the problems of the human mind is incomparably more difficult than setting a broken bone. We can't expect therapists to fail *less* often than medical doctors. But we can expect more transparency and humility than practitioners typically bring to discussions of therapy's limitations.

"In psychotherapy, psychologists help people of all ages live happier, healthier, and more productive lives," declares the American Psychological Association.[31]

There is, alas, no proof that they accomplish any of that in aggregate. *Wanting* to help is just not the same as *helping*.

Therapists Are a Little Touchy about Iatrogenesis

Iatrogenesis isn't news to medical doctors who are professionally obligated[32] to admit their treatments may produce adverse effects.[33] But when I asked therapists point blank whether therapy carried risks, most minimized and many outright denied this.[34] They wanted both to promote therapy as an effective remedy for mental illness and to deny that it carries significant risks.

Why don't therapists typically admit that their methods *can* cause iatrogenic harm?

A group of researchers considered the question and concluded that, unlike the doctor, the "psychotherapist is the 'producer' of treatment," and is "therefore responsible, if not liable, for all negative effects."[35] The therapist often doesn't want to acknowledge that the medicine isn't working—because she *is* the medicine. The admission is a little personal.

Shrinks are badly incentivized where iatrogenesis is concerned. A doctor may decide that a patient would no longer benefit from thyroid medication, discontinue it, and keep the patient. A therapist gets paid by the dose. Once she decides you don't need therapy, she loses a customer.

Actually, it's worse than that: it's in therapists' interest to treat the *least sick* for the *longest period of time*. Ask any therapist what it's like to treat a bipolar or schizophrenic patient. Answer: *extraordinarily difficult.* (Many refuse to treat such patients for this reason.) But sit with a teenager once a week who has social anxiety? The family pays on time, the teen's problems are small, nobody's getting violent during your session. It's little wonder why, having acquired such a patient, a therapist may be reluctant to surrender her.

Most therapists have no idea who has been made worse by their therapy because they make no effort to track side effects. The profession does not require it. Medical doctors (psychiatrists), who once dominated therapeutic practice, generally stopped offering psychotherapy in recent decades.[36] The medical authority they lent to therapy fell to those without medical training.

And since the field of psychology lacks clear guidelines on what qualifies as a therapeutic "harm,"[37] it's unclear how therapists would track damage done by therapy, even if they wanted to. As one group of researchers put it: "a divorce can be both positive and negative, and crying in therapy can reflect a painful experience and therapeutic event."[38]

When iatrogenic risks go untallied, the harms pile up, threatening the well far more than the sick. It isn't hard to see why: Suffer a gunshot wound, and your risk of picking up an opportunistic infection in the operating room is outweighed by the lifesaving treatment you require. Suffer a scratch, and you have nothing to gain from surgery—nothing but risk.

What would we expect to find if we steeped a generally healthy population in a tea of unnecessary mental health treatments? Unprecedented iatrogenic effects. With that in mind, please meet the rising generation.

Chapter 2

•

A Crisis in the Era
of Therapy

At sixteen, Nora[1] sits at the giggly edge of womanhood. Her hair, a cascade of dense brown curls. Her smile, all gums and braces, enlivens whenever she mentions her friends. She is always, always connected to them, she tells me—on Snapchat, all day long, even during class. At her large private high school in Southern California, she sings in the school choir, is a cast member of every play, and is a top student.

On a mild April afternoon, we sit on Adirondack chairs in her mother and stepfather's backyard patio. Nora tosses her hair and recrosses her legs, bare in a flouncy skirt, testing the air with the notion that we are two adults—she, the cuter, more up-to-date model.

"I always have a friend who's going through something super serious," she tells me. "I don't know why it's always that way."

That sounds normal enough for high school girls, so I ask: What are they going through? Anxiety, depression, she ticks off. Trouble with parents. Lots of self-harm.

Like what?

Scratching, cutting, anorexia, she rattles off. "Taking away basic needs. Like, one of my friends will be in the shower and turn it up too hot or too cold."

Okay. What else?

"Trichotillomania."

"Excuse me?"

"Pulling out your hair. That's a big one."

Also known as "hair-pulling disorder," this is the urge to pull out hair from the scalp, eyelashes, and eyebrows, emanating from an uncontrollable need to self-soothe. Dissociative identity disorder, gender dysphoria, autism spectrum disorder, and Tourette's belong on her list of once-rare disorders that are, among this rising generation, suddenly not so rare at all.

Nora is casually au fait with dozens of mental disorders, almost as if she keeps the *Diagnostic and Statistical Manual of Mental Disorders* by her bedside. (She doesn't.)

Given how poorly so many seem to be faring, one might be inclined to suggest that these teens could really use some therapy. Actually, "a large majority" of Nora's friends are already in therapy—many have been for years, she tells me. Several are on psychiatric medication.

Does it seem to be helping?

"I'd say for some, yes. Others?" Nora shrugs. "My friend, I'm not going to say her name—since COVID-19 started, she just got a lot of anxiety. She's been on medication for a few years now. She sees a therapist, and I have to say, she just seems to be getting worse." Nora thinks it over. "She honestly seemed better before medication."

I ask Nora what seems to be troubling her friends. Nora reiterates that they're going through "really hard things," but when I ask her what, she is vague: strained relationships with peers, breakups, disagreements with parents.

By the time I meet Nora, I've interviewed enough adolescents to know that she isn't avoiding the question. Teenage communication today is more constant, largely digital, and, even among teen girls, far more superficial than it was a generation ago. Less baring of souls, more trading of memes. Even to their best friends, they communicate only this: that they are going through something bad and serious, something that will require their friends' sympathy and indulgence.

Some of her friends complain their parents are "emotionally abusive," but when I ask Nora why their therapists haven't called Child Services, she seems unperturbed. Yes, she assumes they're sort of exaggerating. To preserve the friendship, you suspend disbelief.

There's something else. Nora drops her chin, embarrassed by what she's about to confess: "I've noticed with a lot of people who'll use their mental issues—it's almost like a conversation piece. It's almost like a trend."

I reassure her that she's at least the twelfth adolescent to tell me this. She exhales.

What's it like to have so many friends suffering with anxiety disorders and depression? Actually, she tells me, those who don't have a diagnosis feel left out. "You're expected to have these mental issues. And these things that are being normalized—these things are not normal," she says. "I'm surrounded by it, so I think that in some ways, it has become our new normal. How is it possible, with all that around me, for it not also to be inflicted on me—for me not to be depressed about it?"

I ask her why it's depressing to have friends who are struggling. "I know three people who were committed to mental facilities long-term— one who committed suicide," she says. All of them, high school students.

Nora is faring a lot better than most of her peers and many of the young people I interviewed: she has a group of friends, a steady boyfriend, excels at school, and is planning for her future. She is on no psychiatric medication, and is not in therapy.

But she also casually bundles two sets of friends, as if they are one: those whose mental illness is so profound that it requires psychiatric commitment, and those who are seeking explanations for their unhappiness and discovering diagnoses. Like so many young people I talked to, she regards high school friends with "exam anxiety" or "social phobia" as existing on merely one end of a psychological continuum that terminates with the woman who shows up naked to Target.

They Need Therapy, You Say?

The mental health establishment has successfully sold a generation on the idea that vast numbers of them are sick. Less than half of Gen Zers believes their mental health is "good."[2] They do not believe mental health is something that arises typically, in the normal course of a balanced life, but like a boxwood tree, requires constant tending by the gardener you hire to prune it.

The rising generation has received more therapy than any prior generation. Nearly *40 percent* of the rising generation has received treatment from a mental health professional—compared with 26 percent of Gen Xers.[3]

Forty-two percent of the rising generation currently has a mental health diagnosis, rendering "normal" increasingly abnormal.[4] One in six US children aged two to eight years old has a diagnosed mental, behavioral, or developmental disorder.[5] More than 10 percent of American kids have an ADHD diagnosis[6]—double the expected prevalence rate based on population surveys in other countries.[7] Nearly 10 percent of kids now have a diagnosed anxiety disorder.[8] Teens today so profoundly identify with these diagnoses, they display them in social media profiles, alongside a picture and family name.

And if you ask mental health experts if young people, in aggregate, have *undiagnosed* mental health problems, they invariably answer in the affirmative. Meaning, according to experts, *not* having a mental health problem is increasingly anomalous.

We have plied members of the rising generation with more antianxiety and antidepressant medication than any prior. We've afforded them more mental health accommodations in school[9] and in sports.[10] They face less stigma[11] for receiving mental health treatments, and so much more emotional sensitivity[12] from adults in their lives.

From the time they first lurched across the living room rug on unsteady legs, parents treated them to therapeutic parenting. ("I see you're having some *big feelings*. How would you like to express that, Adam? Would you like to stomp your feet? Or grit your teeth?") Their teachers employed therapeutic methods of pedagogy ("Tell me about your drawing, Madison. What does it represent *to you?*") and read them books about how to process their feelings.

A decade ago, a writer for *Slate* noted that instead of using moral language to describe misbehavior, educated parents had begun employing therapeutic language.[13] A-list adolescent heroes from Huck Finn to Dylan McKay suddenly struck us as undiagnosed sufferers of "oppositional defiant disorder" or "conduct disorder." Agency slunk out the back door.

Suddenly, every shy kid had "social anxiety," or "generalized anxiety disorder." Every weird or awkward teen was "on the spectrum" or, at least, "spectrumy." Loners had "depression." Clumsy kids had "dyspraxia."

Parents ceased to chide "picky eaters" and instead diagnosed and accommodated the "food avoidant." (Formal diagnosis: "avoidant restrictive food intake disorder," or ARFID.) If a kid whined about an itchy tag at the back of his shirt or complained that hallway noise kept him from getting restful sleep, his parents didn't tell him to ignore it; they bought tag-free clothing of soft Pima cotton and appointed his room with a soft-sound machine to address his "sensory processing issues." No chiding kids for messy handwriting (that was "dysgraphia"). No telling kids with the blues that it takes time to adjust to a new town or new school (they have "relocation depression"[14]). No reassuring them that it's normal to miss their friends over the summer ("summer anxiety"[15]).

We've all been swimming in therapeutic concepts so long we no longer note the presence of the water. It seems perfectly reasonable to talk about a child's "trauma" from the death of a pet or the routine humiliation of being picked last for a sports team.

In the course of a single month, three zeitgeist-epitomizing stories hit the news: The American Academy of Pediatrics, in 2022, reversed perhaps a century of standard protocol and declared that kids with active headlice should no longer be sent home from school; better to scatter bloodthirsty vermin across the entire student body than that anyone bear the emotional stigma of having been sent home.[16] The *Washington Post*'s "mental health professional" informed readers that having your name mispronounced is damaging to the psyche.[17] And New York University fired a storied organic chemistry professor, author of the field's premier textbook, because holding premed students to the same standards (and grading scale) he'd employed for decades suddenly failed to make student well-being a priority.[18]

"Student Wellness Centers" have sprouted at our most prestigious universities. Our best athletes withdraw from competition to attend to their mental health; and young Hollywood starlets, Prince Harry, and a slew of Grammy winners proclaim the "work" they are doing in therapy against a continuous struggle with anxiety and depression. "Wellness" and "trauma" form the contrapuntal soundtrack against which the rising generation came of age.

Seventy-five years of rapid expansion in mental health treatment and services has landed us here, marveling at the unprecedented psychological frailty of American youth.

The Treatment-Prevalence Paradox

It began with the soldiers returning home from the Second World War.[19] On a scale previously unimagined, GIs had seen—and meted out—death and suffering. Many returned home shaky—some, shattered.

Congress greenlit a dramatic expansion in *preventive* therapeutic services.[20] No longer content to treat the ill, therapists became determined to support the healthy.[21] Between 1946 and 1960, membership in the American Psychological Association quadrupled.[22] Then, from 1970 to 1995, the number of mental health professionals *quadrupled again*.[23] In the United States since 1986, nearly every decade has seen a *doubling* of expenditure on mental health over the one before.[24]

There's a paradox embedded in this tale of exponential expansion. More widely available treatment ought to abate the rate (and severity) of disease.

Take breast cancer, pitiless killer of over forty thousand American women each year. As early detection and treatment for breast cancer improved since 1989, rates of death from breast cancer plummeted. Or maternal mortality: as antibiotics became more readily available, rates of maternal death in childbirth collapsed. Better and more widely available dental care has meant fewer toothless Americans. And as we developed immunizations and cures for childhood illness, child mortality rates nose-dived.

And yet as treatments for anxiety and depression have become more sophisticated and more readily available, adolescent anxiety and depression have *ballooned*.

I'm not the only one to have found something fishy in the fact that *more* treatment has not resulted in *less* depression. A group of academic researchers recently noticed the same. They published a peer-reviewed paper titled "More Treatment but No Less Depression: The Treatment-Prevalence Paradox."[25] The authors note that treatment for major depression has become much more widely available (and, in their view, improved) since the 1980s worldwide. And yet *in not a single Western country* has this treatment made a dent in the incidence of major depressive disorder. Many countries saw an increase.

"The increased availability of effective treatments should shorten depressive episodes, reduce relapses, and curtail recurrences. Combined, these treatment advances unequivocally should result in lower point-prevalence estimates of depression," they write. "Have these reductions occurred? The empirical answer clearly is NO."[26]

I checked with several of the paper's authors. Two confirmed that the same might be said for anxiety. As treatment has become more widely available and dispersed, point-prevalence rates should go down.[27] They have not. And while the authors admit that there was likely more depression in the past than we realized, they argue that there is at least as much, and probably more, depression now.[28]

After generations of increased intervention, that shouldn't be the case. More access to antibiotics should spell fewer deaths from infection. And more generally available therapy should spell less depression.[29]

Instead, adolescent mental health has been in steady *decline* since the 1950s.[30] Between 1990 and 2007 (before any teens had smartphones), the number of mentally ill children rose thirty-five-fold.[31] And while overdiagnosis or the expansion of definitions of mental illness may partially account for this rapid change, it is hard to dismiss or contextualize away the startling rise in teen suicide: "Between 1950 and 1988, the proportion of adolescents aged between fifteen and nineteen who killed themselves quadrupled," *The New Yorker* reported.[32] Mental illness became the leading cause of disability in children.

Yes, the coincidence of these two trends—deteriorating mental health in an era of vastly expanded awareness, detection, diagnosis, and treatment of psychological disorders—may be just that: *coincidence*. It does not unveil a causal arrow. But it is peculiar. At the very least, it may provide a clue that many of the treatments and many of the helpers aren't actually helping.

Therapists will insist that I've got things wrong end up. They are the lifeguards, not the sharks; it's simply that the rising generation has been swimming in shark-infested water, meeting more formidable challenges than any prior generation.

Karla Vermeulen, an associate professor of psychology at the State University of New York at New Paltz, told me that explicitly in our interview. And she says so in her book, where she writes: "No past American generation has faced the *cumulative load of multiple simultaneous stressors* today's emerging adults grew up with"[33] (emphasis is hers).

Therapists *are* helping young people, they insist. Young people today simply face more formidable challenges than did their predecessors. Therapists typically point to three: smartphones, COVID-19 lockdowns, and climate change.[34]

Is It the Smartphone, Dummy?

Tic disorders, gender dysphoria, anorexia, dissociative identity disorder, trichotillomania, cutting: the parade of horribles induced by smartphones could fill a psychiatric manual of its own. If smartphones were a boy who wanted to see your daughter, a generation ago, parents would have taken one look at him and said: *No way am I letting that kid in the door.* The smartphone and the rise of social media offer a compelling candidate for an environmental cause of poor adolescent mental health.[35]

Eight years have slipped by since Twenge and Haidt[36] (and four years since yours truly[37]) first warned the public of the dangers of social media and smartphones to teens.[38] That ought to have provided our eager mental health experts with an obvious mandate: treat social media like cigarettes. Call to restrict smartphones from middle school and high school campuses. Urge companies to place a black-box warning on social media, if they were really feeling feisty.

They didn't. None of the psychological organizations—not the American Psychiatric Association, the American Psychological Association, the National Association for School Psychologists, or the American School Counselor Association—issued any such call to arms. In the last decade, as the average age of a child getting a first smartphone dropped to age ten,[39] these organizations had little to say about it.

They've been preoccupied with their own style and method of intervention. Because any parent can take away a phone, but only a psychologist can diagnose a child or refer for medication. The most important thing they could have done to help improve kids' mental health was something that didn't require their expertise.

In truth, the entire society has dropped the ball when it comes to kids and smartphones. Why have parents continued to supply these devices in ever greater numbers to younger and younger kids? Flip phones are useful in emergency; GPS devices and digital cameras are of higher quality and cheaper than ever before. Why do parents continue to gift $1,000 phones to kids knowing full well that they are linked to a rise in depression, anxiety, and self-harm? The most conscientious of parents *at best* require their kids to dock them in the kitchen and cease their scrolling at bedtime. That's what counts as restricting a device that has been convincingly linked to shortened attention span, insomnia, severe anxiety, and depression.

When I asked parents why they would hand their children a device that puts kids at risk for a wide array of mental disorders, they invariably give one answer: *That's how they make plans with friends. I don't want them to be the only one who doesn't have one.* Therapists typically discourage parents ever from taking away a teen's smartphone, on the grounds that doing so will only sabotage the parent-child relationship.[40]

And while we're asking questions, why did public middle and high schools, en masse, abandon all efforts to police their use *even during class time?*

I spoke to one head of a private high school where students keep their phones with them all day long, even in class (now standard protocol at most high schools). It siphons their attention while they're trying to learn, I said. It keeps them from getting to know each other. They don't talk or make friends in the same way as they might if there were no phones present. And then there's all the ways that social media sabotages their emotional well-being. Why would you allow this?

He nodded amiably until it was his turn to speak. "It keeps them calm," he said.

Nobody has made any serious effort to block teens' smartphone use—not parents, not teachers, and definitely not mental health experts—because smartphones have become one more mental health accommodation we disburse to the young. We know it isn't good for them. We know the long-term consequences run from dark to dire. We know the devices are addictive, sleep-depriving, and pathology-inducing. But for right now, they provide unbeatable palliative care—soothing as any blankie.

If mental health experts wanted to do what was best for adolescents, advising parents against giving young teens smartphones would be a no-brainer. They would say, as a doctor might: *There's no point in bringing your kid here if you're going to let him keep smoking.* They hold themselves out as guardians of youth mental health; they ought to offer the *most radical* advice when it comes to smartphones and our young.

Instead, mental health experts rush in the opposite direction, embracing smartphone use, dismissing smartphones' impact on adolescent depression as exaggerated;[41] offering seminars to teens and their parents on "responsible social media use," which is a little like drug counselors lecturing on the appropriate uses of ecstasy. Mental health experts arrive at schools to warn parents and teens of the "risks" of social media, always careful to weigh these against the many wonderful benefits, and then conclude: *Have at it!*

And for a generation that already struggles with in-person interaction, mental health experts now offer the ultimate morphine drip: therapy, embedded in the smartphone. Some have done away with both voice and video interactions, offering therapy by text message.

If you want to improve a kid's mental health, locking up her smartphone might be a start. At a minimum, smartphones take a teen further from the world of in-person friends and activity likely to bolster her sense of well-being. They are undoubtedly responsible for exacerbating a variety of social contagions, from tic disorders to gender dysphoria. But banish the smartphone and fix a generation? I'm not so sure.[42]

Youth mental health has been in decline, after all, for the last five or six decades.[43] And then there's parents' powerful reluctance to take away our kids' smartphones. What accounts for this fecklessness, in the face of the obvious threat they pose? The very fact that we've been so long aware of their dangers and done absolutely nothing to curtail their ubiquity in adolescent hands requires its own explanation. That we persist in handing these devices to young teens and tweens is itself a symptom of a larger problem.

Didn't Enjoy Your Solitary Confinement?

COVID-19 lockdowns sent numberless kids into punishing isolation. If our mental health experts anticipated the predictable mental health catastrophe of forcing kids into social solitude for over a year, they largely kept the insight to themselves. Not a single one of their major national professional organizations even opposed the lockdowns' continuing into a *second consecutive school year* in the fall of 2020, when a further deepening of kids' isolation might have been averted.[44]

The mental health organizations are not shy about wading into public policy discussion: The American Psychological Association has railed against America's history of systemic racism. "Our nation is in the midst of a racism pandemic," said the APA's CEO in his June 2020 congressional testimony, advocating changes to police tactics.[45]

In this vein, the APA has touted the mental health benefits of affirmative action,[46] and, in a splashy press release, announced its readiness "to help society respond to climate change."[47] But against the pressing and pervasive threat of forced social isolation? Crickets.

How could the experts have missed a mental health calamity so obvious and foreseeable?

Parents protested; they were largely ignored. The mental health–expert complex, with all its institutional heft, declined to offer so much as a public warning to policymakers about the impact on kids.[48] Perhaps they didn't know the lockdowns would be devastating to the young people they were uniquely responsible to help. Whatever the reason for this colossal failure, there's something perverse in their subsequent attempt to use the pandemic lockdowns to wave away the treatment-prevalence paradox, or—worse—to argue for their *greater* role in public policy development and the lives of American kids.

In truth, before the novel coronavirus had escaped China's borders in 2019, nearly a third of Americans between the ages of eighteen and thirty-five said they were experiencing a mental illness.[49] Hospital admissions for nonfatal self-harm were up 62 percent over the previous decade,[50] with nearly 20 percent of girls ages twelve to seventeen reporting having had a major depressive episode in the previous year. Child suicide rates rose 150 percent over the previous decade.[51]

"Climate Anxiety"

Karla Vermeulen wears her hair in a cool pixie cut cropped close to the scalp. The lenses of her square plastic glasses are the size and shape of two Post-its. At the base of her neck, a string of beaded earthenware completes the picture of a no-nonsense researcher. Indeed, Vermeulen outranks almost any American as a credentialed expert in adolescent mental health.

Vermeulen trains therapists and writes books to guide them in the counseling of the rising generation. Her expertise is "disaster mental health"—which is to say, people in crisis. One might say: This is her moment.

When I learned she'd written a book, *Generation Disaster: Coming of Age Post-9/11*, I contacted her immediately. I had assumed a kindred spirit— one who'd studied the same cohort that so completely fascinates me.

Young people *are* resilient and strong, she assured me. They are simply meeting more formidable challenges than any generation before them. "They're dealing with all of these other stressors, but it's all floating on this unstable surface of climate change," she said.

It turns out, *Generation Disaster* may be the most misleading title in the history of the printed word. By "generation disaster," Vermeulen actually means: *This generation is* not *a disaster—not by a longshot.* If anything, *everyone else* is a disaster for being so overly critical of these magnificent, socially conscious young people.

Like Vermeulen, many therapists are convinced that "climate anxiety" is a real and important category of mental health disorder. A cottage industry has arisen to treat it: "climate-aware therapy." What with the polar ice caps melting, tropical disease raging, hurricanes and floods scheduled to land with Noahide vengeance, *of course* young people are depressed! *Nature*, the medical journal *The Lancet*, and NPR all agree:

depression is merely a rational response to the greenhouse gases' smothering fug.

Atlantic editor Franklin Foer intimated the same in a piece about his fourteen-year-old daughter who suffers from anxiety. "I long to build a seawall that can protect her from her fears," Foer writes of his decision to let his daughter skip school to attend a climate change protest inspired by activist Greta Thunberg. "But her example, and Thunberg's doomsaying, have made me realize that my parental desire to calm is the stuff of childish fantasy; anxiety is the mature response. To protect our children, we need to embrace their despair."[52]

But is climate anxiety—dare I ask—rational? And is the best we can offer kids affirmation of their fears?

Actually, while there is little doubt the earth is warming, there's a great deal of reason for environmental optimism; many environmental trends are going in the right direction.

"Deaths from natural disaster have declined over 95 percent over the last century. Actual disasters themselves have gone down over the last twenty years. Disasters are measured strictly as deaths and damages from extreme weather events," said Michael Shellenberger, a longtime environmental activist and author of several books on the environment. "We're more resilient than ever."

The number of people who died from weather-related or climate-related disasters last year was 6,000 *globally,* he pointed out to me. To place that in perspective, 106,000 people will die this year (2023) from drug overdose and poisoning in the United States alone. As for carbon emissions, they slightly declined globally over the last decade.[53]

And yet people are telling surveyors that they feel far more environmental anxiety today, when most trends are going in the right direction, than they ever did in eras past. Where was the outburst of environmental anxiety when we were almost exclusively burning coal to generate electricity or blasting a hole in the ozone layer with CFCs? Or when a blanket of brown-yellow smog blocked Los Angelinos' view of the nearby San Gabriel Mountains? All were known problems, but the mental health diagnosis was nonexistent. That alone may have contained the spread of worry.

Even for adults who are profoundly concerned about climate change, in other words, validating and reinforcing a child's terror about human extinction via climate change is no rational imperative. It is, instead, a very specific choice that an adult makes for her own reasons.

"Embrace Their Despair"

According to Foer and Vermeulen, a parent's job is not to arrest a daughter's fears by placing them in perspective.[54] Not to ply her with soothing pablum—something only dumb kids fall for, apparently—like the idea that the earth is going to be around for a long time. Not to remind her that for gazillions of years the human species has met and mastered every prior challenge, including brutal vicissitudes in climate. Don't reassure her that there are brilliant and dedicated people working very hard to meet the changes brought on by a warming climate. Resist the urge to take the upper hand and let her know that one day, after she finishes her education, she can choose to be one of those scientists. Until then, she has other concerns. Like passing ninth-grade math.

Vermeulen and Foer unwittingly help unlock a recent puzzle. While teen girls have seen a severe mental health decline, those who identify with liberal and left-leaning politics have suffered worst of all.[55] Liberal teen boys evince worse depression than conservative teen girls. That ought to suggest that most of what we're seeing isn't a mental *illness* crisis. It's deeply connected to the values and worldview we've given our kids, the ways they've raised them, the influences around them.

So many progressive parents seem to believe their job is to scare the ever-living crap out of kids when it comes to climate change. Use the phrase "human extinction" at bedtime. As many bedtimes as you can.

I ask Vermeulen if it would ever be appropriate to say to a kid, *Listen, you're really exaggerating the threat of climate change right now. Let's get through the week.*

Vermeulen becomes visibly stricken. "I would never tell someone they were exaggerating. That's very invalidating and not helpful. That's going to raise defenses and make them feel unheard."[56]

But kids toss a lot of worries at their parents, sometimes just to see which ones bounce back. Parents who follow the therapists' direction and embrace their children's despair breathe life into the monster under the bed. In the small number of homes where parents are themselves wracked with apocalyptic fears, it shouldn't surprise us that such fears also menace the child.

Beth, the Psych Nurse: Stop Trying to Make Climate Anxiety Happen

Now in her late thirties, Beth has been a psych nurse for over a decade at a medical clinic serving the students of three Boston-area universities. As alarmed as everyone seems to be about young people's mental health, Beth tells me, it's worse than we know. She routinely sees college kids who can't bring themselves to call her office. They ask a college counselor—or even a parent—to schedule an appointment on their behalf.[57] They claim their "social anxiety" forbids this basic task. But Beth, who writes their prescriptions, tells me that isn't it. They've just never been made to do anything on their own.

As an example, Beth recalled that one college co-ed brought her mom along to the appointment. The mom kept track of her daughter's menstrual periods with an app on her phone.

I asked if the daughter was mentally impaired in some way. No, Beth said. She was just, well, *managed*. Never allowed to fall or fail, standing on two wobbly legs that have barely tested the ground. Then, thrust out from under the family awning for college, university life hits these kids like a hailstorm.

Many college-age young women, Beth says, are smoking marijuana several times *a day*, by themselves, just to mute their pain. She tells me this is new. The marijuana use isn't social; it's compulsive and medicinal.

I asked Beth how many of the thousands of students she treats mention climate change or systemic racism as a reason for their distress. She told me flatly—none. Not a single one. "I don't think anyone ever. Like they might make some an offhanded joke about it?" Beth's answer dovetailed with my work. In my scores of interviews with young people about their mental health, *none* gave climate change as a reason for their or their friends' emotional struggles. All except one (a TikTok influencer) explicitly denied that climate change was an important source of young people's distress.

So what reasons do they give for the pain they feel? Exam stress. Being overwhelmed by the work piling up. Total inability to reach the expectations set by professors who—unlike the public school teachers they had before—may actually fail them if their grades warrant it.

A lot of their distress, Beth says, falls into the category of social interactions gone very bad—things they said or posted online that they later regret and can't seem to stop reliving. The boy who dumps them or leaves their texts "on read." They want to get over it. They believe they can't.

So why, then, do so many therapists and researchers and intellectuals insist that climate change is a primary cause of their distress? And why do young people *tell* researchers that climate change is a reason for their anxiety? Turns out, when young people are not in the throes of severe distress, they offer reasons that will seem rational to the adults around them and garner the sympathy and attention they want or need.[58]

Researchers often graft onto the young whatever explanation seems most rational to them, based on their own political biases. For conservative researchers, the rise of fatherlessness, the decline of marriage, or decreased religious affiliation—all of which coincide with climbing rates of mental illness—might seem rational explanations. For liberal researchers, climate change, school shootings, systemic racism, economic inequality, and the politics of MAGA provide favored candidates.[59]

So, yes, young people today are more worried about climate change than were previous generations, just as schoolkids in 1962 were more worried about nuclear war with Russia than schoolkids today. But there is no extant record of a rash of sixties kids, terrified as they were of nuclear apocalypse, failing to show up for school.[60] For that matter, how did American schoolchildren march off to school on December 8, 1941? And yet they did.[61]

But for therapists who continue to see "climate change" as rational grounds for serious mental disturbance, optimism is not an option. There is no bright side, and it does no good to point out to a young person claiming "climate anxiety" that she may be suffering an emotional parallax. With some notable exceptions, placing an adolescent's worries into perspective is not what therapy does—nor even what it seeks to do. That wouldn't be affirming the patient.

No. We. Can't.

The rising generation is strikingly different from those prior, according to academic psychologist and author of several books on Gen Z, Jean Twenge. It isn't simply the rates of diagnosed mental illness that makes them so distinctive. They are far more obedient to authority, agreeable, and tied to Mom. More politically radical (more likely to favor far-left positions) and much less inclined to self-aggrandizement than, say, millennials. Actually, what seems to motivate a large portion of Gen Z, born between 1995 and 2012, is not hope or optimism or belief in themselves—it's *fear*. They are arguably the most fearful generation on record.

In April 2021, I met Twenge at her San Diego home to profile her for *The Wall Street Journal*. I wanted to learn more about a generation that had already started to seem awfully troubled. We sat on damp plastic chairs, ten feet apart, in her lush backyard while the pandemic raged around us.

Gen Z, Twenge told me, is far less likely to date, obtain a driver's license, hold down a job, or hang out with friends in person than millennials were at the same age. In 2016, high school seniors spent up to *an hour less per day* hanging out with each other than those of the 1980s. They also engage in the least amount of sex (while arguably having it most available)[62] and report having the fewest romantic relationships or romantic encounters.[63] They are reluctant to cross the milestones at which previous generations eagerly launched themselves. As one young person said to me, expressing a sentiment I heard echoed by others, "I was very scared to start college. But I guess everyone was when they were my age?" Actually, I was there. No, we weren't.

They are also far more pessimistic than previous generations—much more pessimistic than millennials, especially. What are young people today so pessimistic about? I asked Twenge.

"Everything," she said. "At their own prospects, the prospects of the world. And you have to ask, what causes what? Is it because the world is so bad, that's why they're depressed? Or do they see the world as bad because they're depressed? It could be either one."

But there's something else, too. In numbers never before seen, young people doubt they have the power to improve their circumstances.

"Locus of control" is the term psychologists use to refer to a person's sense of agency. If you have an *internal* locus of control, you believe you have ability to improve your circumstances. If you have an *external* locus of control, you do not. Instead, you tend to attribute events to things outside of your control, like other people or bum luck.

The rising generation has moved toward an external locus of control, Twenge said. The generation standing at the very beginning of life's journey also believes it can't do anything to improve its lot.

These profound feelings of helplessness, ineffectiveness, and dependency may be symptoms of the generation's depression. Or all may be symptoms of a third cause, something therapy can't cure but could worsen. But today's mental health experts rarely consider that there is any problem facing today's youth to which they are not the invariable solution. So, more therapy, then. How much more? Loads.

Becca: My Therapist Is Helping Me Prepare to Make Friends—in College

When we speak, Becca has just graduated from a large public high school in Santa Clarita, California. She doesn't have a job or a plan to look for one. For now, she's just trying to get into the right mindset before she heads off to university in the fall. She hopes to study—you guessed it— psychology. Her therapist is helping her prepare to make friends.

"It's kind of been a lifelong issue for me. I think it's more of just putting myself out there," Becca tells me. "And my therapist says, specifically, that I should be the one to reach out first. So I've been trying that and especially now that I'm going off to college. I don't know my roommate situation yet, but I'm definitely going to try to talk to them and become closer. It's kind of like a fresh start."

For generations, this mundane fact of life—needing to make new friends in a new place—was the sort of thing young adults simply resolved to do on their own. But Becca's been in therapy since her parents divorced when she was six. You cannot convince her that she does not need a therapist to help her plan, rehearse, and revisit her attempts to make friends.

Perhaps unsurprisingly for someone so close to her therapist, Becca doesn't know her current "best friends" all that well. Becca can't tell me what religion most of her friends are or what their parents do for a living. Nor do they know very much about her. "With my friends, it's mostly, we talk about boys and stuff like that. But with my therapist, I talk about deeper issues, like my anxiety. She gives me methods to help with it, like meditation and just sitting down and thinking about whether it's really worth stressing over."

Advice dispensed by a professional therapist is likely to be more mature and measured than that of another teenager. Parents who foot the bill certainly hope so, at any rate. But it's hardly a clear win. Because your therapist won't call you on your birthday every year for the next thirty.

She won't coerce you into humiliating yourself at a karaoke bar on your twenty-first birthday just because she loves you that much. She isn't going to introduce you to a coworker or harangue her boyfriend into arranging a setup for you, just because she can't stand to see you alone. Your therapist won't hop on a train to attend your bachelorette just so she can toast your misadventures or stand beside you at your wedding, tearily clutching a fistful of peonies. She may promise to understand you, but let's face it: your therapist will not be prized from her hourly billing to celebrate the birth of your child just because it feels so monumental that one of you had a baby.

No, they are the dividend stream of actual friendship. And so many hours logged bearing souls, piling into cars for road trips, narrowly avoiding accidents, and getting lost in bad neighborhoods—they are the invested capital. Therapists care about you in the practiced manner and to the precise extent any professional does a client—for the duration of a "fifty-minute hour," so long as she takes your insurance or you remain cash-flow positive.

The social critic Christopher Lasch once observed that therapy "simultaneously pronounces the patient unfit to manage his own life and delivers him into the hands of a specialist."[64] And I couldn't help thinking of Becca's predicament when I read this from Lasch: "As therapeutic points of view and practice gain general acceptance, more and more people find themselves disqualified, in effect, from the performance of adult responsibilities and become dependent on some form of medical authority."[65]

Therapy for Every Single Child?

The rising generation has already received a lot of therapy. Thanks to artificial intelligence, the rain shower may soon become a flash flood. That's what four different venture capitalists informed me: Big Tech is already revolutionizing mental health, creating apps that will soon have the capacity to provide therapy to *every single child.*

Eager to meet my kids' future therapist, I signed up for myala, a wellness tracker app "available to any student over the age of 16," according to its website. My session began with a "check-in" to assess my current mental state.

Here are six of the first ten questions my therapist-bot asked me:

"How lonely do you feel?"

"How supported do you feel?"

"How worried do you feel right now?"

"How down do you feel right now?"

"How often do you feel left out?"

"How sad do you feel right now?"

You may be wondering, as I did: *What fresh hell is being asked how sad you are, in six different ways, by a string of code incapable of caring if you were flogged in the street?* This series of questions seemed enough to flatten the stuffing of just about anyone. I tried to abandon the survey. It didn't let me.

Turns out, if you're not up for confessing to AI how lonely you feel, you'll get a notification reminding you that you've failed at that, too.

Some of these apps facilitate therapy with an actual person. Some connect teens to therapists who conduct therapy over text, to avoid hassling them with an actual face-to-face conversation (Charlie Health) or to the numberless therapists who will Zoom. There are apps that match up the rudderless with every manner of life coach (BetterUp). Apps that allow little kids ("ages 0–14") and their parents to track their moods (Little Otter).

Many wellness apps have already dispensed with the human-therapist model, making the "therapy" free to any kid with access to an iPad. "Therapy without a therapist" is Big Tech's solution for making therapy scalable—able to meet the bottomless demand of a society obsessed with therapy. Integrating AI may soon cut human therapists out of the loop entirely. And the goal of nearly all of these applications is also mental health startup Talkspace's motto and mission: "Therapy for All." *Every single child.*[66]

Over three billion dollars of capital investment poured into mental health tech startups[67] in just the fifteen months following the onset of COVID-19. Therapy and its iatrogenic effects are being crop-dusted across the entire population.

The decks of promotional materials mental health start-ups show potential investors are unflinching: the poor mental health of the rising generation spells unimaginable business opportunity. They claim that one out of six of children in the United States "has an impairing mental health disorder." Without embarrassment or apology, one internal pitch to investors refers to kids and young adults between sixteen and twenty-six as its "beachhead population."[68]

Before we hand over the delicate psyches of every single child to their totalizing and indiscriminate mental health interventions, it's worth scrutinizing the efforts already underway. At best, they have failed to relieve the conditions they claim to treat. But far more likely: the methods and treatments mental health experts champion and dispense are already making young people sicker, sadder, and more afraid to grow up.

Chapter 3

•

Bad Therapy

When he was two years old, Camilo Ortiz and his parents entered the United States illegally from Colombia. Unable to speak English, ineligible even for public assistance, they moved into a one-room basement apartment in Queens. Ortiz's father devised a series of schemes to support the family—many of them illegal.

When Ortiz was eleven, his parents divorced. When Ortiz was seventeen, his father was caught ferrying $300,000 cash in the trunk of his car. His father was arrested, convicted, and imprisoned for money laundering.

But Camilo Ortiz does not enter our story as a patient. He enters as a tenured professor and leading child and adolescent psychologist. And he has a divergent perspective on how psychotherapists ought to be treating troubled, anxious, and stressed-out kids.

For one, Ortiz worries that a lot of therapy directed at kids is useless. "It's just a pretty easy job to play with kids in your office, so the incentives are all wrong," Ortiz told me. "I could make a great living if I just said, 'Sure, bring your kid in, and I'll play blocks with her and we'll do play therapy.' And that would not do a thing of good for them. And I could have a full caseload as long as I want."

Although he gets several calls a week from parents pleading with him to see their young children in individual therapy, he turns them all down. For most problems, Ortiz says, individual therapy has almost no proven benefit for kids. "The evidence is pretty clear that parent-based approaches are more effective." Meaning, a therapist should treat a kid's anxiety by treating the kid's parents. Parents often unwittingly transmit their own anxiety to their kids. And parents are in the best position to help a child deal with her worries on an ongoing basis.

And yet numberless psychotherapists not only offer individual therapy to young kids, they practice techniques like "play therapy" that have shown scant evidence of benefiting kids. In fact, there's very little evidence that individual (one-on-one) psychotherapy helps young kids at all.[1]

But why doesn't individual therapy work for young kids? If it's good for the goose—why not for the goslings? "Well, let's take an anxious five-year-old," Ortiz says. "Let's say I'm the best therapist in the world and I teach her some amazing techniques for dealing with anxiety, on a Monday at four p.m. So we're supposed to believe that on a Friday, when she's dysregulated, and anxious, at age five, she's going to remember what we talked about, and then be able to institute difficult techniques in a moment of dysregulation?" he asks rhetorically. "I can't get *adults* to do that. It just doesn't work with children." It's far more effective, Ortiz says, to teach the parents who spend many hours a day with their kids the best techniques for, say, getting a child over her fear of sleeping alone.

Also, the power imbalance between therapist and child in the intense context of individual therapy is simply too great, he tells me. Children are easily convinced of things. Think recovered-memory therapy, a dark episode in the history of psychiatry in which therapists inadvertently implanted false memories in child patients.

I met Ortiz at his Tudor revival in Forest Hills, Queens, where he lives with his son, elegant wife, and yappy dog, Pesto. (His daughter was already away at college.) Ortiz looks a little like he just stepped out of a Brooks Brothers catalog. Tweedy and trim, he wears tortoiseshell glasses, slacks, and a half-zip mock neck sweater. His appearance suggests a boyhood poring over Latin declensions, boarding at Exeter, summers in Montauk. Not one mired in privation until a test score in elementary school won him a spot at the prestigious Hunter College High School. There, for the first time, he found himself surrounded "by only very smart kids who had high aspirations for educational attainment." Their ambition was infectious, or at least instructive. He realized he had high ambitions for himself, too.

Today, Ortiz is a professor of clinical psychology at Long Island University, where he trains psychologists and conducts research into treatments for child and adolescent anxiety and depression. So what makes someone a good therapist for adolescents? For one thing, he said, a good therapist doesn't treat therapy with a teen as an annuity. "If your therapist doesn't talk to you about termination [of psychotherapy] during your first session, it's probably not a good therapist."

Ortiz absolutely believes in the ameliorative power of specific kinds of therapies, especially cognitive-behavioral and dialectical behavior therapies (known as CBT and DBT) for remediating specific ailments like tic disorders, affective disorders, and obsessive-compulsive disorder. Ortiz is a cognitive behavioral therapist, and he uses its methods to help families of kids who suffer with conditions like chronic bed-wetting. He has seen it improve the lives of his patients. But he has enough respect for the power of therapy to reject the idea that everyone should be in therapy, a notion Ortiz likens to a surgeon who ventures: *Well, he looks healthy, but let's open him up and see what we find.*

Therapy, when it works for adults, gets its power from the patient's buy-in. But a child or adolescent who enters therapy invariably does so because she was strong-armed by an adult. Sometimes, there is no buy-in at all. A therapist must then flatter or entertain the adolescent, avoiding the unpleasant toil that represents therapy at its best. And if the adolescent still isn't convinced, matters may be made more explicit: *Mom thinks whatever is wrong with you is serious enough to lay out $250 an hour.*

However hard we work to "destigmatize" therapy, the message to any child patient is twofold: *Your mother thinks there is something wrong with you* and *Your problem is above her pay grade.* Almost necessarily, the presence of the intermediary will alter a parent's relationship with her child, whether the parent realizes this or not.

For those tallying iatrogenic risks of one-on-one psychotherapy with children, that's: demoralization (convincing a young person there's something wrong with her) and undermining parental authority (Mom can't handle your problems, so she's hired someone who can—someone who has better judgment about you than she does). All for a process with doubtful chance of working.

Ortiz discloses the risk of iatrogenesis in a waiver to his therapy clients because he *wants* them to be on the lookout for iatrogenic effects; he wants them to avoid harm. "I talk to my clients about the fact that in some percentage of cases, people get worse in therapy. It's not a big percentage, but it can happen," he said.

This struck me as not only sensible but wise. After I interviewed Ortiz, any psychologist, psychiatrist, or therapist I came to trust needed first to take seriously the possibility that therapy can harm. Fortunately, I found my way to forty-five academic psychologists and fifteen psychiatrists, many with international reputations for excellence, all of whom freely acknowledged the possibility of iatrogenesis. (Several had authored books and papers on the subject.)

What does bad therapy look like, I wondered. If a sadist *wanted* to induce anxiety, depression, a feeling of incapacity, or family estrangement, what sort of methods would she employ? How would a malevolent mastermind induct a generation into a tyranny of feelings?[2] Like this.

Bad Therapy Step One: Teach Kids to Pay Close Attention to their Feelings

Yulia Chentsova Dutton heads the Culture and Emotions Lab at Georgetown University. I traveled to DC to meet her in the hopes that she might shed light on why American kids, in particular, seemed to be struggling so mightily with emotional regulation.

"I am an emotions researcher," the pixieish Soviet émigré said as we toured her lab. "Emotions are highly reactive to our attention to them. Certain kinds of attention to emotions, focus on emotions, can increase emotional distress. And I'm worried that when we try to help our young adults, help our children, what we do is throw oil into the fire."

In our three hours together, Chentsova Dutton reviewed with me her cross-cultural research comparing young people's emotional responses to stressors in countries like Japan, Russia, and China. She also showed me the room in her lab where she fixes electrodes to subjects and observes them through a one-way window, while they watch a video designed to deliver psychological provocation. Not at all hard to imagine why she likes her job.

A rich emotional vocabulary can help children describe their feelings. But many of our therapeutic interventions with children, she says, go far beyond supplying one. "We are basically telling them that this deeply imperfect signal"—that is, what they are feeling—"is always valid, is always important to track, pay attention, and then use to guide your behavior, use it to guide how you act in a situation."

Placing undue importance on your emotions is a little like stepping onto a swivel chair to reach something on a high shelf. Emotions are likely to skitter out from under you, casters and all. Worse, attending to our feelings often causes them to intensify. Leading kids to focus on their emotions can encourage them to be *more* emotional.

It troubles Chentsova Dutton that so much therapeutic intervention with kids proceeds from the conceit that children should attribute great import to their feelings. Emotions are not only unstable, they're also highly manipulable, she said, hinting that she could make me feel all kinds of things if she really wanted to. Asking someone a series of leading questions, or making certain statements to them, can reliably provoke certain emotional responses. ("It's just so easy," she said.)

In an individualistic society like ours, we incline toward the erroneous belief that feelings accurately signal who we are in the moment. But in fact, "feelings are responsive to so many cues, and because of that, so often are off."

The anger you feel does not necessarily indicate that you are in the right or that someone treated you unfairly. You may feel envious of a friend, even though you would not actually want what he has. You may feel loved by someone who mistreats you or resent someone who's only treated you kindly. Feelings fool us all the time.

Adults should be telling kids how imperfect and unreliable their emotions can be, Chentsova Dutton says. Very often, kids should be skeptical that their feelings reflect an accurate picture of the world and even ignore their feelings entirely. (Gasp!) You read that right: a healthy emotional life involves a certain amount of daily *repression*.

How is a child supposed to get through a day of school if she's never learned to put aside her hurt feelings and concentrate on the lessons in front of her? How will she ever be a good friend if her own feelings are always, at every instant, front and center? How will she ever hope to function at work?

She can't. She won't. They aren't.

But isn't it a good idea to inquire regularly about kids' feelings?

Therapists, teachers, and parents in America all seem to proceed under the belief that checking in is a little like sticking a thermometer outside your front door: harmless and occasionally helpful.

Michael Linden, a professor of psychiatry at the Charité University Hospital in Berlin, thinks this is a terrible practice. "Asking somebody 'how are you feeling?' is inducing negative feelings. You shouldn't do that."

Why? I asked. If all you're doing is asking, each morning, *How are we feeling today, Brayden?*, isn't the child as free to provide a positive answer as a negative one?

That isn't true, Linden shot back. "Nobody feels great," he said. "Never, never ever. Sit in the bus and look at the people opposite from you. They don't look happy. Happiness is not the emotion of the day."

Linden is a world-renowned expert in the iatrogenic effects of therapy. After I had read one of his papers on psychotherapy's more reckless adventures, we arranged to meet over Zoom. Handsome and cheery, he apparently loves poking fun at Americans—which, I've learned, is something German and Northern European academics find almost irresistible. Linden has a full head of neat gray hair, a broad smile, and a sporting air of disagreeableness.

If you track a person's emotions over the course of a day or even a week, Linden told me, happiness is actually a very rare emotion, statistically speaking. Of our sixty-thousand wakeful seconds each day, only a tiny percentage are spent in a state we would call "happy." Most of the time we are simply "okay" or "fine," trying to ignore some minor discomfort: feeling a little tired, run down, upset, stressed out, irritated, allergic, or in pain. Regularly prompting someone to reflect on their current state will—if they are being honest—elicit a raft of negative responses.

Linden saw my surprise, so he asked me to consider how I was feeling right then, during our interview. I was inclined to say "good," but he jumped in: "You don't feel happy in this moment. You are concentrating on the interview."

He was right. It was five a.m. in California when we spoke, and I am, to put it mildly, not a morning person. I was acutely aware that the three sleeping children one floor above me might, at any moment, wake and interrupt the interview. I disliked how tired I looked on my webcam. Having allotted every spare minute to sleep, I had run out of time to apply makeup. I hadn't downed my morning coffee.

Linden looked relaxed in his merino wool sweater, but I was pale and exhausted, straining to seem sharper than I felt, struggling to catch his meaning through the sharp pickets of his accent. So not "happy," exactly, no. Linden was spot-on. Being more aware of, and precise about, my current feelings elicited primarily negative introspection.

I thought back to Nora's friends and wondered which of them would be helped by paying closer attention to their feelings. Not those who were struggling with profound mental illness. Certainly not those who, according to Nora, were leaning into their diagnoses, exaggerating their symptoms.

But there's an even bigger problem with asking kids, over and over, to reflect on their feelings, Linden told me. It has to do with psychological orientation.

Psychologists have studied the states of mind that tend to make us more successful, whatever the challenge. There are at least two we can adopt: "action orientation" and "state orientation."[3] Adopting an action orientation means focusing on the task ahead with no thought to your current emotional or physical state. A state orientation means you're thinking principally about yourself: how prepared you feel in that moment, the worry you feel over a text left unanswered, the light prickling at the back of your throat, that crick blossoming in your neck. Adopting an action orientation, it turns out, makes it much more likely that you accomplish the task.

Our best coaches know this instinctively. Consider the way they motivate a team before the game: *We can do this!* they say. *Wiggins, you're gonna cover number eleven like you're his shadow. Tyler, watch the penalties. Defense—you're gonna put relentless pressure on their QB, I want to see hurries and sacks. Offense, head up, stay composed, nice clean blocks.* Focus, focus, focus on the task ahead!

They do not say: *Let's take a moment to hear how each of you is feeling. Tyler, we'll start with you. Still bummed about your parents' divorce?* If you want to win—if you want to accomplish anything—among the worst things you can do is attend to your disappointments, discomforts, and painful relationships right now. No winning head coach asks his players to consider their feelings at halftime because thinking about yourself shatters your ability to get things done.

"State orientation keeps you from being successful in anything," Linden said.

I asked Linden what he would expect to see in a society where kids were constantly encouraged to heed their feelings.

"If you start your day by asking yourself whether you are happy, the result can only be that you're not happy. And then you think you need help to become happy. And then you go to a psychotherapist and he'll make you *really* unhappy in the end."

But why can't the answer always be "I'm happy"?

Because it will never be true, Linden says. And time spent answering this question only pushes us further from any tangible goal and the satisfaction of having completed one.

Bad Therapy Step Two: Induce Rumination

We all have a friend who has spent way, way too much time obsessing over her ex. That's rumination, a style of thinking characterized by brooding on past injuries and personal problems. Venting may produce relief, but rehashing the same hurt can become pathological.[4] It is also one of the most significant iatrogenic risks of therapy.

Leif Kennair, a world-renowned expert in the treatment of anxiety, depression, and obsessive-compulsive disorder, studies disorders of rumination. A professor of personality psychology at the Norwegian University of Science and Technology, Kennair has also written a book (sadly, in Norwegian) rigorously detailing the ways therapy can become counterproductive.

"Trying to get the patient to consider their past and how it went wrong, and what could have gone better and how should it be different, what can happen, what's the most likely outcome and so on—a lot of these different interventions are actually worry- and rumination-increasing interventions," he told me over Zoom. Instead, when patients present with depression or generalized anxiety disorder, therapists "should be doing worry and rumination *discontinuing* interventions."[5] Meaning, a good therapist should do what cognitive behavioral therapists do: prove to a patient that rumination is an unproductive mode of thought and train them to stop.

By the time I spoke to Kennair, several therapists had assured me that there was no proof that young people today were more depressed than were prior generations. I asked Kennair how we could be sure that young people weren't simply more "open" about their poor mental health?

Kennair's response was elegant and astonishing: being overly prone to talking about your emotional pain *is itself* a symptom of depression. "If you do this"—habitually give voice to your negative thoughts or personal

problems—"you're co-ruminating at least. But I believe they are ruminating more. And rumination is *the* major predictor for depression."

Bad Therapy Step Three:
Make "Happiness" a Goal but
Reward Emotional Suffering

Hang around families with young children for an afternoon, and you'll
hear parents check that their kids are *enjoying* their ice cream, *excited*
about school the next day, that they *had fun* at the park. In so many ways,
we signal to kids: your happiness is the ultimate goal; it's what we're all
livin' for.[6]

According to the best research, we have it all backward. If we wanted
our kids to be happy, the last thing we would do is to communicate that
happiness is the goal. The more vigorously you hunt happiness, the more
likely you are to be disappointed.[7] This is true irrespective of the objective conditions of your life.

"We know that chasing positivity for yourself is actually associated
with low psychological function—that it's associated with more depressive symptoms," Chentsova Dutton told me. "We know that people who
are really strongly desiring to be happy are not particularly happy and
that the desire to be happy serves as a vulnerability factor."

Consider your grandparents. My grandmother, who grew up poor,
took genuine delight in life's peculiar deliverances: a scoop of chocolate
ice cream; a simple family birthday party with an unsightly homemade
cake; *tchotchkes* with Hebrew lettering turning up in a remote country
antique shop. Each produced in her the spasmodic glee of someone who
never expected that her own life would be filled with happiness.

By insisting that happiness be their goal, we place kids in a cruci-
ble. On the one hand, "chasing positivity" tends to make them more
depressed. Then feeling depressed gets socially rewarded, Chentsova

Dutton said. So, kids are naturally "amplifying their signal of how much they suffer."

Cody, a senior at a public high school in Brooklyn, told me the same. A generation ago, kids might have identified with what Cody calls their "strengths": the jock, the popular kid, the math team member, the beauty queen. But today, that's verboten. "Identifying with your strengths now isn't seen as too cool because some people may manipulate you into thinking that you're privileged because of it."

What's wrong with identifying with your struggles? "Well, I see that they don't try to solve it."

Cody took pains to explain that he wasn't talking about the severely depressed—just the average kid. Once they get the validation from other students for their mental health crises, "they don't break out of that rut," he said.

Bad Therapy Step Four: Affirm and Accommodate Kids' Worries

All Mason will eat is buttered noodles. Harper is afraid of dogs. Would you mind crating your dog during our visit? Or, from the therapist: Sounds like your kiddo has testing anxiety. I'll write her a note, so that the school gives her untimed tests. Sound familiar?

Therapists aren't the only ones who affirm and accommodate children's anxiety. Parents do this all the time. But therapists do so while purporting to treat it. "Therapists can inadvertently project the message that clients need to be very worried about anxiety-producing stimuli," Ortiz told me. "We have found that therapists who are themselves anxious people tend to be over-protective in their interventions with clients."

It may bring a child short-term relief for a therapist to agree that dogs *can be* scary and brainstorm strategies for avoiding the chocolate lab next door. But this may also reify the worry, intimating that coming across a dog is like encountering a mountain lion: an emergency worthy of full-blown evasive action. So, yes, therapists can reinforce a child's or adolescent's outsized fears. Therapists can make kids' anxiety worse.

A core tenet of therapies like CBT is that a kid's extreme aversion to, say, dirt may be based on the false belief that dirt is harmful. The best way to demolish this maladaptive belief is for your kid to have direct and repeated contact with precisely the thing she is afraid of.[8] If your kid is afraid of dogs, you prompt her to pet a dog.[9] For a germophobic patient with obsessive-compulsive disorder who is washing his hands a hundred times a day, the therapist might insist the patient touch a toilet and, eventually, stick his hand into a messy toilet bowl. Ortiz once led a patient to do this and then wipe his hand on a pillow and sleep on it.

"Once they can do these pretty outrageous kinds of exposures, then the regular fears that they typically worry about don't seem so big. Touching your own door handle once you've stuck your hand into a toilet bowl pales by comparison."

"Exposure therapy" is CBT's escalating method of encouraging patients to confront things that make them uncomfortable. It is among the few therapies with an evidentiary track record of benefits. Although a great many therapists claim to use CBT methods, a fraction of them are trained in its rigors or practicing its evidence-based methods.[10]

School psychologists and counselors so often do the opposite: solidify a child's worry through affirmation and accommodation.[11] They intervene with the teacher, ostensibly on a child's behalf, to lighten the homework load or to provide tailored assignments if the standard curriculum seems to cause too much stress. None of this encourages the development of a child's natural resources for coping with her worries or overcoming stressful situations.

Accommodation deprives children of the opportunity to vault a challenge and renders them "actually less capable," Ortiz said. Force a kid to sleep in a house beset by the normal sounds of snoring siblings, whistling of winds, or creaking of joists, and eventually she will sleep. She'll realize, more importantly, that she *can*.

We all need practice sitting with discomfort, Ortiz emphasized—emotional as well as physical. If we get the necessary practice, we become better at tolerating it. If we don't, we may become *worse* at it. And yet so many adults are intent on deleting all irritation and inconvenience from children's lives as if they were toxins.

I asked neuropsychologist and author Rita Eichenstein why we're seeing so many phobias and so much anxiety among kids today. "There's sensory deprivation. The minute the kid goes home from the hospital, they're in a car seat, facing backwards," she said. "The pristine nursery. That's all quiet now. They're all using sound machines. They're not getting dirty. They're not outside in the dirt. They're not getting that normal chaos."

Banishing normal chaos from a child's world is precisely the opposite of what you would do if you wanted to produce an adult capable of enjoying life's intrinsic bittersweetness, the small pleasures you might never notice if your life were a theme park, all cotton-candy jingles and frictionless rides.[12] And yet, consider how we proceed. We beg doctors to give our kids antianxiety medications, teachers to give them untimed tests. We purchase plastic visors so bathwater never runs over our toddlers' eyes, and carefully remove sesame seeds from their hamburger buns.[13] We aren't just driving ourselves insane. We're making our kids more fearful and less tolerant of the world.

Bad Therapy Step Five: Monitor, Monitor, Monitor

In decades past, parents primarily fretted over *physical* dangers to kids: stranger danger, crossing the street, and the like. But as parenting took a therapeutic turn, and we began to worry about emotional damage, we realized we could *never* look away. After all, a kid who breaks an arm lets out a scream. But a child who's been traumatized by teasing makes no sound. We required much more intel, round the clock. We needed adult eyes on our kids: therapists, school psychologists, and counselors ready to conduct infrared thermal imaging of our kids' emotional lives. We expected them to monitor and report back to us.

"Kids today are always under the situation of an observer," said Peter Gray, a professor of psychology at Boston College and author of the classic introductory textbook on psychology. "At home, the parents are watching them. At school, they're being observed by teachers. Out of school, they're in adult-directed activities. They have almost no privacy."

It took only a moment's reflection to realize this was true and a dramatic departure from the experience of previous generations. At school, my kids have "recess monitors," teachers who involve themselves in every disagreement at playtime and warn kids whenever the monkey bars might be slick with rain. On the bus, "bus monitors." After school, so many kids I know head to scheduled activities—bouldering or ukulele or jiujitsu—presided over by an adult.

One might be inclined to think this an improvement over letting kids tromp around the world unsupervised. Adults generally model better behavior than kids do. Parents give better advice than friends. Teachers are likely to insist on fair rules and curb bullying. And *all of them* will ensure that no kids experiment sexually or with drugs. More monitoring is better, isn't it?

Actually, Gray said, adding monitoring to a child's life is functionally equivalent to adding anxiety. "When psychologists do research where they want to add an element of stress, and they want to compare people doing something under stress versus no stress, how do they add stress? They simply add an observer," Gray said. "If you're watched by somebody who seems to be assessing your performance, that's a stress condition."

In the last generation, we came to think of unsupervised time as dangerous—a host site for childhood trauma, bullying, and abuse. Better that a recess monitor establish clear rules for schoolyard kickball and insist that everyone play fairly than a kid ever feel left out. Better to hire bus monitors than risk some kid taking another's lunch money. Better that parents track their teens' whereabouts with an app than ever wonder where they are—or trust them to get home safely. But this incessant monitoring has infested childhood with stress.

True, teens can't engage in sexual activity if they're being watched. But they can't engage in intimacy, either, Gray pointed out. Put another way, a supervised "playdate" is no play at all—not if you're referring to the evolutionary activity that confers vast psychosocial benefits and teaches us to get along with other humans.

Real play, of the developmentally beneficial sort, involves risk, negotiation, and privacy from adults:[14] the fort or treehouse built to block adults' view. Instead, Gray warns, we are living through a "play deprivation experiment" in which teachers and parents and therapists endlessly instruct children on feelings and emotions—but rarely afford them the space or privacy to develop the capacities that are the subject of their endless preaching. "We have removed the things that are joyful to children, and we have substituted things that are anxiety-provoking, and they would be anxiety-provoking for you and me too," he said.

Things that are joyful to children: danger, discovery, dirt. Games whose rules they invented with that ridiculous cast of characters they call friends. Their hearts aren't fooled by Mom's carefully arranged simulacra: the hypoallergenic, nontoxic "slime" she begs all the kids to make with her from a kit that arrived from Amazon. *Isn't this fun? It's so gross! Right, girls?!* Harmless enough, but it doesn't help a kid blow off steam or test her limits or negotiate relationships with peers. It doesn't help her learn about herself and, in the process, discover what sorts of activities or people she might one day come to love.

Bad Therapy Step Six:
Dispense Diagnoses Liberally

Your five-year-old son wanders around his kindergarten classroom distracting other kids. The teacher complains: he can't sit through her scintillating lessons on the two sounds made by the letter *e*. When the teacher invites all the kids to sit with her on the rug for a song, he stares out the window, watching a squirrel dance along a branch. She'd like you to take him to be evaluated.

And so you do. It's a good school, and you want the teacher and the administration to like you. You take him to a pediatrician, who tells you it sounds like ADHD. You feel relief. At least you finally know what's wrong. Commence the interventions, which will transform your son into the attentive student the teacher wants him to be.

But obtaining a diagnosis for your kid is not a neutral act. It's not nothing for a kid to grow up believing there's something wrong with his brain. Even mental health professionals are more likely to interpret ordinary patient behavior as pathological if they are briefed on the patient's diagnosis.[15]

"A diagnosis is saying that a person does not only have a problem, but is sick," Dr. Linden said. "One of the side effects that we see is that people learn how difficult their situation is. They didn't think that before. It's demoralization."

Nor does our noble societal quest to destigmatize mental illness inoculate an adolescent against the determinism that befalls him—the awareness of a limitation—once the diagnosis is made. Even if Mom has dressed it in happy talk, he gets the gist. He's been pronounced learning disabled by an occupational therapist and neurodivergent by a neuropsychologist. He no longer has the option to stop being lazy. His sense of efficacy, diminished. A doctor's official pronouncement means he cannot improve his circumstances on his own. Only science can fix him.[16]

Identifying a significant problem is often the right thing to do. Friends who suffered with dyslexia for years have told me that discovering the name for their problem (and the corollary: that no, they weren't stupid) delivered cascading relief. But I've also talked to parents who went diagnosis shopping—in one case, for a perfectly normal preschooler who wouldn't listen to his mother. Sometimes, the boy would lash out or hit her. It took him forever to put on his shoes. Several neuropsychologists conducted evaluations and decided he was "within normal range." But the parents kept searching, believing there must be some name for the child's recalcitrance. They never suspected that, by purchasing a diagnosis, they might also be saddling their son with a new, negative understanding of himself.

Bad Therapy Step Seven: Drug 'Em

First comes diagnose, then comes medicate. But if Lexapro, Ritalin, and Adderall were the solution, the decline in youth mental health would have ended decades ago.[17]

Altering your child's brain chemistry is about as profound a decision as you'll ever make as a parent. But for many child psychiatrists and far too many pediatricians, it involves little more than a pro forma signature and tearing off a sheet gummed to a prescription pad.[18]

Steven Hollon holds a named professorship in psychology at Vanderbilt University, where he studies the etiology and treatment of depression. "You want to be very careful starting children and adolescents on antidepressants," he told me. He's even more adamant about antianxiety medicines like Xanax and Klonopin. "Anything that makes you feel better within thirty minutes is going to be at least psychologically and physiologically addictive, and it probably is going to be both."

I asked Hollon if, absent a severe psychological crisis, we should be interrupting adolescent development by introducing antidepressants. "Evolutionary biologists would say no. An evolutionary biologist would say it's part of life. You learn to deal with grief, you learn to deal with loss," he said. We need to develop those capacities for our own survival. "The things you can learn to do—sometimes they hurt a little bit, it's scary at times. But the things you can learn to do, you're better off learning to do those things than relying on a chemical substance."

With children and adolescents, there's far less proof of antidepressants' efficacy than for adult patients.[19] The evidence base is far smaller than it is for adults.[20] And kids are, by definition, a moving target, undergoing changes so rapidly that doctors run the risk of medicating for circumstances soon to be in the rearview mirror.

There are the meds' morbid side effects, imposed on a teen who is already struggling: weight gain, sleeplessness, diminished sex drive, nausea, fatigue, jitteriness, risk of addiction,[21] and, of course, a sometimes-brutal withdrawal.[22] Suicidality remains a side effect of antidepressants for reasons that are not well understood.[23]

But possibly the grimmest risk of antidepressants, antianxiety meds, and stimulants is the *primary* effect of the drugs themselves: placing a young person in a medicated state while he's still getting used to the feel and fit of his own skin. Making him feel less like himself, blocking him from ever feeling the thrill of unmediated cognitive sharpness, the sting of righteous fury, an animal urge to spot an opportunity—a romance, a position, a place on the team—and leap for it. Compelling him to play remote spectator in his own life.

Many adults, accustomed to popping a Xanax to get through a rough patch, are tempted to extend that same accommodation to their suffering teen. But the impact of starting a child on psychotropic medication is incomparably different. Every experience of a child's life—so many "firsts"—will now be mediated by this chemical chaperone: every triumph, every pang of desire and remorse. When you start a child on meds, you risk numbing him to life at the very moment he's learning to calibrate risks and handle life's ups and downs. When you anesthetize a child to the vicissitudes of success and failure and love and loss and disappointment when he's meeting these for the first time, you're depriving him of the emotional musculature he'll need as an adult. Once on meds, he's likely to believe that he can't handle life at full strength—and thanks to an adolescence spent on them, he may even be right.

If you can relieve your child's anxiety, depression, or hyperactivity without starting her on meds, it's worth turning your life upside down to do so. ·

Bad Therapy Step Eight: Encourage Kids to Share Their "Trauma"

"Really good trauma-informed work does not mean that you get people to talk about it," physician and mental health specialist Richard Byng told me. "Quite the opposite."

Byng helps ex-convicts in Plymouth, England, habituate to life on the outside. Many of these former prisoners endured unspeakable abuse as children and young adults. And yet, Byng says, the solution for them often includes *not* talking about their traumas.

One of the most significant failings of psychotherapy, Byng says, is its refusal to acknowledge that not everyone is helped by talking about their problems. Many patients, he says, are harmed by it.

"If you know that someone's been traumatized, what I tend to do is just acknowledge it very lightly," Byng told me. "Very lightly just acknowledge that, yeah, part of why you're like this is because some bad stuff's happened. And we'll put it aside. But I'm trying to talk about what's going on in the present."

Not every kid who's experienced serious adversity will be helped by "sharing" their traumas? The act of talking about your past pain does not necessarily relieve it? Discussing a traumatic experience, even with a trained therapist, can sometimes increase suffering? This is my shocked face.

Therapists would better serve patients if they adopted a humbler approach, Byng says—one that "acknowledges that some people don't want to talk about things. That acknowledges that some people will just need to go off and be on their own, but also that some need support and that it's hard to know what people need and what's going to be helpful."

But many teachers, counselors, and therapists today presume the opposite: *Kids cannot possibly get on with their lives until they have thoroughly examined and disgorged their pain.* In the Academy Award–winning film *Good Will Hunting*, the protagonist (played by Matt Damon) can escape his traumatic past and get the girl only after he has thoroughly explored his history of child abuse with his therapist (played by Robin Williams). In packed theaters across the country, hearts swelled, tears rained down, and the American mind renewed its faith in the curative miracle of talk therapy. Outside of Hollywood, rehashing sad memories often creates more problems than it solves.

There are therapies, like dialectical behavior therapy, that take a better approach than the model that insists that you can only be cured if you are compelled to "talk about it." This better approach, in Byng's view, involves "accepting you've been harmed and acknowledging that only you can make a difference," without pressing people to talk about their pain. But he admits "that's quite difficult to pull off."

And yet it's often what's best for patients. A dose of repression again appears to be a fairly useful psychological tool for getting on with life— even for the significantly traumatized among us.

Rarely do we grant kids that allowance. Instead, we demand that they locate any dark feelings and share them. We may already be seeing the fruits: a generation of kids who can never ignore any pain, no matter how trivial.

Bad Therapy Step Nine:
Encourage Young Adults to Break Contact with "Toxic" Family

Clinical psychologist and author Joshua Coleman has devoted his entire practice to a phenomenon known as "family estrangement": adult children cutting off their parents, refusing to speak to them, even barring them from seeing the grandkids. A large-scale national survey confirms a recent increase in this phenomenon: almost 30 percent of Americans eighteen and older had cut off a family member.[24]

Are the ostracized parents typically abusive? No, Coleman said; in general, he doesn't believe they are. From his own practice, Coleman has observed that adults who were abused as children very often blame themselves for the abuse. "Often, they're more interested in salvaging whatever they can of parental love."

So what gives? Why do so many young people today seem to have a hair-trigger for yeeting the 'rents? I don't care how annoying she is, you don't cancel Mom just because her needling gets under your skin. (You hang up on her, wait five minutes, call back, act as if nothing happened, and casually ask her to pick up your sons from soccer practice.)

When parents confront the adult children who've cut them off, Coleman tells me, the most typical explanation they give is: "'Well, my therapist said, you emotionally abused me or you're emotionally incestuous. Or you have a narcissistic personality disorder.' The parents, of course, respond defensively, and that just feels like proof positive to the adult child."

Coleman added, "I've wanted to write an article for the longest time with a title something like, 'Your Biggest Threat to Your Relationship with Your Child Isn't Parenting. It's the Therapist They're Going to See at Some Point.'"

One of the most damaging ideas to leach into the cultural bloodstream, according to Coleman, is that all unhappiness in adults is traceable to childhood trauma. Therapists have made endless mischief from this baseless and unfalsifiable assertion.

This is precisely how therapy often encourages young people to look at their lives. If your career isn't going well, if you're having trouble in relationships, if you're dissatisfied with your life, commence the hunt for hidden childhood traumas. And since parents are ultimately responsible for your childhood, any unearthed "childhood trauma" inevitably reads as an indictment of parents.

Family estrangement is a major iatrogenic risk of therapy not only because it typically produces so much desperate, chronic distraught to the cut-off parents. It also strips the adult child of a major source of stability and support—and for generations after. Estrangement means grandchildren raised without the benefit of loving grandparents who pick them up from school or temper their parents' foul moods. Worse, it leaves those grandkids with the impression that they descend from terrible people. People so twisted and irredeemable, Mom won't let them in the house. Even the homeless guy outside Walgreens gets a wave and a dollar every once and a while. But the people I come from? They must have done something unforgivable.

Children learn that all relationships are expendable—even within the parent-child dyad. Mom cut off her own parents. There's just no good reason to believe she wouldn't do the same to me if I did something to upset her, too.

Bad Therapy Step Ten:
Create Treatment Dependency

Therapists can do harm to someone's agency and belief in themselves, Dr. Byng told me. Treatment dependency is a common iatrogenic risk of therapy. "I think that's probably the simplest explanation of the problem: that we're just teaching people that they're not adequate humans."

A patient inducted into the habit of consulting with the therapist may become convinced she cannot *ever* act without the express approval of an authority figure. A young person trained by adults to seek approval before undertaking small risks won't feel capable of meeting the challenges we consider intrinsic to adulthood—making a new friend, grappling with a breakup, choosing a college major.

My friend Evelyn runs a major lab at one of America's premier biomedical research institutions. Each year for the last fifteen, she reviews hundreds of applicants to hire a select few recent college graduates for a year of research. The candidates hail from the nation's top universities, where they typically aced all of their premed requirements. Some have been published in academic journals. Suffice it to say, these kids are no slouches. Whatever the struggles of their generation, Evelyn's hires represent the crème de la crème of having their shit together.

Last year, when I called Evelyn for her birthday and mentioned the topic of my book, she grew suddenly animated. In the last decade, she's observed a marked change in young adults.

"They are very afraid. They're afraid to be wrong. They're afraid to crystallize an idea in the lab and then test it. They're afraid not to be 'amazing.'" She sounded frustrated. "It's almost like they'd rather not start than find out that they're not amazing. The amount of fear—" She stopped for a moment to consider her own, younger children. "That's what I don't want to raise."

I ask her how she knows it is *fear* that constrains them and not, say, inexperience or prudence. She knows it's fear, she says—because they tell her. "A huge percent of my mentorship conversations with them are about their psychological state and their experience in the lab and how they're doing emotionally." They regularly update her on their mental health, expecting she'll want to know. She does not know precisely how they came to this idea—that providing mental health updates is an important part of cellular research—but she's learned to roll with it.

When Evelyn was in high school, she was running her own experiments at the National Institute for Health, under the supervision of a cell biologist. Now, she can't get *college grads* with far better academic grounding to do the same. "They could do any research they wanted," she says. "I would love it if they would run their own experiments." Though they have the foundational scientific knowledge to succeed in medicine, she says, they lack all traces of gumption. Compared with the young people she hired a decade ago, "they have no agency," she says.

I can hear in her voice a surge of exasperation. "I said to one of them, 'Are you here to hand me the syringe of saline when I ask for it? Is that *really* what you want to be here for? You can have resources: go do some science.'"

She sounds harsh, but she really isn't. She's gentle and kind and nurturing. She absolutely loves to kindle scientific curiosity and is possessed of ample reserves of patience. She suggested to one intern that he design his own experiment and run it. His response? "'I'm working up to it. First, I want to get my skills together.' I mean, what's 'working up to it'?" she says. "*Six months later*, you're going to do an experiment?"

"It sounds as if they're childlike?" I venture.

"Yes!" she says. "They are 'in training.' They are 'getting ready.' They're saying 'I'm getting these skills. I'm going to launch—I promise,'" she says. "The level at which they are satisfied with what they are producing is very low." Meaning, they hold themselves to the standard of a much younger, much less accomplished student.

What Evelyn describes is precisely what "treatment dependency" looks like. Leery of trusting herself, a patient will develop an "external locus of control" and be reluctant to attempt the sort of reckless chance from which romantic adventure and professional success might otherwise be born.

Emotional Hypochondriacs

Bad therapy encourages hyperfocus on one's emotional states, which in turn makes symptoms worse. This reminded me of a few people I've encountered who seemed to suffer from hypochondriasis. The girl on the soccer team who almost never made it onto the field but was always nursing a mysterious sports injury, arriving at school with a soft cast or neck brace or crutches, tenderness no X-ray could explain. Or the young social justice activist I interviewed who was on disability and kept rescheduling our conversations for "migraines" or Lyme disease or a litany of other, always-changing frailties.

Was it possible that mental health experts were turning young people into emotional hypochondriacs? For that matter, what *is* hypochondriasis?

According to Arthur Barsky, Harvard Medical School psychiatry professor and world expert in hypochondriasis (now known as somatic symptom disorder or illness anxiety disorder), hypochondriasis is an anxiety disorder. Hypochondriacs have anxiety about their health and physical symptoms.

Hypochondriacs are not wimps, and they are not imagining their pain. But nor do they necessarily have *more* pain than other people. They are simply overly attentive to the normal pains we all feel.

"The hypochondriac interprets his normal bodily sensations unrealistically, believing they are a sign of disease,"[25] Barsky wrote in his book, *Worried Sick*. That hyperfocus—a kind of anxiety about the body—is enough to amplify physical symptoms.

"Women are terrified of breast cancer. They will examine their breast so frequently, that it starts to get tender. And they say, 'Well, Jesus! It must be inflamed,'" Barsky told me. "What they're doing is actually making it worse." The most effective treatments for hypochondriasis,

Dr. Barsky said, are behavioral modifications that force the sufferer to stop mentally and physically attending to her pain.

I asked Barsky which hypochondriacs are most resistant to treatment.

Those who have turned their distress into what he calls an "organizing principle." They join online groups devoted to their mysterious illnesses, stop going to work and rearrange their social lives as a shrine to their symptoms. They require nothing short of a rescue mission: something to shift their focus from themselves and tear them from this self-destructive mental loop.

Bad therapy does precisely the opposite. It engenders intensive focus on feelings, amplifies emotional dysregulation, increases a sense of hopelessness, of incapacity and a paralytic helplessness against a rising sea of feelings.

And far from confinement to the psychoanalyst's couch, bad therapy is today practiced on almost every kid—by therapists and just as often by nontherapists. The epicenter of bad therapy in your children's life is, most likely, their school.

Part II

Therapy Goes Airborne

I can't think of a content area that needs more social-emotional learning than mathematics.

—*Ricky Robertson, educational consultant*

Chapter 4

•

Social-Emotional Meddling

The first time anyone suggested my then seven-year-old daughter had "a lot of anxiety," I was not at the pediatrician, but at a parent-teacher conference. "She's looking at the clock a lot at the end of the day," the assistant teacher piped up. "She seems to have a lot of anxiety about missing the bus. We thought you should know."

It seems unlikely that any teacher a generation ago would have scrutinized a second grader's clock-checking at the end of a nine-hour school day, much less have sprung this banal observation like a magician's reveal, at parent-teacher conferences.

I knew that this was the first year my daughter was taking the bus without her older brothers, so there was no one to alert the driver if she failed to board on time. But also, her grandfather hates to be late; her father hates to be late; *I* hate to be late. Worrying over punctuality is very much within the norm of our family. And yet, a teacher who had met my daughter only a few months before informed me that this was grounds for concern, airily implying that I ought to get her tested.

Most American kids today are not in therapy. But the vast majority are in school, where therapists and non-therapists diagnose kids liberally. According to a survey of physicians in the Washington, DC, area, teachers were *most likely* to be the first to suggest an ADHD diagnosis in children.[1] Probably for this reason, one of the premier nonprofits devoted to adolescent mental health, the Child Mind Institute, provides an online "symptom checker" specifically to help a parent *or teacher* inform herself about "possible diagnoses."[2]

I began to wonder what else schools were doing in the name of improving kids' "mental health." I was in luck. Each year, the state of California sponsors a three-day public school teachers' conference to showcase its vast array of emotional and behavioral services. Immediately, I registered.

That is how, in July of 2022, I came to join more than two thousand public school teachers at the Anaheim Convention Center, right next to Disneyland.[3] Ankle tattoos winked over fresh pedicures, Anne Taylor cardigans abounded, and the occasional mohawk sliced indoor air cool enough to crisp celery.

We talked "brain science" based on a YouTube video many of us had seen.[4] It explained that the brain is like a hand, with the thumb folded into the palm. "Our amygdala is really important in serious situations," said the voiceover. This sounded right. We felt like neuroscientists.

We lamented the burdens placed upon school counselors, now part of an expanded psychology staff, which oversees every public school the way diversity officers dominate a university. We were leery of these new bosses, but we had to admit, they had a big job to do. Our kiddos were bonkers. (The word we were careful to use was "dysregulated.") Counselors now routinely monitored the social-emotional quality of our teaching, sniffed out emotional disturbance in our students, and decided what assignments to nix or grades to adjust upward.

We talked about the need to give kids "brain breaks," the salvific power of "Mindfulness Minutes," and the importance of ending each day with an "optimistic closure." Our purview was the "whole child," meaning we were expected to evaluate and track kids' "social and emotional" abilities in addition to academic ones. Our mandate: "trauma-informed education." We pledged to treat *every kid* as if she had experienced some debilitating trauma.

Subsequent interviews with dozens of teachers, school counselors, and parents across the country banished all doubt: Therapists weren't the only ones practicing bad therapy on kids. Bad therapy had gone airborne. For more than a decade, teachers, counselors, and school psychologists have all been playing shrink, introducing the iatrogenic risks of therapy to schoolkids, a vast and captive population.[5]

"Emotions Check-Ins": Constantly Taking Every Kid's Emotional Temperature

Forget the Pledge of Allegiance. Today's teachers are more likely to inaugurate the school day with an "emotions check-in."

Ask kids: "How are you feeling today? Are you daisy bright, happy and friendly?" school counselor Natalie Sedano advised our assembled conference room of teachers. "Or am I a ladybug? Will I fly away if we get too close?"

This prompted great excitement in the audience, and teachers jumped up to share their own "emotions check-ins." One teacher shared a wellness check-in she learned from a teacher training. Every day, she asks her kids if they feel it's a "bones" or "no bones" kind of a day, borrowing the verbiage from a viral TikTok video in which a pug owner shares the mood of his thirteen-year-old pug, Noodle. If Noodle sits upright, it's a bones day! If he collapses, it's a no-bones day.

"That is so fun!" Sedano enthused. "Love it! Thank you!"

No one betrayed a worry that having kids peg their day as "no bones" at the very start might tend to lock a kid into feeling it was a "bad day" all day long. (I tried to goad a few of my table companions to consider that maybe all this feelings focus was a little much; no dice.)

But I couldn't help remembering what I'd learned from Kennair and Linden. They would have said that this unceasing attention to feelings was likely to undermine kids' emotional stability.

If we wanted to *help* kids with emotional regulation, I asked Kennair, what would we communicate instead? "I think I'd say: worry less. Ruminate less," Kennair said. "Try to verbalize everything you feel *less*. Try to self-monitor and be mindful of everything you do—*less*."

But there's another problem posed by emotions check-ins: They tend to induce a *state orientation* in kids, potentially sabotaging kids' abilities to complete the tasks in front of them at school.[6]

"If you want to, let's say, climb a mountain, if you start asking yourself after two steps, 'How do I feel?,' you'll stay at the bottom," Linden said.

Many psychological studies back this up.[7] An individual is more likely to complete a difficult task if she adopts a *task orientation*—a focus on the job ahead. If she's thinking about herself, she's less likely to complete it.

We were only at the very beginning of the school day, and already things were looking grim. But I resolved to give these mental health experts a chance. After all, they were only trying to help.

The School Psychologist Would Love to Talk to You

Few schools today believe that they can get by without a full psych staff, typically comprising a school psychologist, team of school counselors, and handful of social workers. Student outbursts that might once have earned a kid detention, suspension, or a trip to the principal now prompt a scheduled visit with a counselor or school psychologist.

In 2022, California announced a plan to hire an additional ten thousand counselors in order to address young people's poor mental health.[8] A recent California bill, likely to pass, allocated $50 million for the hiring of additional squadrons of social workers and mental health professionals in public schools.[9] Meaning, however much in-school therapy kids have already received, they likely will soon be getting much more.

California school psychologist Michael Giambona provides individual therapy sessions to his middle school students during the school day. He also routinely runs interference with kids' teachers on kids' behalf.

"My teachers have special training in working with individuals with behavior needs and mental health needs," he told me. "So they know how to handle situations. And we meet weekly, and we talk about what's going on with each student and how we can approach them and support them when they need it."

That all sounded promising—adults trained to address kids' specific disorders and prepared to tailor the classroom experience accordingly.

But there's a problem with in-school therapy, an ethical compromise, which arguably corrupts its very heart. In a remarkably underregulated profession, therapists still have a few ethical bright lines. And among the clearest is—or was—the prohibition on "dual relationships."

As psychologist and author Lori Gottlieb explains, "The relationship in the therapy room needs to be its own, distinct and apart,"[10] she writes. "To avoid an ethical breach known as a dual relationship, I can't treat or receive treatment from any person in my orbit—not a parent of a kid in my son's class, not the sister of coworkers, not a friend's mom, not my neighbor."

This ethical guardrail exists to protect a patient from exploitation. A patient may reveal her deepest secrets and vulnerabilities to her therapist. Anyone possessing this much knowledge of a patient's private life may be tempted to exert undue power. And so the profession makes "dual relationships" off limits.

Except that school counselors, school psychologists, and social workers enjoy a dual relationship with every kid who comes to see them. They know all a kid's best friends; they may even treat a few of them with therapy. They know a kid's parents and their friends' parents. They know the boy a girl has a crush on, what romantically transpired between them, and how the relationship ended. They know a kid's teammates and coaches and the teacher who's giving him a hard time. And they report, not to a kid's parents, but to the school administration. It's a wonder we allow these in-school relationships at all.

The American Counseling Association appears to have noticed the obvious problem. In 2006, it revised the *ACA Code of Ethics.* While still prohibiting sexual relationships with *current* clients, it decided that "nonsexual" dual relationships were no longer prohibited—especially those that "could be beneficial to the client."[11]

As school counselors and psychologists came to see themselves as students' "advocates," they slipped into a dual relationship with their students: part therapist; part academic intermediary; part parenting coach.[12] Today, school counselors and psychologists commonly evaluate, diagnose, and treat students with individual therapy; meet with their friends; intervene with their teachers; and pass them in the lunchroom. A teen who has just spent a tear-soaked hour telling the school counselor her deepest secrets might reasonably be fearful of upsetting anyone with that much power over her life.

But are school counselors and social workers exerting undue influence over kids?

Over the past two years, so inundated have I been with parents' stories of school counselors encouraging a child to try on a variant gender identity, even changing the child's name without telling the parents, that I've almost wondered if there are *any* good school counselors. One parent I interviewed told me that her son's high school counselor had given him the address of a local LGBTQ youth shelter where he might seek asylum and attempt to legally liberate himself from loving parents.

There are good school counselors; I interviewed several. But the power structure's all wrong. Grant a leader the powers of a monarch, and he may gift his subjects freedom—but what's to tether him to his promises? That's placing a whole lot of trust in an individual counselor's conscience.

You might respond at this point: *Fortunately, my child has never been to see the school counselor.* But more likely, *you don't know.* In California, Illinois, Washington, Colorado, Florida, and Maryland, minors twelve or thirteen and up are statutorily entitled to access mental health care without parental permission. Schools are not only under no obligation to inform parents that their kids are meeting regularly with a school counselor, they may even be barred from doing so.[13]

As long as a parent has not specifically forbidden it, a school counselor may be able to conduct a therapy session with a minor child without parental consent.[14] School counselors are encouraged to make "judgment calls" about what information, gleaned in sessions with minor children, they may keep secret from the children's parents.[15]

Even in states that require parents to be notified of their kids' in-school therapy, school social workers remain free to meet informally with a child and inquire about her sexual orientation, gender identity, or parents' divorce; such conversations often do not count as "therapy."[16]

The Group Therapy Behemoth: Social-Emotional Learning

Ever since her school adopted social-emotional learning in 2021, Ms. Julie[17] routinely began the day by directing her Salt Lake City fifth graders to sit in one of the plastic chairs she'd arranged in a circle. *How is each of you feeling this morning?* she would ask, performing a more intensive version of the "emotions check-in." One day, she cut to the chase: *What is something that is making you really sad right now?*

When it was his turn to speak, one boy began mumbling about his father's new girlfriend. Then things fell apart. "All of a sudden, he just started bawling. And he was like, 'I think that my dad hates me. And he yells at me all the time,'" said Laura, a mom of one of the other students.

Another girl announced her parents had divorced and burst into tears.

Another said she was worried about the man her mother was dating.

Within minutes, half of the kids were sobbing. It was time for the math lesson; no one wanted to do it. It was just so sad, thinking that the boy's dad hated him. What if their dads hated them, too?

"It just kind of set the tone for the rest of the day," Laura said. "Everyone just was feeling really sad and down for a really long time. It was hard for them to kind of come out of that."

A second mom at the school confirmed to me that word spread throughout the school about the AA meeting–style breakdown. Except that this AA meeting featured elementary school kids who then ran to tell their friends what everyone else had shared.

Thanks to social-emotional learning, scenes of emotional melee have become increasingly common in American classrooms. In 2013, the *New York Times* reported on a near identical scene that took place after a California teacher conducted a similar social-emotional learning session with his kindergarteners.[18]

"With children especially, whatever you focus on is what will grow," Laura said. "And I feel like with [social-emotional learning], they're watering the weeds, instead of watering the flowers."

Advocates of social-emotional learning claim that nearly all kids today have suffered serious traumatic experiences that leave them unable to learn. They also insist that having an educator host a class-wide trauma swap before lunch will help such kids heal. Neither claim is well-founded.

But the predictable result is precisely what Ms. Julie saw: otherwise happy kids are brought low and a child seriously struggling has his private pain publicly exposed by someone in no position to remedy it.

When I first heard the term "social-emotional learning," I assumed a hokey but necessary call for kids to get a grip. Or maybe it was the new name for what they used to call "character education": treat people kindly, disagree respectfully, don't be a jackass. Proponents insist it arrives at those things, albeit through the somewhat circuitous route of mental health.

Sometimes described by enthusiasts as "a way of life,"[19] social-emotional learning is the curricular juggernaut that devours *billions* in education spending each year and upward of 8 percent of teacher time.[20] (Many teachers say they try to ensure that social-emotional learning happens *all day long*.)[21] Through prompts and exercises, social-emotional learning (SEL) pushes kids toward a series of personal reflections, aimed at teaching them "self-awareness," "social awareness," "relationship skills," "self-management," and "responsible decision-making."[22] (At least one variant, "transformative SEL," embeds kids' soul-searching in straight-up Marxism, according to a bracingly honest admission by a California town's department of education.[23])

Seventh-grade teacher Kendria Jones's "deep commitment" to social-emotional learning means sharing her own upbringing at the hands of a drug-addicted mother.[24] She tells her eleven- and twelve-year-old students what it's like to be a single mom after the death of her son's father. "I'm very vulnerable with them," she told *Education Week*.

Interestingly, were Jones an actual therapist, such self-disclosure would be considered unethical. Anytime a therapist might be inclined to share her personal history in order to gratify her own need, she must abstain in order to prioritize the client's needs.[25] And here's where things get tricky: teachers aren't actually trained in psychotherapy, and they aren't bound by its ethical guidelines, either. Setting up an "emotional sharing" session may sound good, but typically, therapists perform this function under ethical guidelines so that they don't inadvertently exploit or betray their patients.

Sometimes when a kid plunks himself down on the rug for morning circle, he is in no mood to exhibit a painful experience no matter how much it might expand the class's emotional horizons to hear that Austin walked in on his parents having sex. This leaves teacher-therapists with a problem: How to get kids to dish about their emotional lives when they don't want to?

One presenter at the conference, Amelia Azzam, a regional mental health coordinator for Orange County Public Schools, told a story that seemed to answer this quandary. She knew of a teaching assistant who trailed a seventh grader to lunch. She "goes out to lunch where this young student sits, and she always says 'hi' to him. And she has casual interactions with him." And one day, he told her that his dad was getting out of jail. "Nobody else knew that," Azzam said.

Good therapists know that it may be counterproductive to push a kid to share his trauma at school. Good therapists are trained specifically to avoid encouraging rumination. But school staff who play therapist rarely seem aware that they might be encouraging rumination as they stalk a kid at lunch, waiting to see if he'll open up about his father's incarceration minutes before a history test.

"Sometimes people who don't talk, who don't share—that's not resilience," educational consultant Ricky Robertson told the audience of teachers. "That's emotional amputation."

Sarah: School Staff That Play Therapist with My Kids Are Playing with Fire

Sarah is a teacher married to a doctor, raising three kids she and her wife adopted out of foster care. All three kids suffered sexual and physical abuse before the state removed them from the home of their biological mother. Each has a significant learning disability.

One of their daughter's first memories is of eating kitty litter from the box. Describing what he saw when he removed the kids from their biological parents' home, "the detective cried on the stand," Sarah told me.

Sarah and her wife pay for qualified therapists to work with each kid on an ongoing basis. A source of constant heartache to Sarah is that she must send them to public school, where so many teachers and counselors are eager to play amateur therapist.

"My kids don't need to be ashamed about their background. They didn't do anything wrong," she said, her voice like an overtightened guitar string. But teachers who engage kids in social-emotional lessons "don't understand the ramifications of the words that they use that can make a child feel less than, in just a simple assignment, whether it's social-emotional or not. By trying to do the right thing, they actually hurt my kid."

"How do they hurt your kid?"

"Because they don't understand the gravity of what her situation is."

When teachers casually pry into Sarah's kids' past pain for the benefit of class "unity" and empathy development, it puts at risk all the work her children have done in actual therapy to cope with the memories of their early childhood and cordon them off, for the length of a school day. "It's not right," Sarah said, referring to teachers' constant invitations that kids share their traumatic experiences.

To justify the need for this "trauma-informed care"—and the full-court press to persuade kids to divulge their traumas—several educators offered me the example of a student whose father died that morning. Would that be a good day to insist that Hayley take her algebra test? No, it would not. The only way for a teacher to know whether to postpone the algebra test is by prompting an entire class of kids to take turns sharing their trauma.

One wonders how educators get away with a pretext so transparent. But succeed they do. For more than a decade, they have been quietly increasing and expanding their interventions, transforming every school into an outpatient mental health clinic, staffed largely by those with no real training in mental health.

I asked Christine, a public school teacher and administrator for two decades in Oregon, why teachers are being told to assume that on any given day, one of their students may have suffered a catastrophic loss. Wouldn't that be a little like greeting each kid, every morning, with an armful of bandages—assuming one of them had just survived a head-on collision?

"Oh, no, you're preaching to the choir," Christine said. "I think you should recognize kids come in from different places, and they may have had an argument with their parents before school. But that doesn't invalidate their opportunity to learn."

In a prior era, educators widely believed that the *best* thing you could do for a disadvantaged kid was to maintain high expectations for his conduct. Teach him that whatever chaos exists at home does not diminish the order that the grown-ups will establish at school. Encourage him to take refuge in the reliable expectations with which his teacher will greet him each day. And—especially when he has given you *no* indication that he needs any special exception made for him—do him the honor of assuming he's capable of delivering.

For those ticking off bad therapy steps, schools are racking up quite a few: inducing state orientation with emotions check-ins. Encouraging kids to focus on their feelings, which can cause bad feelings to perseverate. Treating kids with in-school therapy, which can introduce all kinds of iatrogenesis, especially where it does not abide an ethical "dual relationship" boundary.

It gets worse from there.

Social-Emotional Learning: Teaching Resilience by Treating Every Kid as Irreparably Broken

Social-emotional exercises typically invite kids to marinate in a time when they were sad, scared, or vulnerable. One of the most popular social-emotional curricula, Second Step, for instance, instructs eighth graders to divulge the following:

- "Have you ever stayed overnight in the hospital?"

- "Has someone close to you died?"

- "Have you ever lost a championship game or important competition?"

- "Do you attend religious services?"

- "Have you ever worried about the safety of a loved one?"

- "Have you ever been really embarrassed?"

- "Have you ever changed schools?"

- "Have you ever been teased?"[26]

Lest you think that teachers might be sated with a simple "yes or no," the exercise directs: "For every 'yes' answer, follow up with the question 'What was/is it like?'" *How did it make you feel?*

Although kids are asked to involve their parents in the assignment, many parents would naturally respond: *Why on earth is this the school's business?* Parents know that many school employees are mandatory reporters, for whom Child Services is but a phone call away. It's reasonable to assume that some parents will refuse to help, and the kid will complete the assignment on her own.

Whatever children divulge, teachers can easily store. Companies like Panorama Education provide the software that allows teachers to record their own observations of students' social and emotional capacities and whatever they may have learned from the regular, unofficial group therapy sessions. In this way, an incident once confessed may follow a child for the rest of her academic life. As in, *"I'm just meeting you now, in the eleventh grade, but it says here—" [click, click] "you and a cousin engaged in inappropriate touching in kindergarten. Would you like to talk about it?"*

SEL Should Be the Goal of Every Class—Yes, Even Math Class

Kids cannot possibly learn until their social-emotional needs are met. And kids' social-emotional needs clearly are *not* being met. Ergo, "social-emotional" learning must be injected into every single subject.[27]

Giambona recited the theory for me, which was becoming increasingly familiar: If these kids are having panic attacks in class, they can't learn. "It doesn't matter if you're teaching them great writing skills or you're teaching them about World War II—they're not going to access it," he said.

True, if a kid's mid-emotional meltdown, it may be hard for him to concentrate on algebra. But for all emotional vicissitudes that don't quite reach fugue state, couldn't *To Kill a Mockingbird* provide a worthy distraction?

Social-emotional learning enthusiasts happily disrupt math or English or history because, to the true believers, education is merely a vehicle for their social-emotional lessons—the corn chip that carries the guac straight to a kid's mouth. "I can't think of a content area that needs more social-emotional learning than mathematics," Robertson told our assembled conference room.

But how would a teacher manage to make social-emotional learning the goal of a math class? To discover the answer, I sat through a presentation titled "Embedding SEL in Math."

Our mock lesson commenced with—you guessed it—discussion of our feelings about math. "Anxiety!" more than one teacher volunteered. The presenters showed us a series of kindergarten-level "math problems" that prompted us to look at a bunch of shapes and asked: "Which one doesn't belong?" At the end, they revealed the correct answer: *They all belong. No wrong answers! Everyone wins!* See, that wasn't hard.

I began to wonder whether this wasn't some sort of ploy by the Chinese Communist Party to obliterate American mathematical competence. I turned to the high school math teacher next to me and asked her how she could possibly incorporate this sort of approach into Algebra II. She stared back at me, a frozen rictus pinned to the corners of her mouth. She seemed to think Big Brother was watching us.

The only feeling apparently never affirmed in social-emotional learning is mistrust of emotional conversation in place of learning. A decent number of kids actually show up hoping to learn some geometry and not burn their limited instructional time on conversations about their mental health with the math teacher. But from every angle, such children could only be made to feel errant and alone.

In the minds of social-emotional learning advocates, healthy kids are those who share their pain during geometry. That is how a teacher knows they are emotionally regulated. They are willing to cry for the benefit of the class.

Teaching Kids How to Be a Friend (and Other Useless Meddling)

Many social-emotional lessons purport to teach kids how to be friends. One lesson for fourth graders includes tips for parents: "Talk with your child about your views on friendship."[28] And "If your child has a fight with a friend or claims not to like a friend anymore, discuss what happened." The authors may think kids are basket cases, but they believe parents are imbeciles.

The materials even include a script for parents to offer their kids. "Say: 'I'm sorry. Will you be my friend again?' Say: 'I really like you and want you to be my friend again.' Say, 'I'm sorry your feelings were hurt.'"

The problem? It's not at all clear that making friends is the kind of skill human beings *can* learn from a lecture or handout.

"There's at least two different brain systems for learning," Georgetown University psychologist and neuroscientist Abigail Marsh told me. "There's semantic learning, for example, learning information out of books that then becomes part of your sort of explicit memory." The study of, say, the American Civil War is a good example of this kind of learning—best done through reading about it (not starting one).

Explicit and implicit learning represent different neural processes.[29] Explicit or semantic learning works for applying the quadratic equation: it is *intentional*, rules-based, requires conscious effort to master, and it typically fades if it is not routinely engaged or tested.[30]

Implicit learning involves different neural processes and is acquired principally by *doing*: zipping up your pants or buttoning them, hitting a ball, and brushing your teeth are of this sort. They aren't typically learned through a book, the memory of how to do them stays with us even without testing, and when we perform them, we don't consult the steps involved at all.

Long before human beings could solve the quadratic equation, the survival of our species has depended on our being awfully good at forming friendships. Parents may have provided a small amount of guidance, often in the form of morality tales—just as schools once did, long before educators thought friendship-making required a poky lady at the front of the class pushing a social-emotional curriculum.

Kids of every previous generation made friends without explicit instruction. Why does this area of a child's life suddenly require the oversight of the school counselor? Interpersonal skills are principally acquired through the real-life theater of trial and error, Kennair told me. Emotional regulation is learned that way, too. You get a bad grade on a test. You throw a fit and cry. Classmates shoot you weird looks and shy away from you. The next time, you study harder, or learn to take the disappointment in stride.

You can't learn emotional regulation from a lecture, Kennair said. You learn how to handle the disappointment of not making the basketball team by *not making the basketball team*. Not from classroom instruction.

Social-emotional learning exercises often assume that by discussing a hypothetical disappointment, kids can skip the painful experience and arrive straight at maturity and social competence. But there is no way to gain friendship skills except by attempting to make a friend. There is no real way to learn to overcome failure except by struggling and, eventually, managing to do it.

A Sneak Attack on Parental Authority

One social-emotional learning lesson makes plain what so many others merely imply: *Teens should spy on their parents and report back to their teachers.* No, really.

In a Second Step exercise titled "Homework: I Spy . . ." seventh graders are encouraged to play a game that might as well be called *Hero of the Soviet Union.* "You are a private investigator," it prompts. "You have been hired by an unnamed source to 'spy' on your family. The source wants to find out all the various feelings that one or more of your family members have while doing activities at home. You won't be able to talk to your family (you don't want to blow your cover!) so you'll have to use your keen skills of observation."[31]

Go ahead, rub your eyes and read that one again.

The exercise continues: "Start with one person. Write down what you observe about his or her facial expressions, body language, tone of voice, and what he or she says. Then guess based on these clues what he or she might have been feeling. Then try the same activity with another family member."

But the writers of Second Step were not born yesterday. Think they'd just leave this smoking gun lying around for any skeptical journalist to expose? The exercise concludes, rather coyly: "When you've completed the sheet, show it to an adult in your family and see if he or she can guess who you were spying on."

Like any seventh grader is dumb enough to tell mom he was spying on her, writing down her private comments for the benefit of the school counselor. That would only lead to a "disagreement with an adult family member," which the materials ask kids to report on in the very next lesson.[32]

Many of the social-emotional exercises ask students to consider typical conflicts they might have with their own parents. In one example, the father of an eighth grader, Willa, "has a rule that he needs to know where she is and that she has to ask permission before she goes anywhere. Willa thinks that since she's in eighth grade, she doesn't have to do this anymore. Her dad should trust her more."[33]

There's a lesson in which Mom and Grandma disagree on how much screen time a child should get,[34] a lesson in which an "adult director" of an after-school activity (an obvious stand-in for Mom) insists that a child complete homework before joining the fun,[35] and a lesson in which a mom insists that her teen daughter may not wear jeans to a wedding.[36]

Kids are encouraged to dish about their families, evaluate the parent's rule in each case, and pass judgment on its reasonableness. The school counselor floats above it all like a high priestess and asks, in so many ways: *How does that make you feel? Do we think parents are right in this instance?*

The best "social-emotional" result, we're told, is a compromise, the "win-win" scenario in which parent and teen each meet the other halfway: *How about jeans and a fancy top?* Rarely, if ever, do the lessons contemplate that a parent's rule should simply be followed. The conceit is that parents and children exist on equal footing (though, of course, the school counselor presides over both).

Never do the materials seem to consider that undermining a child's relationship even with imperfect parents creates psychological damage all its own. How is a child supposed to feel secure after you've undermined her faith that her parents know what's best or have her best interests at heart?

The casual denigration of parents to their children turns out to be a signal feature of social-emotional learning. Mom and Dad are only "caregivers," service providers, and incompetent[37] ones at that, who might even be harmful to their kids' mental health. They present the obstacles to children's flourishing, like "parent negativity."[38] "Yet parents and caregivers with positive intentions don't always know where to start—or how to help—when it comes to social-emotional learning," notes Panorama Education.

This isn't merely teachers' lounge banter, public servants blowing off steam while abusing the communal microwave with a Tupperware of tuna casserole. It's why they're always sending out "tips" to parents on how to talk to our kids about the news or even life events. It's the reason they've created an entire social-emotional "at home" lessons component—for parents to practice with kids. All predicated on the belief, to borrow the language of one lesson, that parents are often "roadblocks" to kids' flourishing.[39]

A Second Step exercise for middle schoolers, for instance, includes this example: "Vera wants to join an elite superpower squad." Can you identify roadblocks she might face? "Internal roadblocks" include "self-doubt." "External roadblocks" include "other students say she's not good enough" and "my parents tell me I can't practice at home."[40]

Likely for this reason, schools have increasingly encircled themselves in a zone of secrecy. Try asking your kid's school for their social-emotional workbook; notice how hard it is to obtain a copy of one. One teacher told me that counselors at her middle school were encouraging kids to stop by the counseling center for informal therapy sessions never logged or reported to parents.

I asked Elizabeth, a middle school science teacher in Grants Pass, Oregon, whether she had ever seen teachers or counselors report loving, good parents to social services based on social-emotional discussions with kids? "Yes," she said, without hesitation. "Counselors do. Administrators do."

Social-emotional learning turns out to be a lot like the Holy Roman Empire. Neither social, nor good for emotional health, nor something that can be learned. It seemed certain that schools would continue teaching it for decades.

I thought back to the wrenching scene from Ms. Julie's class and the boy who headed home that day, excruciatingly exposed. Perhaps kids treated him with sympathy or even pity after that. But is that what he wanted?

Social-emotional learning enthusiasts would argue that the entire class benefited from the hands-on lesson in sensitivity and kindness. But notice what else happened that day: in the name of "social-emotional learning," educators took the boy's private pain and repurposed it as a "teachable moment."

I wondered when it would occur to that boy, if it hadn't already, that he had been used.

Chapter 5

•

The Schools Are
Filled with Shadows

When my twin sons were in the fifth grade, one came home from school with an announcement: "Mr. Bryan hates me."

"Who?"

"The assistant teacher. He only cares about Isaac. If *Isaac* raises his hand, Mr. Bryan tells the teacher to call on him. If *Isaac* has a question, he answers it. If *I* have a question, Mr. Bryan just completely ignores me."

Although the school had sent out lists of the assistant teachers, I'd never heard of "Mr. Bryan." I assured my son that there was no way an assistant teacher cared only about one student. He must be imagining things.

But my son hadn't had a bad interaction with an assistant teacher. He'd seen a shadow. Our school was full of them.

In private schools, they are called "shadows," but in public schools you'll hear them called "ed techs," "paraprofessionals," or "parapros." Part body man, part special ed teacher, shadows are hired privately by parents or supplied by public schools to stick closely to one particular kid, ostensibly to smooth the kid's acclimation to class.[1]

More than a decade ago, shadows made it mercifully possible for kids with autism or severe learning disabilities to remain in a classroom with neurotypical kids and avoid the stigma of being sent out to "Special Ed."[2] They still do this—only they now provide the service to children with a far broader set of behavioral needs.

Today, public schools assign shadows to follow kids with problems ranging from mild learning disabilities to violent tendencies, and private schools advise affluent parents to hire shadows to trail neurotypical kids for almost any reason. To help a kid make friends on the playground, to soothe a kid wriggling in his seat, to help a kid *succeed* and have fun at school. *Do you think now might be a good time to raise your hand? Why don't you share your snack with Paige? How about complimenting Ella's doll? That's enough hugging—Sebastian might not like to be touched.*

More monitoring, more dependence on an adult, less practice handling themselves, less inducement to believe that they *can*. But is there also less stigma? While a lot of teachers gaslight the class about which adult is a kid's "shadow" (*Mr. Bryan is our new assistant teacher!*), many of the elementary school kids I talked to seem to figure it out anyway. He's the guy in the *Star Trek* T-shirt loping behind Brayden on the way to the monkey bars.

If hiring an actual shadow exceeds your school's budget, the school psychologist will often recommend handing a kid a fidget toy as an alternative means of soothing him. The theory apparently proceeds as follows: *All kids possess a finite number of fidgets. If a kid has a surplus, he can siphon some with a toy, leaving him with a smaller, more manageable quantity of fidgets.*

That killer reasoning notwithstanding, I needed to see these things for myself. I bought about a dozen and piled them on my desk or affixed them to my desk chair. The prickly inflated rubber seat cushion that allows a squirmy kid to bounce in place. The giant rubber band that straps onto chair legs—sort of a mouth harp for your feet. The fluorescent accordion tubes that let out a hilarious groan when you expand and contract them. The cubes with clickers and buttons on each side, to depress and roll, and flip back and forth. The rubbery prickle balls that look like sea anemones. The Gumby fingers, if Gumby had had fingers and not merely green paddles.

"You're doing it all wrong," my son said when he saw me turning these over on my desk, depressing the buttons and moving the levers a few at a time. "You're using it like a middle-aged woman."

I asked him to show me how the kids use them in class. He took the dodecahedron and began to rub it manically, turning it over, his head leaning over the project as if it were powered by his concentration. He looked like a boy participating in one of those Rubik's Cube competitions, where geniuses from Asia spin the jumbled cube together in a matter of seconds.

How does anyone pay attention in this environment? I asked my kids.

Stupid question. They don't.

When researchers put fidget toys to the test to see whether they improved attention in kids, they found that when fidget spinners were used, there was an initial decrease in activity level, followed by *poorer attention overall* for the kids who used them.[3] Dr. Ortiz summarized the findings for me: "Probably a waste of money, and maybe the effect is the exact opposite of what adults are looking for."

It felt as though we'd hit upon a theme for many of the mental health accommodations at school: unhelpful at best; destructive at worst. And now, thanks to experts, ubiquitous.

Accommodation and Avoidance

The theory of academic accommodation is simple and humane: Does it really make sense to require a kid with dyslexia to complete the verbal section of an SAT exam in the same time as a kid without dyslexia? Or, worse, to hold him back when he fails to meet grade-level expectations for reading comprehension?

Those exigencies once formed the bulk of academic accommodations. They are now the tail on the elephant.[4] School counselors—students' in-school "advocates"—lobby teachers to excuse lateness or absence, forgive missed classwork, allow a student to take walks around the school in the middle of class, ratchet grades upward, reduce or eliminate homework requirements, offer oral exams in place of written ones, and provide preferential seating to students who lack even an official diagnosis.

Sheryl, a high school English teacher in the Wisconsin public school system, told me that she is no longer permitted to lower a student's grade for handing in an assignment late. Her principal requires her to accept any homework from students, as long as it's submitted by the end of the semester—and sometimes, by the end of the year. "I had a multitude of kids trying to turn in 18 weeks' worth of work right before the semester ended," she said.

But doesn't that create an unconscionable pileup of work for a teacher to grade? Yes, it does. She once dreamed of becoming a teacher. Now, at thirty-one, she's already making plans to quit.

The psychological justifications for requesting these accommodations are often vague. "'I was having a rough day and dealing with my gender identity'—this happens all the time," said David, a public high school orchestra teacher, explaining how accommodations have been abused. A quick meeting with a counselor is sufficient to purchase two extra weeks to hand in an assignment or obtain any other academic dispensation.

David is a handsome thirtysomething, earnest and excitable as a youth pastor. His hair is high-and-tight auburn, with a neatly trimmed beard to match. He speaks openly of his own closeted confusion as a gay high school student. But he's very grateful that his teachers never allowed his emotional turmoil to become an excuse for failing to master the violin.

Lowering expectations for perfectly able kids who claim vague mental distress, he says, is doing them harm. "One of my seniors, she'll come in, like, 'I just can't play today. I'm having a really tough, tough Mental Health Day.' And I mean, if I had said that to any of my orchestra directors, it would have been like, 'I'm sorry, get your instrument. We're having rehearsal. I'm sorry that you're having an issue right now. The violin, or viola, or whatever you play will help you.'"

David believes helping his students perfect an instrument is far better for their sense of well-being and their feeling of accomplishment than whatever else might be achieved by allowing them to avoid hard work. But once a school counselor gets involved, he says, any "accommodation" demanded, no matter how unreasonable or unnecessary, becomes nearly impossible for a teacher to oppose.

On the advice of her son's high school counselor, Angela, a member of a television production crew, let her highly intelligent but anxious son, Jayden, obtain an accommodation so that he could take untimed tests for his last three years of high school. The counselor was kind and Jayden seemed to need the extra time for math tests. But instead of spurring him to work harder, or easing his emotional burden, the accommodation seemed to erode his will to try.

"I really regret it because he used it as a crutch. Like, 'Oh, I can't turn the paper in on time because I have a 504 [right to accommodation for a disability],'" Angela said. "We thought we were helping, and I realized all these things are not helpful."

Restorative Justice: A Friendly Powwow with the School Bully

In 2021, Stephanie's twelve-year-old son, Oscar, began seventh grade at 75 Morton, a Manhattan public middle school that turned out to be a lot like juvie. Oscar avoided drinking water during the day; he was terrified of the bathroom. "Guys would go into the bathroom and have fights and write all kinds of nasty stuff on the bathrooms," Stephanie told me. "There was poop on the floor."

School violence erupted so often that year that the students started a Snapchat group named "75 Morton Fights" to catalogue the brawls.[5]

"There were these really violent fights. I'm not talking about girls slapping another girl. I'm talking about three girls grabbing another girl by the hair, pulling her down on the ground, kicking her in the head and the ribs and face-punching," she said.

One boy slammed Oscar's head with a metal locker door three times. The third time, it cut his cheek. Had the wound been a centimeter north, he might have lost use of his eye.

None of Oscar's bullies was even suspended, according to Stephanie, and by then I knew why: "restorative justice."[6]

In 2014, President Obama issued a Dear Colleague Letter threatening schools with loss of funding if they continued to suspend and expel a disproportionate number of minority kids. This presented schools with a quandary: How do you maintain order without punishment? The Dear Colleague Letter spelled out the solution: "restorative practices, counseling, and structured systems of positive interventions."[7] Violent kids were rebranded as kids in pain. Schools stopped suspending or expelling them. And a newly invigorated era of mental health in public schools was born.

"Restorative justice" is the official name for schools' therapeutic approach that reimagines all bad behavior as a cry for help. Its central practice is the restorative circle, a ritual of obscure Native American origin in which a teacher directs students in conflict to sit in a circle of their peers and take turns sharing their pain. To signify whose turn it is to talk, they pass around a "talking piece" or totem, which consists of anything from a gemstone to a popsicle stick with googly eyes. (So much for the reverent tribute to Native Americans.)

Because this is quasi-therapy, teachers often explicitly call for secrecy from those "outside the circle" (i.e., parents). "What is shared in a circle stays in a circle," one teacher advises others to tell their students, on the education blog *Edutopia*. "There is no sharing beyond the classroom of anybody else's story. Protect each other's story."[8]

But what if actual bullying occurs? What if one kid slams another kid's head repeatedly into a locker? Bully and victim are brought together in a restorative circle to confront each other and share their pain for the benefit of the class.

California public elementary school teacher Ray Shelton believes restorative circles are abusive. "It puts a lot of the responsibility on the victim. Because they have to face the person who hurt them and talk with them and deal with them when they may not want to," he said. "It just revictimizes them, you know?" The offender is compelled to apologize in front of the class. But the victim is pressed not only to accept the apology but to offer one of her own—for whatever she may have done to provoke her attacker.

Worst of all, it does not seem to curb violence. In 2021, a six-foot-tall seventh grader in Chattanooga threw another kid through a plate-glass window and received only an in-school suspension—"essentially a time-out," according to Rhyen Staley, who was then a middle school teacher at the school. Later that year, the student threatened to stab another kid and was only, finally, suspended after screaming repeatedly at another seventh grader that he was going to "fucking kill her."

Several teachers told me that thanks to restorative justice, public schools no longer hold back or expel kids in any but the most extreme circumstances. Until they commit egregious acts of criminality, violent kids are kept in school and assigned shadows, under the therapeutic ethos: *treat*, don't punish. Nikolas Cruz, a student at Marjory Stoneman Douglas High School, had committed violent and menacing acts for years. He was assigned a shadow—his mom.[9] "The Parkland shooter" later took seventeen lives.

Every teacher I spoke to confirmed that the approach is failing. Therapeutic techniques are no substitute for a system that punishes violence.

"The problem is people are afraid to speak out against it, especially those on the inside," Staley said. "One, because they take it on faith that it's going to work, they just need to give it more time. And then the other thing is, they're afraid to lose their jobs by speaking out against it." Staley told me he has left teaching, partially in response to the chaos he was forced to mutely observe.

A RAND meta-analysis showed that schools that implemented restorative justice fell apart. At the middle school level, academic outcomes worsened in schools with restorative practices. There was no reduction in incidents of violence or weapons violations, no fewer suspensions for male students, nor even reduction in arrests at these schools. "This, of course, raises the question of whether restorative practices can be effective in curbing the most violent behavior, at least within a two-year implementation period," the authors wrote.[10] A question the terror-stricken, nonviolent students at school would presumably like to see answered.

"Restorative justice destroys and ruins schools," Wisconsin middle school teacher Daniel Buck told me. "Because if kids know that they can get away with something without a consequence, they're going to do it."[11]

Delinquency is up. Chaos reigns. The system that elevated emotional harm to physical harm wound up excusing physical harm in the name of emotional well-being.

Therapeutic Anarchy

Kelly spent seven years as a public middle and high school counselor in upstate New York until 2021, when she decided she couldn't take the bedlam anymore. Students slammed doors in her face and catcalled her in the hallways. Students walked out of class to roam the school whenever the mood struck. Provided they claimed their mental health required this, all disruptive behavior was excused or explicitly welcomed.

Kelly protested, but as she soon learned, she was an outlier. Academic accommodations like "anytime passes" allowed any student claiming to be "in crisis" to trade class for a session with the counselor. Students exploited a system that seemed to regard them as incapacitated. "They would use it during their least favorite class," Kelly said.

Schools across the country are reporting far worse behavioral outbreaks in recent years. "Ask anyone who has worked in some of America's failing public schools and nearly all of them will tell you the same thing: The biggest problem isn't the quality of the teachers," one teacher wrote in the *New York Post* in 2018. "It's the behavior of the kids: angry, disruptive, disrespectful kids whose behavior is out of control."[12] Every public school teacher I interviewed said the same: kids' behavior has deteriorated over the last decade.

Christine, who oversees social-emotional programming in high schools in Oregon, said that rates of student dysregulation have exploded since at least 2016. "Kids having utter meltdowns, tantrums, screaming, yelling, throwing things, crying, threatening to kill themselves, cursing at teachers, just general bad behavior," she recounted.

Teachers I talked to all noted a rise in tantrums, violence, screaming in a teacher's face, throwing objects around the classroom, slamming doors, catcalling, all in the last decade. Kids seem to exercise no control over their behavior, teachers told me. And a large part of the problem, they said, is a school regime that demands no self-discipline from students, believing such expectation unreasonable if not unevolved.

"If I stop them and try to correct some intonation, they'll just throw the bow on the ground as a fourteen- or fifteen-year-old having a temper tantrum," David, the high school orchestra teacher said. "They throw temper tantrums a lot."

But how did he know that the students acting out weren't simply in need of meds? Most of them are already on antidepressants, he told me. He knows this because they discuss their meds openly and also because their medications are sometimes listed on internal files shared with teachers.

Because his music classes draw from all four grades of high school, David regularly has over a hundred students per year. In contrast to the students he taught a decade ago, he says, far more students today are either emotionally unpredictable or zombified. "It's like you're talking to a potted plant most of the time."

Kids, at best, seem unhelped by the therapies and meds and accommodations showered upon them. They can't or won't control their emotional outbursts. They can't or won't get their homework in on time. In greater numbers than teachers ever remember seeing, they can't or won't *do* for themselves.

David offers me two recent examples to prove his point. At his students' first concert of the year, a succession of boys approached him with their clip-on ties in hand, unsure how to fasten them. They weren't asking how to tie a Windsor knot, he wanted me to know. *They wanted him to affix their clip-on ties.* "One of the moms looked at me. She'd seen me doing this all day long, and she's just like, 'These kids are helpless.' They're literally fifteen and sixteen years old. And it's like you're dealing with an eight- or nine-year-old."

At another recent competition, David was stuck in meetings, so he told his high school students to get themselves lunch. One sixteen-year-old boy came to him and told him he didn't know how. "There's a Chipotle right across the street," David said. The boy had money with him. But he didn't know how to procure lunch for himself. He had made it sixteen years without ever having entered a shop alone and bought himself a sandwich.

The Grand Justification:
Childhood Trauma

After educational consultant Ricky Robertson used the word "trauma" a half dozen times in one conference breakout session of the three-day conference I attended, I whispered to my seatmate that we should start a drinking game. Luckily, we didn't have booze or the game would have ended with two fatalities. Over the course of the hour, Robertson would use the word "trauma" 105 times.

Part diagnosis, part MacGuffin, no concept was more often invoked at the public-school teachers conference than the notion that all these kids had experienced an "adverse childhood experience" or "ACE," colloquially known as "their trauma."[13] In the minds and imaginations of many of today's educators, the best way to help disadvantaged kids is by assuming that all kids have suffered harm and treating them *en masse* with blanket mental health interventions, as if therapy were fluoride to be dumped in the drinking water.

The idea that it is even possible to count a kid's adverse childhood experiences to determine her damage originates with a famous study, which purports to show that children with four or more of the following childhood circumstances tend to have below-average physical and mental health outcomes later in life.[14] The ACEs are:

1. Physical abuse

2. Sexual abuse

3. Emotional abuse

4. Physical neglect

5. Emotional neglect

6. Mental illness

7. Divorce or parental breakup

8. Substance abuse in the home

9. Violence against mother

10. Incarcerated household member[15]

The ACE study argues that these factors are common, interrelated, and have a cumulative detrimental impact on mental and physical health outcomes. If you grew up with a drug-addicted mom who suffered from mental illness and sexually abused you, you might be more likely to suffer addiction or homelessness, chronic illness, or fall prey to domestic violence or suicide. The study suggests that, on average, as ACE scores rise in a population, the concentration of inflammatory markers in the population's blood also rises. The challenge and utility for public health researchers became obvious: lower the ACE scores from one generation to the next and watch all sorts of public health problems dissipate.

Harvard Medical School psychiatry professor Dr. Harrison Pope, in a telephone interview, called the ACE study of childhood trauma "a classic example of a methodologically flawed study."

If you want to find out whether trauma causes some pathology, there is a rigorous way to proceed: *prospectively.* You find children who have suffered trauma and document the trauma on the spot. Then you send in researchers blinded to which group suffered actual, documented traumatic experiences to check in with the subjects ten or twenty years later and note if the subjects demonstrate a larger incidence of illness and psychopathology than similarly situated people who have not suffered trauma.

But if you proceed retrospectively, as the ACE study does, if you only select adults and ask about their *history* of trauma, the group you survey is very likely to be selected in a biased fashion. Adults who know they are suffering in the present are motivated to find explanations in their past and are highly suggestible to whichever ones the researcher finds interesting. With any group of people suffering from psychopathology, there are also likely to be a great many confounding variables—factors other than trauma that may have caused the current problem. Confounding variables include genetics, for instance, and all the influences that an alcoholic parent might unwittingly let in the door (like bad adults).

But even if the ACE study *did* show that populations that had experienced various kinds of trauma in childhood, on average, tended to manifest various health risks as adults—that isn't primarily how the study has been used. The ACE study—which has been cited more than thirty-two thousand times since it was published in 1998 in more than 150 journals—has taken on a life of its own. It is routinely used as a diagnostic screener with individual children, as if one could simply count up a child's ACEs and predict her future maladies.

One of the authors of the original study, Robert Anda, recently worried aloud that his study was being misused. The ACE categories are "crude" measures, never intended to apply to assessments of *individual* risk, Anda said in a lecture. Researchers citing the study often fail to consider the variability of human response to stressors experienced in childhood. Some kids will weather difficult circumstances just fine.

"It's not appropriate to apply that average risk from a big epidemiologic study to an individual person because it's an average of that wide scatterplot of actual exposure to the biologic of adversity," he said. "Unlike recognized public health screening measures, such as blood pressure or lipid levels that use measurement reference standards and cut points or thresholds for clinical decision making, the ACE score is not a standardized measure of childhood exposure to the biology of stress."[16]

The ACE categories include having an "incarcerated household member." Across a population, that may be one valid indicator of elevated risk for future health problems. But it cannot apply at the individual level because it does not distinguish, for instance, between these two cases: one in which a child's single mother and sole caregiver is thrown in jail for dealing heroin; and another in which a child's Uncle Marv, who lives with the family, is imprisoned for Medicaid fraud. On the individual level, there are dramatic prospective differences in likely outcomes of those two kids. One is placed in foster care, knowing his mother is a drug dealer. The other thinks of wacky Uncle Marv and shakes his head.

The danger of conflating the two scenarios, which occurs when schools attempt to apply ACEs as a screening tool for individuals, is— you guessed it—iatrogenesis. Schools are likely to overestimate the risk faced by an individual. "If you overestimate risk, you may refer people to treatment and services that they don't need that not only may waste their time but may have some risk involved," Anda told his audience.

The scandalous misuse of the concept of ACEs by the educational establishment to dial down expectations of millions of American kids, in fact, proceeds from an earlier choice by the study's authors. The name "ACE" itself is a giant red herring. Anda claims it is a "measure to show how adversity accumulates to increase risk" in a population. In fact, it does nothing of the kind.

The study does not show that immigrants to America, whose lives are full of "adversity," are more likely to saddle their kids with mental and physical illness long term. Of course they are not. That's because most ACEs of the original study are not simply measures of adversity, at least not as the word is commonly used; they're measures of *dysfunction*.

Poverty, the struggle to gain employment, the stress of working several jobs at once, of never fully understanding the society you inhabit; the unresolved longing for your home culture, mother tongue, and family of origin—they are *adversity*. The pain of never fitting in at school, wearing all the wrong clothes, bearing the burden of your family's high expectations; the guilt of how much they've struggled so that you can live in America: that's *adversity*. And none of it accumulates to produce poor long-term outcomes. (There is good reason to believe that it may even produce *better* outcomes for children.)

The difference between adversity and what I'm calling dysfunction matters. A child whose mother is addicted to heroin is not *merely* emotionally abused or neglected. He isn't merely someone whose mother was often late picking him up from school, too tired at night to ask about his day.

A child whose mother is a heroin addict or regularly beaten by a boyfriend knows that every time his mother is late to pick him up at school may signal that she is somewhere dead or dying. *And he may be right.* Even the most minor inconsistencies on his mother's part may foretell worse things to come: relapse, criminality, the chance that she will soon abandon him. Every time his mother stumbles through the door, she ushers in the menace of whatever or whomever she might have brought home.

Perhaps children who have suffered what the original researchers called "ACEs" need special care. Some of them may find it difficult to shake the torment that trails them to school. The question, for such kids, might not be whether they should receive mental health support but *what kind.*

That is far from the majority of kids, and it is dangerous to conflate those who have suffered years of sexual abuse or been intentionally starved or burnt by the parents who are supposed to love them with those who have faced "adversity." Growing up with a stepfather who beats or rapes you is nothing like feeling the pressure to take a job after school because your parents are struggling to pay the bills. It's nothing at all like getting up early to prepare lunches for your younger siblings because your father, a good man who works three jobs, isn't yet home from the night shift. It's not even like losing a loving father to cancer. If your parents beat you or sexually molest you, as far as your upbringing goes, their presence in your life introduces danger, uncertainty, and emotional torment of the severest and most unpredictable sort. That is vastly and qualitatively different from the pain of losing a loving father whose memory and example you cherish still.

Educators add to the list of ACEs freely, whenever the mood (or convenient political cause) strikes, and assume the same long-term poor health consequences. Over the course of the three-day conference, I heard about "the generational and historical trauma of colonization," the trauma of "kids that are immigrants or refugees" and have had to take on adult-level responsibilities for their families; the trauma of pollution, climate change, and of course the "historical trauma" of being born black in America.

"Fifty percent of kids in a typical US classroom have experienced two ACEs. That's not including the pandemic," Robertson intoned to the assembled room of teachers.

"Everything's 'trauma,'" Christine, the Oregon public school teacher told me. "The trauma of having to wake up every day and be black and know that there's white supremacy out there—that's 'trauma,'" she says skeptically. She ticks off a few traumas that educators are supposed to hunt for. "The trauma of knowing that your parents are stressed about maybe not having a house, the trauma of a divorce, of suicide, of not feeling like you have your gender identity recognized."

Christine is black. She does not believe that having grown up black in America renders a child the victim of psychological trauma. But her view apparently sets her in opposition to the white counselors in her public school.

"I think we are destroying our children by telling them they can't get over whatever hurts. And I'm not saying that there isn't racism. I'm not saying that there aren't people who do really bad things and are horrible. But what I'm saying is that it's not serving our children to say that they're constant victims," she said.

And yet Christine believes that's precisely the message educators deliver through their "trauma-informed" and "social-emotional" interventions. "You're basically saying that everyone who's black is stupid, overly traumatized, has no ability to be successful. It's insane on a level where I don't even recognize the people I work with half the time. But I also recognize that all of us who are like, 'This is crazy,' are fearful to say anything."

Kids from Troubled Backgrounds Have the Most to Lose from Accommodation

Psychologist and writer Rob Henderson spent much of his childhood in foster care. Today, he writes eloquently about children who have suffered the most abject circumstances. What they need is also the thing so few adults in their lives are willing to supply: high expectations. "People think that if a young guy comes from a disorderly or deprived environment, he should be held to low standards. This is misguided. He should be held to high standards. Otherwise, he will sink to the level of his environment," Henderson writes.[17]

He marshals a number of peer-reviewed psychological studies to show that "young men will only do what's expected of them." Those from stable, affluent families require less external pressure to motivate them. Those who've lived through troubled circumstances need *more*. In fact, Henderson suggests that they would be much better served by getting an education than being swaddled in excuses and opportunities to avoid obtaining one.

There is no good reason to believe that most kids are traumatized. The best research indicates the opposite: even among victims of heartbreaking circumstances, resilience is the norm.[18] Disturbing events are best understood as "*potentially* traumatic," meaning they may leave no lasting psychological imprint at all, and certainly not necessarily a negative one.[19]

Without clear evidence to the contrary, the best working assumption would be that a child who comes to school from less-than-ideal circumstances *can* regulate her emotions, *can* complete her math assignments, *can* meet high expectations. And when in doubt, treating her as though she *can* may be more likely to encourage the result that she *will*.

Educators are careful to toss out mention of "resilience," but the picture they paint is of irremediable psychological frailty. When they do talk about "resilience," they most often talk about "helping kids build resilience." But resilience is not typically something that experts *help you build*—it's a process that occurs on its own, through the normal course of facing life's challenges and surmounting them.

The same is true of emotional regulation. You fail, you are cut from the team. And lo and behold, you're still alive! Ready to face another challenge, perhaps by preparing harder next time. Or choosing a different path entirely—one better suited to your tastes and talents.

As for a culture of victimhood? "That's an anti-resilience culture," Kennair told me. By treating kids as if they bear an incipient defect, educators are very likely doing real harm. It's no wonder so many kids feel powerless to make positive changes in their lives. They've been told, over and over, by educators: *You can't.*

Chapter 6

•

Trauma Kings

My maternal grandmother—the most optimistic, can-do woman I've known—entered the world a matricide. In 1927, her mother died giving birth to her, a fact two of her less forbearing older siblings rarely let her forget. For the first few years of her life, a series of indifferent cousins in DC and Philadelphia were called upon to nurse and house her. Never given enough milk, my grandmother's teeth grew in gray. Scanty nutrition stunted her growth.

Her widowed father could not raise her, though stories varied as to why. Whispers followed her, in Yiddish, that a relative molested her while she lived in his home. Others claimed that her father—a Russian immigrant, bereft, undereducated and overwhelmed—simply liked the racetrack too much.

When my grandmother turned six, she had her first real stroke of good luck. Her eldest sister, Clayre, met a boy. At eighteen, Sammy's shoulders spanned a doorway, the top of his head closing in on the transom. He had not much more than a third-grade education. But in 1930s

America, that mattered less than size of his hands, the strength of his arms, the fierceness of his hunger for work. He'd been supporting his own family since he was eight; two more hardly seemed like an imposition. Clayre married Sammy, and they took my grandmother in and raised her.

When she was sixteen, my grandmother attended a Saturday night slumber party with some girls from her high school class. Sunday morning, the girls took a bus to the East Potomac public pool for a swim. A terrible headache followed my grandmother home. Within hours, the pain had spread to her neck. When my grandmother couldn't touch her chin to her chest, Clayre summoned the family doctor, who confirmed a diagnosis of spinobulbar polio. He ordered my grandmother into isolation at Gallinger Hospital.[1] Clayre burned all of my grandmother's clothes.

Around the time Sammy's giant feet stomped the beachhead at Normandy, my grandmother turned seventeen in an iron lung, straining to breathe and unable to swallow. Family visits were mimed through a hallway window: a wave, a smile, a blown kiss. The dreaded illness lasted a year until, one day, my grandmother's tongue and pharynx enlivened enough to negotiate a teaspoon of water. Nurses crowded her bedside to witness her first sips.

If she mourned the loss of an entire year of high school, my grandmother never mentioned it. Her unpublished memoir records the day she left the hospital on a stretcher. "I remember how beautiful the sky looked, and the white floating clouds and the pure smell of fresh air as they put me into the ambulance, and I headed home."

During her junior year at George Washington University, my grandmother met Buddy, a Jewish boy from Virginia who had spent the war teaching better-sighted, less mathematically inclined Army Air Corps cadets what they needed to know. They married, and together she and Buddy raised three kids. Over the years, they housed a series of down-on-their-luck relatives and foster kids with whom she had good reason to identify. She completed law school at night and became one of the first female judges in Maryland history.[2] And until the last year of her life, at ninety-four, her sharp mind softened with age, she held fast to a feeling that would not leave her: every day alive was a miracle.

But in this respect, my grandmother was not remarkable. You likely know people of that Greatest Generation who emerged from similar privations and believed the same. My motherless grandmother endured poverty, polio, and world war. And yet it would have never occurred to her to respond to a survey in the way an apparently typical American young man born in 1990 recently did. "I've grown up in the 21st century, where disasters happen every 20 minutes."[3]

Or another young man responding to the same survey, born in 1999, who somehow managed to drag himself out of bed to offer this sunny thought: "We have no future and no hope. We are the end of history."

We know precisely how my grandmother's generation thought about the war and political turmoil of their age because they kept diaries, wrote letters, and contributed to magazines like *Seventeen*, an upstart publication at the time. A surf of 1940s-era issues of *Seventeen* reveals a generation of "teenagers"—a word that had only just come into existence—lusty and headstrong and critical of the generation that had led them into economic hardship and war.

They decry their parents' and teachers' racial prejudice and religious intolerance. They are full of cheek, convinced they could—and would— bring a far better world into existence than the one their parents had given them. ("We couldn't do any worse than they have, anyway," wrote one teen girl in a letter printed in the magazine.)[4] If patriotic hopefuls was merely a part they played, then America's young method actors managed at last to convince themselves.

Most American generations endured national hardships. But there was no rash of suicides among young southerners during the Civil War nor during Reconstruction. None among teens during the Great Depression, though they did see suicide among the adults of the time.[5] Nor was there a rash of suicide among young adults following Pearl Harbor, when so many of them were sent off to war. Not during the Cuban Missile Crisis, when the world might actually have blinked out like a Zenith TV on the fritz, nor during the endless waves of disillusionment that accompanied the Vietnam War. The Boomers who fancy themselves having confronted some of the ugliest chapters in American history—segregation, Vietnam, Watergate—are usually the first to acknowledge that they could, and did, initiate a positive change.

The majority of those who watched the towers fall on 9/11 did not develop post-traumatic stress disorder.[6] This was true even among those who lost family members to that barbarous act of mass murder. Resilience and trauma researcher George Bonnano of Columbia University conducted a series of studies to learn from those who witnessed the 9/11 attacks or lost loved ones in it. His research team found that after the initial shock of the attack, the most common pattern evinced by those who lost loved ones or directly witnessed the attack was: "a stable trajectory of healthy functioning across time."[7] Resilience, in other words.

For thousands of years, we expected most people who suffered even colossal misfortune to bounce back. Researchers confirm that the vast majority of those who suffer even severe hardship, left to their own devices, will be able to do just this:[8] pull themselves up, get back on the horse, try again. Some even posit that we can be made *better off*—stronger, smarter, more determined, more grateful—by the thousand natural shocks of a bumpy childhood.

Then something changed. We surrendered our faith in the native human ability to surmount hardship—and told our kids that they could not possibly recover, let alone emerge stronger. "I think one big problem with the field of academic psychology is that it has become limited to the privileged and the wealthy," Camilo Ortiz said. Very few mental health experts have ever been poor, much less weathered forced migration or the incarceration of parents,[9] as Ortiz did. It's easy for them to exaggerate the degree to which minor upsets scar adolescents' psyches.

Therapists nevertheless grabbed the reins of the culture and breathed life into a specter that haunts us still: "childhood trauma."

A Bunch of Broken Toys

Today, school counselors and psychologists would invite a motherless girl like my grandmother into their offices, inquire about her family life, and ensure that all of her teachers knew she'd been through something very hard. They would hunt for minute signs that she wasn't coping, and because she was a bright girl, she would catch their meaning: she was damaged. Because she had no mother, because her family was poor, because they were immigrants, because she had survived abuse and a nearly fatal illness, adults would be watching her for signs of trouble. Their expectations for what she could handle, what she might achieve, would be dialed way down. In the parlance of today's school counselors, she was *at least* a "four ACEs kid," clobbered by four adverse childhood experiences, which should spell all kinds of physical and behavioral problems.

No one today would dare punish a girl with my grandmother's biography for bad behavior or dock her grade if she failed to complete an assignment. Hadn't she been through enough? Just coping would be a miraculous achievement for this traumatized young lady. If their eyes didn't broadcast this message, surely her regular check-ins with the school counselor would.

We are, as a culture, enthralled by the notion of childhood trauma—wary of inflicting it, eager to spot it. Books that insist we all have hidden trauma from our childhoods live on bestseller lists. They do not budge.

And what a relief it is to discover our own! *So that's why I'm needy; why I can't get to work on time; why I struggle to maintain relationships.* It lets us off the hook. It isn't that we overlooked significant character flaws in romantic partners or that we've furnished our lives with accoutrements of chaos—drugs, social media, and porn. No, the source of our unhappiness is our childhood trauma, akin to a disease—another undeserved impairment. Trauma hangs above our heads like a low ceiling. How much can we possibly grow? We can't. Nor can we throw open the door and step out of the cramped space; trauma has nailed our shoes to the floor.

The great Israeli sociologist Eva Illouz notes that the trauma narrative is plotted backward—from present adult dissatisfaction to the epiphany of a childhood spent in a dysfunctional family. "What is a dysfunctional family? A family where one's needs are not met. And how does one know that one's needs were not met in childhood? Simply by looking at one's present situation," Illouz writes. "The nature of the tautology is obvious: any present predicament points to a past injury."[10]

Like fortunes told by readers of palms and tarot cards, the childhood trauma explanation for adult dissatisfaction is unfalsifiable. (It can never be disproved.) How do we *know* we didn't fail in our jobs or relationships because of the unresolved pain of having been spanked by Dad or screamed at by Mom or bullied in junior high? We don't. We can never know. The idea is slippery, it evades serious judgment, and because it both seems to explain all of our troubles and lets us off the hook for fixing them, it slides down so easily.

High Priest of the Church of Trauma

Bessel van der Kolk has been called "the world's most famous living psychiatrist."[11] His canonical book, *The Body Keeps the Score*, has sold three million copies and dominated the *New York Times* bestseller list for hundreds of weeks, like an Olympic athlete competing in a high school sport. Virtually everywhere I went while researching this book, I met people who told me that the book had changed their lives.[12] From van der Kolk they learned that their bodies stored the trauma of their childhoods, frozen in perpetuity like a spear-toting caveman at the Museum of Natural History.

Van der Kolk, who still hosts trauma workshops, has become a guru to millions. Silky gray hair complements a seductive insistence that he keenly feels your pain. A Northern European accent brings to mind—if not Freud, precisely—someone ambiguously serious about matters of the mind. Van der Kolk even spent a few years at Harvard as an associate professor of psychiatry before he lost his affiliation with Harvard Medical School and transferred to Boston University.[13]

All of that would suggest that his theory about childhood trauma—which he terms "the hidden epidemic"—ought to be taken very, very seriously. The catch? According to several of the greatest academic psychologists and psychiatrists alive today, van der Kolk's theory amounts to a bill of goods.

Does the Body Keep the Score? Literally, No. Figuratively? Also, No.

Van der Kolk published his mega-seller in 2014, but it's based on an idea first articulated by van der Kolk in a 1994 paper of the same name.[14] The "memory" of "trauma"—he argues—is "encoded in the viscera, in heartbreaking and gut-wrenching emotions, in autoimmune disorders and skeletal/muscular problems."[15] Traumatic memory can be stored anywhere—in the brain's hippocampus, which assails us with worry; in the shoulder that aches; in the white blood cells that fail to turn up. Autoimmune disorders, anxiety, depression, ADHD, asthma, migraine headaches, fibromyalgia, even cancer can all proceed from childhood trauma, according to van der Kolk.[16]

In 1994, van der Kolk invited eight subjects who claimed to be haunted by memories of traumatic events into his lab. He prompted them to recall the experiences while each lay inside a PET scanner that tracked brain activity. He expected bright spots in the amygdala, which is activated by intense emotion. But according to van der Kolk, their amygdalae seemed to go into overdrive, as if their bodies were faced with a *present* threat. He also noticed a decrease in activity in the Broca's area of the left brain, a speech center.[17]

"When something reminds traumatized people of the past, their right brain reacts as if the traumatic event were happening in the present," he surmised. "But because their left brain is not working well, they may not be aware that they are reexperiencing and reenacting the past—they are just furious, terrified, enraged, ashamed or frozen."[18]

From these studies, a narrative was born. Any of us could be thrown into this "fight-or-flight" state by "body memories" that we can't always access or articulate. And if we found ourselves suddenly enraged or terrified for reasons we couldn't explain, we now knew why: trauma memory.

"What has happened cannot be undone," van der Kolk writes. All you can do is work with a therapist to unearth and revisit your trauma. "What *can* be dealt with are the imprints of the trauma on body, mind and soul; the crushing sensations in your chest that you may label as anxiety or depression; the fear of losing control; always being on alert for danger or rejection; the self-loathing; the nightmares and flashbacks; the fog that keeps you from staying on task and from engaging fully in what you are doing; being unable to fully open your heart to another human being."

In a time when so many people feel lost and dissatisfied with their lot, van der Kolk comes along and offers secular absolution: It's not your fault. Trauma made you this way.

Can't concentrate? Trauma! Trouble forming relationships? Trauma! Tightness in your chest? Trauma! Cancer, substance abuse, sexual promiscuity, stroke, irritable bowel syndrome? Trauma, trauma, trauma, trauma![19]

Van der Kolk bases many of his claims on studies of combat soldiers who suffered PTSD. Captivated by his idea that we're all damaged, people who have never seen any combat (or, really, any brutal experience) discover their hidden traumas, reasoning backward from a disappointing adult life to the parent who failed them.

He relays the story of a twenty-six-year-old man named Mark who found himself unable to connect emotionally to others and deeply suspicious of any woman who showed interest in him. In a group therapy role-play session led by van der Kolk, Mark revealed that at the age of thirteen he'd overheard his father having phone sex with his aunt. Years later, after Mark's mother died, Mark's father married the aunt. Mark was invited to neither the funeral nor the wedding. Suddenly, the memory had become vivid to Mark: "You asshole, you hypocrite, you ruined my life," Mark screamed at the participant standing-in for his father.

"Secrets like these become inner toxins—realities you are not allowed to acknowledge to yourself or to others but that nevertheless become the template of your life," van der Kolk writes, mingling the language of biology ("toxins") with that of emotions.[20]

Many Americans will recognize the notion that forgotten or buried childhood experiences can produce devastating "inner toxins" that must be drained by recovering the lost memory under psychotherapy or hypnosis. According to van der Kolk, there is a "wealth of evidence that trauma can be forgotten and resurface years later."[21] The idea once wore slightly different clothes and traveled under a more discreet name: "repressed memory."

The Most Serious Catastrophe Since the Lobotomy

Harvard University psychology professor Richard McNally has called repressed memory therapy "arguably the most serious catastrophe to strike the mental health field since the lobotomy era."[22] The repressed memory scandal of the 1990s resulted in false accusations and high-profile convictions, later overturned.[23] It represented perhaps the most notorious rash of therapist-led iatrogenesis in twentieth-century America. At its center stood a psychiatrist named Bessel van der Kolk.

In the 1990s, van der Kolk was both a chief architect and major proponent of the idea that our bodies hold onto buried memories of trauma, which require a therapist to unearth. He traveled the country testifying for the prosecution in repressed memory cases,[24] facing off against memory experts like Elizabeth Loftus and Harrison Pope, who insisted that the whole idea wasn't good science. "Van der Kolk's testimony was crucial to putting innocent people in prison," wrote Mark Pendergrast, a science journalist who has covered the false memory scandal extensively.[25] Van der Kolk's 1994 paper, also titled "The Body Keeps the Score," supplied scholarly heft to these prosecutions. To this day, van der Kolk has never disavowed the theory; an entire section of his book is dedicated to the "Science of Repressed Memory."[26]

Harvard professor of psychiatry Harrison Pope has long been among the most prominent and vociferous critics of van der Kolk's theory of repressed memory. Following a pummeling by the likes of Pope, Mc-Nally, and Johns Hopkins psychiatrist Paul McHugh, the theory "has practically vanished among scientists writing in the peer-reviewed literature," Pope told me in our email correspondence. But the idea has made a powerful resurgence in the popular imagination, thanks in part to its promotion by therapists transfixed by the notion of childhood trauma.

I asked McNally if he was surprised to see van der Kolk's book spend more than 150 weeks on the *New York Times* bestseller list, where it sits like a Delphic oracle convincing trusting readers that their brains, bodies, and lives lie in tatters because of repressed childhood trauma.

"I thought the memory wars were over. You know, we won," McNally told me candidly. "God, here we go again."

Trauma Salesmen

Gabor Maté is a family physician turned trauma guru who charged the public $33.09 to watch a livestream of his therapy session with Prince Harry. In a recent bestselling book, *The Myth of Normal*, Maté reveals, like a secret too long withheld, that we are all damaged goods. And we all need help—the help of therapists.

"An event is traumatizing, or retraumatizing, only if it renders one *diminished*, which is to say psychically (or physically) *more limited* than before in a way that *persists*," Maté writes. Trauma creates a disconnect from our bodies. If you find yourself with a "diminished capacity to feel or think or trust or assert yourself"; if you find that holding your pain and sorrow leads you to need to "escape habitually into work or compulsive self soothing or self-stimulating"; if you feel "compelled either to aggrandize yourself or to efface yourself for the sake of gaining acceptance"; if you struggle to "experience gratitude for the beauty and wonder of life"; this "might well represent trauma's shadow on your psyche, the presence of an unhealed emotional world, no matter the size of the *t*."[27] (I'll bet you can guess what the *t* stands for.)

Note that this list describes just about any of us at times, which is why the conclusion that no one is normal should be unsurprising. Maté offers the classic anything-and-its-opposite symptoms checklists (e.g., the need to self-aggrandize or self-efface), with the result that virtually anyone can stumble into diagnosis and decide: *I must have suffered childhood trauma.*

Almost anything, according to Maté, may be a symptom of body- and mind-wrecking trauma. Even niceness. "Time after time it was the 'nice' people, the ones who compulsively put others' expectations and needs ahead of their own and who repressed their so-called negative emotions, who showed up with chronic illness in my family practice, or who came under my care at the hospital palliative ward I directed,"[28] Maté writes.

"It struck me that these patients had a higher likelihood of cancer and poorer prognoses. The reason, I believe, is straightforward: repression disarms one's ability to protect oneself from stress."[29]

Gabor Maté's observation that his nice patients had more cancer (and worse prognoses) is certainly arresting, if macabre. Whether there's any statistical validity to it is a different story. It's plausible that people who compulsively put others' needs ahead of their own might also fail to make time for routine mammograms and colonoscopies or tend to neglect the onset of cancer symptoms. But Maté thinks he's found a different cause: repression.

In fact, Maté goes much further. Not only do we carry the trauma we personally experienced, but we harbor the trauma our parents or ancestors did as well. "Trauma is in most cases multigenerational," Maté writes. "The chain of transmission goes from parent to child, stretching from the past into the future. We pass on to our offspring what we haven't resolved in ourselves."[30]

"Normal" has always been a null set, Maté tells us. Even he is damaged. A decade ago, Maté's colleague and comrade, van der Kolk, told him so at a work conference. Over lunch, van der Kolk peered into Maté's eyes and said: "Gabor, you don't need to drag Auschwitz around with you everywhere you go."

It's a revelatory moment for Maté, who survived the Holocaust as an infant in the care of a stranger and then with an aunt until his parents could recover him. "In that instant, Bessel saw me. Despite all my positive engagements with life, despite the love and joy and immense good fortune that have also been my portion, that self-directed hopelessness was an ever-lurking shadow, ready to obliterate the light whenever I experienced a setback or discouragement, and even in innocent, unguarded moments."[31] Apparently, van der Kolk is allowed to tell even Holocaust survivors to "get over it" when it comes to their trauma. No one else is.

This idea of "trauma's shadow on your psyche" has profoundly changed the practice of psychotherapy, education, and how we raise our own children. With their palette of science-ish suggestions and compelling metaphors, Maté and van der Kolk have painted for us a world whose every surface is tinged with trauma's hues. And the notion that every one of us carries the damage of even our ancestors' childhoods has become an indelible feature of our societal self-portrait.

Several of the academic psychologists I spoke to think this view is wholly misguided. They wanted me to know that this theory runs contrary to the best research. In fact, their work showed that the opposite was true: resilience—not permanent traumatic response—is the norm. Even for kids subjected to desperate hardship—poverty, alcoholism in the family, family instability, and parental mental illness—studies showed that in all but the most persistently dire circumstances, they typically demonstrate resilience.[32]

"Memories are not stored 'in the body' [that is, in muscle tissue], and the notion of 'body memories' is foreign to the cognitive neuroscience of memory," McNally has written, in a paper refuting van der Kolk.[33] When you've experienced a potentially traumatic event, you're particularly likely to remember it explicitly. There's no evidence that even survivors of the worst traumas hold memories implicitly or that those memories can be stored outside of the central nervous system.[34]

The idea that we carry in our bodies the trauma of our younger selves—much less the trauma of our ancestors—may be a PR campaign in search of a product. Academic psychologist Martin Seligman, winner of the APA Award for Lifetime Contributions to Psychology, has reviewed and summarized the studies on childhood trauma this way: "The major traumas of childhood may have some influence on adult personality, but the influence is barely detectable. . . . There is no justification, according to these studies, for blaming your adult depression, anxiety, bad marriage, drug use, sexual problems, unemployment, beating up your children, alcoholism or anger on what happened to you as a child."[35]

Meanwhile, many of my own friends were utterly convinced by the idea of which I was becoming increasingly suspicious: that our bodies are invisibly tattooed with trauma. That any harsh word we uttered or punishment we gave our children—any moment when we allowed them to feel in doubt of our approval—would leave lasting emotional scars. And, most dubiously, that children are *helped* by teachers who treat them as if they were recent survivors of the trenches at Verdun.

Elementary School Kids Are Not Combat Vets

In 2001, van der Kolk helped found the National Child Traumatic Stress Network, which now has more than 150 centers nationwide. The network created trauma-informed programs in schools, juvenile justice systems, and child welfare agencies and helped bring "trauma-sensitive teachers" into the classroom.[36]

Van der Kolk's Network taught a generation of teachers to reason from brain scans of PTSD sufferers to children with adverse childhood experiences. "Our goal in all these efforts is to translate brain science into everyday practice,"[37] he wrote.

But it doesn't work. According to James McGaugh, distinguished emeritus professor of neurobiology at the University of California, Irvine, it is a mistake to reason from PTSD victims, who suffered a traumatic occurrence, to kids who grow up in terrible circumstances. The two are entirely different phenomena, from a neuroscientific perspective. "He mixes up the conditions occurring during the formation of an emotional experience with that of sustained trauma over a long period of time," McGaugh told me, about van der Kolk.

As far as the brain is concerned, there is a world of difference between suffering a sudden shock—seeing your unit decimated by an IED—and the grinding torment of growing up with an alcoholic father. We may call them both "trauma," but from a neurobiological perspective, they are entirely disparate kinds of events.

"It's a very different thing to talk about a trauma over a long period of time, let's say a rejected child," McGaugh said. And it's a mistake, if not dishonest, to make neuroscientific claims about kids who suffered a bad childhood based on our work with soldiers who survived a discrete and sudden shock.

Brain scans of soldiers and accident victims with PTSD do not necessarily tell us anything about the brains of kids who have suffered neglect or ongoing abuse by a parent. It's a mistake to extrapolate from one to the other. Kids who have suffered neglect or ongoing abuse need help and support. Conflating them with combat vets does not bring them any closer to getting it.

Brain Studies Don't Prove
Trauma Permanently
Alters Your Brain

People are complicated—the brain, endlessly so. And every psychiatrist I spoke to emphasized to me that we really don't know very much about how the brain works. True, a child who's been sexually assaulted and beaten and has an incarcerated parent may be more likely to suffer a heart attack or fall prey to addiction as an adult. The essential question is: *Why?* We don't have any proof that traumatic experiences *cause* heart disease or addiction. Both cardiovascular disease and drug addiction may be produced by the unhealthy behaviors a child adopted while she was young.

As Dr. Pope explained to me in our telephone interview, van der Kolk's reasoning—including the impressive-seeming brain studies on which it is based—suffers from fatal methodological flaws. Van der Kolk's PET studies purport to show areas of brain difference (and damage) proceeding from childhood trauma. Like the ACEs study, van der Kolk's PET studies are riven by selection bias, information bias, and confounding variables.

Selection bias occurs when a certain type of subject is over-included in a study. A patient suffering a current psychopathology who also survived childhood sexual abuse might be more likely to end up in a study exploring the connection between the two. That study may find a stronger relationship between those two variables than is warranted, simply based on the subjects included.

Dr. Pope offered this devastating, if quirky, analogy. In the nineteenth century, many doctors believed that excessive masturbation could cause mental illness, perhaps even insanity. Suppose, Pope says, we are contemporary psych researchers sent via time machine to the nineteenth century, along with access to today's tools. On our journey, we recruit twenty adults who have been diagnosed by their old-timey physicians as suffering from "masturbation-induced mental illness." We put our subjects through a battery of modern tests and compare the results to those of twenty adults who have no mental illness at all. What are we likely to find? According to Pope, the patients with "masturbation-induced illness" will likely have diminished capacities for attention and short-term memory. "They may show neuroendocrine abnormalities, such as higher cortisol levels, or changes in other hormones from the pituitary gland or the hypothalamus in the brain. They may even have smaller hippocampi," he writes.

The nineteenth-century doctors seem pleased that we have confirmed their diagnosis of masturbation-induced insanity. But of course our "finding" is a mirage created by selection bias. "We have merely shown that a group of people selected because they were ill, differ from a group of people selected because they were well. We cannot logically extrapolate from this observation to say that masturbation caused the abnormalities we have observed," Pope said.

Likewise, the brains of adult PTSD and addiction sufferers van der

Kolk and Maté describe may indeed have higher cortisol levels or smaller hippocampi. It may also be true that many of these patients suffered adverse childhood experiences. For reasons distinct from the infliction of childhood trauma, kids who grow up with parents who are addicts may be more prone to become addicts themselves (greater access to drugs, lower expectations that they avoid drugs, and, of course, DNA). None of those brain markers would prove that the trauma of having been raised by addicts produced the differences in their brains.

Information bias occurs whenever respondents' current knowledge alters their recollection of an earlier event. Unsurprisingly, adult subjects who *know* they currently suffer from a psychopathology are more likely to "recall" having suffered childhood trauma and to identify it as the cause.

Pope offered me the example of a well-known study conducted at Harvard of approximately a hundred women who had given birth to infants with congenital malformations and a comparison group of women who had given birth to normal infants.[38] The surveyors asked these women whether they recalled using hormonal birth control or being subjected to other exposures during pregnancy before they knew they were pregnant.

The mothers of the babies with birth defects, desperate to explain the problems with their children, were much more likely to recall that, yes, they had used hormonal birth control during the pregnancy. But in fact, when the investigators went back and looked at the medical records, there was virtually no difference between the two groups of mothers in the rate of birth control use during pregnancy.[39]

"It was caused entirely by the fact that if you had a congenitally malformed infant, quite naturally, you're going to go through everything that you could possibly remember, trying to seek an explanation. And as a result, you have a bias in favor of reporting all of these adverse effects in the past," Dr. Pope said. So, too, if you ask adults wrestling with addiction or struggling to hold down a job if they happen to have suffered adverse childhood experiences, they are prone to decide that they have.[40]

And, finally, childhood trauma studies, including these brain scan studies, are beset by *confounding variables*—exogenous reasons for whatever purported correlations are observed. Excessive salt consumption was long thought to cause high blood pressure because, it turns out, people who eat a lot of salty snacks are often also obese and drink alcohol. The variables of alcohol consumption and obesity obscured the relatively weak relationship between sodium consumption and blood pressure.

The same may turn out to be true of brain scan studies cited by van der Kolk that seem to show brain differences in individuals with prolonged histories of traumatic stress. Having sustained traumatic stress in your life and possessing certain brain differences might both be the result of a third variable, say, poor prenatal care, or particular genes (like genes that may have inclined you and your parents toward addiction). In fact, subsequent studies of Vietnam vets have shown that small hippocampi are a risk factor for *developing* PTSD, not the result of wartime trauma.[41] The trauma gurus may have fully reversed the real arrow of causality between smaller brain structures and PTSD.

These methodological flaws aren't unique to the work of trauma researchers; all retrospective surveys—in which participants are polled about their past—suffer from these. That's why the proper way to conduct a study on the long-term effects of childhood trauma is to create a prospective, or *forward-facing*, study, Pope says.

Let's imagine you're designing a study to determine whether children who suffer abuse go on to physically abuse their own children. Your graduate students suggest that you interview the local prison population, specifically those convicted of physically assaulting their own children, about the circumstances of their childhoods; the study could be finished in two months, they say. But you're aware that their suggestion is beset by all three flaws: selection bias, information bias, and confounding variables. Could you build a study that avoids them? Yes, indeed.

First, you would collect data on children who are verified to have suffered potentially traumatic childhood experiences. Then, as a control, you would collect data on kids of the same age, sex, and from roughly equivalent socioeconomic and environmental backgrounds who have *not* suffered similarly. Years later, your study would follow up with kids of both groups when they had reached adulthood, careful to use researchers who do not know which camp a respondent belongs to. Finally, you'd examine the results. It's a mind-boggling amount of work, conducted over many years, but it's the only methodologically sound way of arriving at a valid, unbiased result.

This is precisely what Cathy Widom did. In the 1980s, Widom, a professor of psychology and expert on child sexual abuse, wanted to test whether adults who had been abused as kids were *more likely* to physically abuse their own kids. "I decided that I would get documented cases of abuse and neglect—court cases for children between the ages of zero and eleven—so I could establish the temporal relationship between abuse and neglect and these outcomes,"[42] she later explained. Widom's study recruited 908 kids, then matched these kids with 667 other children who lived in the same neighborhoods and attended the same schools but about whom there was no documented proof they had suffered abuse.

Years later, Widom followed up with the now-adult children and many of their progeny. She hired researchers to interview them, but she didn't tell the researchers which camp any subject fell into. She found that parents who had suffered physical abuse, sexual abuse, or neglect during their childhoods were *no more likely* to physically abuse their own children.[43]

We want to believe things happen for a reason—and we'd like to be able to pin that reason down. To say: "*This* is why I feel so crummy." Psychologists call this propensity "effort after meaning."[44] If a mother is grappling with the shock of learning her preschooler has autism, it might lend the diagnosis a sense of comprehensibility for her to conclude that childhood vaccines are the reason. We don't want to be Job, at a loss to explain "Why me?" after cruel misfortune offers no one to blame. We might find it satisfying to think back to the pain our parents caused and imagine our medial prefrontal cortices all lit up.

But we have no proof that childhood trauma *causes* specific adult mental health problems. Studies that purport to show this are riven with sources of bias.[45] What we can say is that childhood trauma is *neither* necessary nor sufficient to produce adult psychopathology.

But then why do so many people think that *The Body Keeps the Score* explains them so completely? Take an adult woman, an office worker, who is chewed out by a boss and finds herself speechless, frozen, and trembling. She feels that she has been sent into a "fight-or-flight" response. The whole experience, and especially her distinctive physical reaction, reminds her acutely of being eight years old and subject to her stepfather's abusive tirades. She reads about "body memories" and thinks: *Yes! This is what I felt.* Her body itself seems to be recalling the trauma.

But as Professor McNally illuminated for me, fear is a normal, evolved biological adaptation to imminent threat: a boss screams in your face, your heart races. That is not a "body memory" but rather the conventional physiological response to danger. That you make the connection to your past may strike you as proof that you have been traumatized. But, of course, you have no idea whether adults with very different childhoods, when treated shabbily by a supervisor, wouldn't evince the same response. Your reaction may not be more profound than the reaction of those who were raised very gently, by parents who never raised their voices at all. Your bodily symptoms may not manifest more powerfully than similarly situated adults without the despicable stepfather.

Our office worker, sadly, might also find herself recalling her screaming stepfather in the *absence* of any imminent threat, along with a full-blown physiological fear response to the awful memory. McNally addressed that scenario as well: such reactions are bodily expressions of the memory of the earlier episode. That isn't the body "keeping the score" and preserving the memory, but the body's response to the recollection.[46] The memory is in the mind, readily accessible; there's nothing repressed to unearth, no séance required to call it forth, and no buried treasure that awaits a therapist's shovel.

What about unexplained physical symptoms, like pain? Surely *that* must proceed from trauma? Researchers have conducted rigorous studies to determine whether abused children experience more pain as adults. In one investigation, researchers identified child survivors of documented abuse or neglect and followed up with them decades later. The same was done with a similarly situated control group, where no abuse was documented.[47] The researchers found that, when interviewed as adults, both groups showed essentially identical levels of pain symptoms, indicating that there was no relationship between childhood abuse and medically unexplained pain in adulthood. Even more interestingly, when asked *retrospectively* whether or not they had been abused, the participants with adult pain were much more likely to report childhood abuse than those without pain. In other words: childhood trauma doesn't result in higher incidence of unexplained pain. But adults in pain are more likely to report childhood trauma. If researchers had relied solely on retrospective reports, they would have erroneously concluded that childhood trauma (and perhaps the resulting "body memories") led to increased levels of idiopathic pain in adulthood.

Why did I become a drug addict when none of my friends did? Why do I suffer inexplicable physical pain? Why did my marriage fall apart? It's natural to want an explanation. If your life is not as you wish it were, it isn't your fault. Something done to you in your past *made you that way.* That's how the snipe hunt for childhood trauma begins. "Memories," once dredged, are rarely independently verified, and the resulting theory of childhood trauma becomes unfalsifiable. If you think you've been damaged, you are.

Why would verifying or validating the memories be necessary? Because the events represented in those bad childhood memories may not have happened at all, or may not have happened in the way you remembered.[48] Even if they happened, they may not have been significant to you at the time. Perhaps the remembered event, raked from your mental riverbed, had no impact on your life until a therapist placed the loupe of your focus upon it, suggesting it had the power to clarify your adult woes.

The Memory Queen

When I arrived at the California doorstep of Elizabeth Loftus, the world's most decorated memory researcher, she couldn't find her car keys. She invited me to join her on a frantic hunt through her impeccably arranged academic housing—a tiled galley kitchen, Formica countertops wiped clean; tidy office fitted with floor-to-ceiling bookshelves, braced by a rolling ladder. To the garage, where, doubled over the driver's seat, I rooted through her glovebox.

"We need a memory expert!" I joked, after a brief internal debate over whether she'd appreciate the teasing.

She was kind enough to laugh.

(In the end, she found them in a pocket of a different handbag. I drove us to lunch.)

Now in her seventies, Loftus has been called the most important female academic psychologist of the twentieth century.[49] Her contributions to the field of memory routinely place her on lists of "Top 100 most influential contributors" to her field, alongside Freud, Skinner, and Piaget. And what she taught us is this: our memory is not like a video recording of the events we've lived through.[50] It's a "constructive" process, susceptible to alteration and suggestion, even years after the fact.

"Memory works a little bit more like a Wikipedia page," she has said.[51]

"You can go in there and change it—but so can other people." Interviewers can press people—children especially—to believe all sorts of things through leading questions.[52] False memories can be just as vivid and apparently veridical as accurate ones.

"Children are more susceptible than adults," Loftus told me over lunch. "But basically anyone can be led with the right amount of suggestion. Not every person all the time, but any group of people can be led to remember things that didn't happen with suggestions."

Through her psychological experiments, she has demonstrated that people will remember a car as having traveled at a higher speed if the questioner uses the word "smashed" to describe the accident, and even to misremember broken glass at an accident scene where there wasn't any. When Loftus added stress to her subjects, she found the same. Members of the military who underwent a prisoner-of-war interrogation, if fed misleading information, misidentified their interrogators and sometimes fingered individuals who hardly resembled their interrogators at all.

In the 1990s, armed with her research, she faced off against van der Kolk in courtrooms—Loftus, testifying on behalf of the accused. Defense lawyers for Harvey Weinstein, Bill Cosby, Jerry Sandusky, and the Duke lacrosse players falsely accused of rape in 2006 have all called upon her expertise at trial. Like the attorneys themselves, she hasn't always been popular for having participated in the defense.

And just as defense attorneys believe even bad people are entitled to zealous advocacy, Loftus believes even bad people ought to be convicted on the basis of solid evidence. Accusations suddenly recalled twenty years after the fact are so often riddled with error, they must be tested, no matter how shocking the accusation or vile the accused.

Her voice thickens with emotion as she talks about due process and the unfairness of convicting a defendant based on a mosaic of fact and fiction. In a time when even law professors have learned to keep their mouths clamped shut in the face of a cultural stampede to "believe women," I wondered how she manages to care so much about the quality of evidence used to overcome the presumption of innocence.

She thinks it over for a beat before her warbly alto picks up. "I'm not like other people. And I don't know how. I mean, for a long time, I've cared about the falsely accused. And it's not because I was falsely accused. I think when I was a teenager, I probably did most of the things I was accused of." Her mouth twists with regret or consternation, as if exasperated by her teenage self.

"I do have another hypothesis though," she says. "Well, when your childhood is filled with a mother who drowned when you were fourteen, an aunt you saw dying in an iron lung when you were twelve from myasthenia gravis, your house burns down and you lose just about everything—" She shrugs. Like Ortiz, Loftus believes her own childhood adversity deepened her perspective, placing her in a unique position to help others. She rejects the notion that hardship on its own makes you sick.

As a child, Loftus was sexually abused by a babysitter. Later, in high school, a boy forced himself on top of her, before she struggled to escape. She knows that these experiences are frightening and does not doubt that they occur. But merely asserting them, she believes, should not be enough to secure a conviction. The veridicality of the memory *matters*. It matters even when the person on trial is a bad man.

And she knows, personally, how easy it is to be fooled by a false memory. Many years after her mother's death, she came to "remember" having discovered her mother's body in the family pool, after a relative strongly suggested to her that she had. Later, the relative called to say that he'd been mistaken; it hadn't been the teenage Elizabeth who'd made the tragic discovery after all.

Flighty and labile as an actor, memory is also creative, impressionable, and fundamentally inconstant, she says. Kids especially are easily led by questioners; social influence and reinforcement can powerfully deter-mine answers children provide.[53] "These therapists can signal even inad-vertently when they're interested in what you're saying or look bored when they're not interested. And people will respond because they want the therapist to be interested. They want the therapists to like them. They want the therapist to spend time with them and enjoy them," Loftus said. If therapists and teachers and parents are *looking* for childhood trauma when they question children, kids are likely to supply it.

Is Any of This Good for Kids?

Let's put aside, for a moment, the highly controversial theory that trau-matic experiences create a "body memory," stored, mysteriously, outside of the central nervous system—in the neck, shoulder, elbow.[54] Put aside the dubious idea that we inherit the historical trauma of our ancestors through epigenetics, as Maté and others have suggested.[55]

Put aside the unproven idea that traumatic childhood experiences typ-ically commandeer the emotional life of an adult, interfering with her ability to maintain good relationships, hold down a job, react normally to ordinary stressors, and become the sort of citizen the rest of us can de-pend upon. The vast majority of adults have managed to do just that—rise above childhood pain, focus on the present and future, and carry on. Put aside the fact that, until very recently in human history, nearly all markers of what we now call "childhood trauma" were just facts of life: hunger, loss of a parent or sibling, war, even occasions of physical abuse.

Is it a good idea to convince millions of adults that childhood hardship causes lasting damage to their bodies and minds? Van der Kolk's exper-tise lies in PTSD and battle-worn soldiers who saw the grisliest combat. PTSD exists, and for its sufferers, it may make sense for a therapist to treat them with some of the methods van der Kolk promotes.

But does it make sense to regard all children—children born today, gently raised in Brentwood and Park Slope and Lincoln Park—as if they are likely to have suffered similar shocks? Is it a good idea to tell young children—explicitly or just by obvious, obsessive implication—that they may be marred by traumatic injury? Should we, as a society, be sponsoring the therapist-led (and ersatz therapist–led) quests to uncover hidden traumas in our children?

"I don't think so," Loftus said. "Because if you believe there's a buried trauma there and you engage in all these practices to try to get it out, you're sometimes in the process going to create trauma memories that aren't real—if it's anything like the cases that I investigated and studied and wrote about."

I ask her if treating all kids with the presumption that they may have experienced trauma is likely to cause them to reframe their childhoods—recasting them in a darker or scarier light. "Well, if you're rewarded for coming up with horror stories, I mean, that's a basic Skinnerian [idea]," she said, referring to the behavioral-conditioning studies promoted by B. F. Skinner.

"The reinforcement increases the behavior and punishment reduces it. So if you're getting reinforced for thinking about traumatic experiences, you're going to increase the behavior."

Loftus says this can happen in group therapy settings as well. A kind of one-upmanship arises, in which participants exaggerate their pain to match the pathos of what others shared.[56] Participants encouraged to throw themselves into their own hyperbole may come to believe it.

"It's a little like memory poker," Loftus said, borrowing a phrase she owes to a colleague. "I'm going to match your memory and raise you with my even more bizarre and more lurid and more interesting memory.' That kind of thing goes on because if somebody is saying, 'Well, I really think I have hidden trauma, I just can't remember,' that's kind of boring for the group, when you're sitting next to somebody who's telling you about satanic ritual abuse." Group sharing sessions may cause kids to 're-member' things that never occurred, Loftus said, or to alter their memo-ries of things that did, kicking up the drama a notch or two.

It's one thing to treat children who recently suffered a *bona fide* tragedy with additional sensitivity and accommodations. But "trauma-informed care" and "trauma-informed education" simply presume the injury and commence the treatment. Iatrogenic effects are bound to follow.

Trauma-Informed Culture

Many of today's most prominent psychodynamic therapists pay lip ser-vice to "resilience," but their mood is low and their forecast calls for end-less storm. They are the proud inheritors of van der Kolk's idea that the body keeps the score. They decry the "impact of childhood trauma" and refer to our "trauma body (perpetual fight or flight)."

Consider *New York Times* bestselling therapist and advice-giver to seven million Instagram followers Nicole LePera, "The Holistic Psychol-ogist," who promises to deliver "the power to heal yourself." Her You-Tube videos have collected over ten million views. She dispenses her advice, free of charge, in tweets that routinely garner millions of views. Here is just one gem, among the numberless, all to similar effect:

"Do you struggle in relationships, fear abandonment, and don't like asking for help?" begins one thread. "You might have been parentified."[57] Parentified?

She defines it: "Parentification is an 'invisible' form of trauma that is often not recognized in our society. It occurs when parents look to their children to provide emotional support, and to run parts of the household. It's a role reversal."

LePera offers a symptom checklist to aid with self-diagnosis:

Adults who've been parentified can struggle with:

- communication skills

- inability to understand their emotions

- inability to meet their own needs

- hyper-independence ("I can do it all alone")

- fear of asking for help or accepting it

- emotional immaturity/high reactivity

- defensiveness in relationships

- codependency patterns

- patterns of self betrayal

- low self worth

- lack of sense of self

See yourself somewhere in this list? Almost everyone will.

Given her vast experience battling lousy therapists, I asked Loftus what a prospective patient should look out for to avoid the quacks. Her immediate suggestion: beware symptoms checklists. "'Do you trust people too much or do you trust too little?' 'Do you drink too much or are you totally abstinent?' All these checklists where you're supposed to see if you have these symptoms, chances are you were sexually abused as a child. And anybody can find themselves on that list," Loftus said.

Like so many of today's popular, trauma-informed therapists, LePera not only promotes symptoms checklists that cast a wide net. She sprinkles diagnoses on her public. There are five major ways in which your parents may have parentified you, she informs readers. By treating you as a peer; by being overworked; by struggling with addiction; by being withdrawn; or by being an immigrant.

Being an immigrant automatically puts you on the list? She explains:

"Parents who sacrifice and bring their child to another country for a better life are forced to rely on their children for help with language, paying bills, or understanding cultural norms. Children play adult roles out of necessity."[58] Some might think those parents who sacrificed so much for their kids are pretty great, as far as parents go. But in the trauma world, they are inflictors of "invisible trauma."

A favorite faux diagnosis of so many therapists, "complex PTSD," was roundly rejected by the editors of the *DSM*—despite efforts by psychiatrists like van der Kolk, a leading proponent of its inclusion.[59] Nonetheless, popular psychotherapists like LePera promote this diagnosis as if it were a recognized disorder.[60]

It isn't. The candidate diagnosis was rejected because—according to Allen Frances, a psychiatrist and professor emeritus of Duke University School of Medicine—the symptom pattern was so broad it overlapped with most other disorders, the traumas it described were so common as to cover most patients, it was based on poor research, "people pushing it [were] not respected" in the field, and it was "too easily sold as explain-all to gullible therapists/patients."[61] In other words, it represented one more attempt by the mental health experts to pathologize *everyone*.[62]

"Do you feel numb, shut down, disconnected from yourself and get stuck procrastinating?" asks LePera in another Twitter thread, viewed over five million times. "You're not lazy. You're not unmotivated. This is a trauma or stress response."[63] Or, perhaps my favorite LePera tweet of all time: "If you procrastinate, it's not because you're lazy. It's because your body is in a threat state."[64]

One wonders how she could possibly know this. (I reached out to LePera's booking agent to request an interview; alas, I did not hear back.) Is she not aware that laziness is one of humanity's most natural and ubiquitous states of surrender? LePera's large audience unquestionably contains a great many lazy people, as does any cross-section of society. A lot of people are lazy, but no one likes to think that they are. In the universe of trauma-loving psychologists, diagnoses proliferate and blame-shifting grinds on.

Hungry for Data

Kids and teens show up to school excited to play Magic: The Gathering, dangle from monkey bars, trade jokes with friends. They aren't always game for a rap session with the school shrink or forthcoming about their "adverse childhood experiences." But public school mental health experts can't collect the funds to underwrite their full array of treatments unless they can somehow *prove* kids are traumatized.

If only there were some way to surveil kids—for their own good, of course. Find out what goes on in their homes. Learn just a little more about their families. Peek, ever so discreetly, into the gray kinks of their brains.

We can't lure every middle schooler into an fMRI scanner. (If only!) Surely, there must be some other way to induce schoolchildren to divulge, in granular detail, every pixel of their trauma.

Chapter 7

•

Hunting, Fishing, Mining: Mental Health Survey Mischief

When your husband arrives at work, his employer hands him a survey. *The purpose is just to find out how everyone's doing,* he's told. The answers are entirely confidential. *But please take it seriously.* Here are a few of the questions:

- How often does your spouse give you a meaningful act of affection?

- Do you feel emotionally supported by your spouse about the things that matter most to you?

- How recently did your spouse offer you an unsolicited compliment?

- How often does your spouse say "thank you" and touch you, after something you did for her?

- Do you ever fantasize about a different sexual partner? How often?

- Have you ever hidden a prior sexual relationship from your spouse?

Think this would have no impact on your marriage? No alteration in his assessment of whether you're meeting his needs?

Compare those questions to the survey questions Colorado administered to elementary schoolkids, asking them to rate their level of agreement or disagreement:[1]

- I can tell my parents the way I feel about things.

- I like to do things with my family.

- I usually have dinner with my family.

- I feel close with my family.

- I spend time with my family doing things like shopping, playing sports, or working on school projects.

- My parents notice when I do a good job and let me know.

- Besides my family, there is an adult who I can trust.

- Important people in my life often let me down.

Surveys have become such a ubiquitous part of adult life, hitting our screens after every internet purchase and Uber ride, it's easy to dismiss them as an innocuous waste of time. But those are the surveys you ignore. There is another sort, too.

Mandated by state agencies and primarily authored by the Centers for Disease Control and Prevention (CDC), ostensibly to assess student mental health, surveys are presented to public school children with all the seriousness of a standardized test. They pry into the most private details of teenage experimentation and family life: alcohol consumption, drug use, and sexual orientation, along with the de rigueur inquiry into race and gender identity. They ask kids whether they feel loved by their parents or supported by their schools, and a series of very specific questions on what types of self-harm they have tried.

School systems use the results to justify ever-increasing demands for mental health resources—i.e., more funding.[2] Parents are technically allowed to "opt out" of these surveys, but in several states, consent is presumed.[3] Results of many of the surveys are uploaded to the CDC's Youth Risk Behavior Surveillance System, the federal program devoted to monitoring kids' risky behavior (and, it turns out, their parents').

I may never have seen these surveys if not for Parents Defending Education. Founded in 2021, the nonprofit has submitted hundreds of FOIA requests and amassed an impressive trove of surveys routinely presented to elementary through high school kids around the country. The organization was kind enough to share their database with me.

By some cheeky coincidence or gambit, the categories of the survey questions neatly track the very ones prohibited by federal statute. Perhaps sensing that school authorities might grow awfully curious about the most intimate details of their students' lives, Congress passed the Protection of Pupil Rights Amendment (PPRA) in 1978, and subsequently expanded, currently prohibits schools from inquiring about eight matters:

1. Political affiliation or beliefs of the student or the student's parent

2. Mental or psychological problems of the student or the student's family

3. Sex behavior or attitudes

4. Students' illegal or self-incriminating behavior

5. Critical appraisals of kids' family members

6. Privileged communications between a student and a therapist or priest

7. Students' religious beliefs or practices

8. Family income[4]

How do the federal government, local schools, and state health organizations brazenly ask about topics verboten under federal law? Provided the surveys are voluntary and anonymous, courts have ruled[5]: *They're kosher!*

More surprising than the surveys' extensive array of questions about middle schoolers' sexual orientations and gender identities is their blithe disregard for criminal law. The 2021 and 2023 Youth Risk Behavior surveys, authored by the CDC, asks middle school children: "How old were you when you had sexual intercourse for the first time?"[6]

A. I have never had sexual intercourse

B. 8 years old or younger

C. 9 years old

D. 10 years old

E. 11 years old

F. 12 years old

G. 13 years old or older

There's a word for "sexual intercourse" had by children at any of the ages listed above. It's "rape."

But our public health officials carry on, apparently unconcerned, as if it's utterly natural for adults to ask prepubescent children about their sexual adventures. The obvious implication—sure to be caught by the kids themselves—is that adults expect kids as young as eight to have interesting sex lives.

Like a high school dropout egging on younger kids toward delinquency, the surveys inquire about drug and alcohol use—students' own, and their family members'. Much of what students might cop to in these surveys could constitute admission of a crime.

The 2021 Florida High School Youth Risk Behavior Survey, authored by the CDC, for instance, asks: "During the past 30 days, on how many days did you carry a weapon such as a gun, knife or club on school property?"[7] Several other surveys ask middle school students for detailed admissions about their drug use and how easy it might be for them to obtain illegal drugs—methadone, fentanyl, and marijuana,[8] or prescription painkillers not prescribed to you. ("Hydros," "Oxy," "Gabbies," or "Trammies" lists the Georgia Student Health Survey,[9] apparently authored by the marketing department of MS-13.)

Mental Health Assessments

For our purposes, the most interesting survey questions are those that peel back young skulls to examine social and emotional fitness and history of trauma. There are extensive questions about suicide. In 2021, the Florida High School Youth Risk Behavior Survey asked kids fourteen and up this utterly standard question set of social-emotional questions:

- During the past 12 months, did you ever feel so sad or hopeless almost every day for two weeks or more in a row that you stopped doing your usual activities?

- During the past 12 months, did you ever seriously consider attempting suicide?

- During the past 12 months, did you make a plan about how you would attempt suicide?

- During the past 12 months, how many times did you actually attempt suicide?

- If you attempted suicide during the past 12 months, did any attempt result in an injury, poisoning, or overdose that had to be treated by a doctor or nurse?[10]

Not to be outdone by the state high school survey, the Florida Middle School Health Behavior Survey of 2021, authored by the CDC, gamely inquires:

- During the past year, did you do something to purposely hurt yourself without wanting to die, such as cutting or burning yourself on purpose?

- Have you ever participated in a game or challenge, by yourself or with others, that involved getting dizzy or passing out on purpose for the feeling it caused? (This game or challenge is also called the Choking Game, the Fainting Game, Pass Out, Knock Out, Tap Out, or Black Out.)

- During the past year, did you ever feel so sad or hopeless almost every day for two weeks or more in a row that you stopped doing some usual activities?

- Have you ever seriously thought about killing yourself?

- Have you ever made a plan about how you would kill yourself?

- Have you ever tried to kill yourself?[11]

You might be wondering: *What sadist put this in front of middle school children?* "Have you ever seriously thought about killing yourself?" is typically the sort of taunt one teen texts to another, or a troll writes on social media. Any seventh grader who isn't already au fait with "the

Fainting Game" or "Black Out" surely will want to educate herself. Mental health experts who would slide this list of questions onto the desks of eleven-year-olds—to satisfy the state's or school's curiosity—really ought to be kept away from children.

But we're far from done! Sixth graders in Georgia were presented with these questions in 2022, which reads like a script of Hannibal Lecter's devise, to induce mental illness in a patient:

During the past 12 months, if you have seriously considering [sic] harming yourself on purpose, what was the most likely reason? Check all that apply:

- I have not seriously considered harming myself on purpose

- Demands of schoolwork

- Problems with peers or friends

- Social media

- Family reasons

- Being bullied

- School grades or performance

- School discipline or punishment

- Argument or breakup with a partner/girlfriend/boyfriend

- Dating violence

- Drugs or alcohol

- Other[12]

The Florida surveys inquire about precisely what measures high school students have taken to lose weight—options that range from fasting to abusing laxatives.[13] Surely no high school girl will overlook this concise list of weight-loss tips.

School psychologists swear up and down that questioning adolescents about whether they have considered suicide (and how often) does not increase the likelihood that they will attempt it. But even if no adolescent attempts suicide after extensive questioning like this, there can be no doubt that it normalizes suicide for them. If you were a kid in high school, you might even think nearly everyone was contemplating self-destruction.

There is some research backing the claim that surveys about suicide don't increase suicidality—though the research does not necessarily account for the sheer quantity of suicide talk deluging today's middle and high school students: suicide hotline numbers plastered in public middle and high school bathrooms and stamped on every high school student ID card in South Carolina, Arizona, Illinois, and California.[14] Nor does available research indicate whether constantly asking kids to report on their self-harm (and providing a Britannica of popular methods and rationales) might tend to implant fresh options in young heads.

But the surveys themselves betray a different view. The 2022 Illinois Youth Survey for eighth graders, for instance, concludes with this: "If any survey questions or your responses have caused you to feel uncomfortable or concerned and you would like to talk to someone about your feelings, talk to your school's counselor, to a teacher, or to another adult you trust." If you don't feel comfortable talking to those adults, the survey directs students to various suicide, sexual assault, and crisis hotlines.[15]

The Washington State Healthy Youth Survey offers a similar warning and invitation to call a crisis hotline.[16] The Wisconsin middle school and high school surveys conclude the same way: noting that the survey may have induced sufficient distress that a student will want to talk to a school counselor, social worker, "or some other trusted adult."[17]

At least in the minds of the administrators, the surveys tend to produce emotional disturbance in kids. Which might make you wonder why they're administering these in the first place.

Critical Appraisals of Family Members

Perhaps the most seditious of survey questions press kids to critically appraise and report on their own families. The Arizona Youth Survey of 2022 asks middle and high school students to "think about the people you consider to be your family (e.g., parents, stepparents, grandparents, etc.)" while responding to the following with one of "NO!, no, yes, YES!"

- People in my family often insult or yell at each other.
- We argue about the same things in my family over and over.
- If you drank some alcohol without your parents' permission, would you be caught by your parents?
- My parents ask me what I think before most family decisions affecting me are made.
- Do you feel very close to your mother?
- Do you feel very close to your father?
- Do you share your thoughts and feelings with your mother?
- Do you share your thoughts and feelings with your father?
- Do you enjoy spending time with your mother?
- Do you enjoy spending time with your father?[18]

While asking students in a neutral way about suicide may or may not encourage thoughts of suicide, asking them to dwell on the state of their relationships is a different matter entirely. As anyone with a frenemy knows well, well-placed questions about the nature of your life and relationships can make you feel a lot worse.

Consider this statement and question, posed to eighth through twelfth graders in Arizona:[19]

- My parents notice when I am doing a good job and let me know about it.

- How often do your parents tell you they're proud of something you've done?

Or this series, presented to seventh to twelfth graders (age thirteen and older) in Indiana:

- How often do your parents tell you they're proud of you for something you've done?

- Would your parents know if you did not come home on time?

- If I had a personal problem, I could ask my mom or dad for help.

- How wrong do your parents feel it would be for you to: use methamphetamines? . . . use heroin? . . . use prescription drugs not prescribed to you? . . . steal something worth more than five dollars? (Answer choices include: "Very wrong," "Wrong," "A little bit wrong," "Not wrong at all.")[20]

Then there are the questions that, if matched with a student, might prompt a call to Child Services. Consider these, given to eighth graders in Illinois, which ask:

- How many days each week do you take care of yourself after school without an adult being there?

- Think of those days that you are home after school without an adult being there. How many hours a day do you usually take care of yourself after school?

- If you drank some beer, wine, or liquor (e.g., vodka, whiskey, or gin) without your parents' permission, would you be caught by your parents?

- If you go to a party where alcohol is served, would you be caught by your parents?

- When I am not at home, one of my parents/guardians knows where I am and who I am with.

- My parents/guardians ask if I've gotten my homework done.

- Would your parents/guardians know if you did not come home on time?[21]

Or from a Missouri Student Survey Questionnaire given to sixth graders, which asks:

- How often do people in your family insult or yell at each other? Never (1) Not very often (2) Some of the time (3) Most of the time (4) All of the time (5).[22]

Put aside, for a moment, the ever-present risk that these highly personal details about a child's family or mental health might be subject to a security breach[23]—and a child's private mental health information spread or sold across worlds unknown. Even if the responses never trickle into the public sphere, the surveys break and enter the private, sacred zone of family. That quirky, cozy den where you forgive your mother for forgetting to ask how your book report presentation went because she works hard and she's tired and even cranky occasionally, too. You don't think much of it when your parents leave you home for an hour while they run to the drug store or market or even go on a date because you're twelve and have a phone you can use if you have a problem.

Surveys betray an ontology—a view of the world and what objects furnish it. And in the world of these surveys, trauma is rampant—if not universal. Abuse and neglect visit every home. Drug use is pervasive, even among middle schoolers. Eight-year-olds have "had sexual intercourse." A sea of torment rises to drown all the children of the world.

No doubt, there are children who are abused, neglected, who use drugs in middle school, and are raped. No one would deny that. Every decent human being wants to help those kids. These surveys do not help those kids. (They are anonymized, after all.) These surveys simply present to all children the ontology of a darkly degraded world and convince them that they inhabit it.

At best, these questions invite criticism of a child's relationship with her parents. They invite the surveyed individual to find that relationship wanting. They push a child to consider that she may not be as loved, emotionally supported, or properly cared for as she would otherwise have believed.

And with all this aspersion cast on families by the mental health industry, we just might have a surprising number of young people deciding they were profoundly neglected or emotionally abused. We might have a young generation cutting off contact with loving parents in startling numbers.

How Mental Health Surveys Hurt Students

An intake form at a psychiatric hospital asks prospective patients the following:

- During the past 12 months, did you ever feel so sad or hopeless almost every day for two weeks or more in a row that you stopped doing some usual activities?

- During the past 12 months, did you ever seriously consider attempting suicide?

- During the past 12 months, did you make a plan about how you would attempt suicide?

- During the past 12 months, how many times did you actually attempt suicide?

- If you attempted suicide during the past 12 months, did any attempt result in an injury, poisoning, or overdose that had to be treated by a doctor or nurse?[24]

Just kidding. These are a standard series of questions administered to public high school kids in several states, all for the sake of tracking their wellness.[25]

As are these, administered to middle school kids in Delaware:

- During the past 12 months, did you ever feel so sad or hopeless almost every day for two weeks or more in a row that you stopped doing some usual activities?

- Do you ever feel sad, empty, hopeless, angry, or anxious?

- When you feel sad, empty, hopeless, angry, or anxious, how often do you get the kind of help you need?

- During the past 12 months, did you do something to purposely hurt yourself without wanting to die, such as cutting or burning yourself on purpose?

- Sometimes people feel so depressed about the future that they may consider attempting suicide or killing themselves. Have you ever seriously thought about killing yourself?

- Have you ever made a plan about how you would kill yourself?

- Have you ever tried to kill yourself?[26]

The authors of these surveys will insist that the questions are posed neutrally, but many seem to presume levels of distress and depression that ought to be relatively rare in middle school. ("When you feel sad, empty, hopeless, angry, or anxious . . .") Others provide new information. ("Sometimes people feel so depressed about the future . . .") And in aggregate, all seem eager for assent.

Why, then, were so many academic psychologists quick to deny that such surveys could negatively impact their respondents? At last, one took pity on me and told me the truth: *You know, we're all reliant on mental health surveys for our work,* he said. What he meant was: *We can't admit that surveys might harm the surveyed—we'd lose our chief tool.*

I realized I needed to talk to an academic psychologist with years of clinical and research experience who was neither dependent on surveys nor subject to the fear of students and administrators that bedevils even tenured professors. I reached out to Jordan Peterson. We met over Zoom. A pale-blue Oxford billowed over his wiry frame. Peterson seemed upbeat and well-rested, volleying my questions as he fed himself thick pieces of rib eye with knife and fork.

I began by telling Peterson about the surveys, quoting from actual questions, and repeating so many academic psychologists' insistence that there is no proof that asking kids repeatedly about self-harm will encourage them to attempt it. That's what they had told me: no proof whatsoever.

"They just don't know the relevant literature," he said. It is true, he allowed, that a one-time survey given to adolescents as a screener for suicide showed no short-term increase in depressive affect, as measured *two days later.*[27] But that study, conducted twenty years ago, scarcely replicates the experience of adolescents today, barraged by questions about their penchant for self-harm.

Because suicide and self-harm are so contagious among teens, Peterson said, adults must be extremely careful not to ask kids leading questions. "Like, 'When was the last time you thought about cutting your wrists?' Do you know how much information there is in that statement?"

He ticked off the embedded implications. "First of all, the information is—'Well, people do this.' The next piece of information is: '*You* could be doing this.' The next piece of information is: 'It's so likely that you're doing this that I can just ask it as a casual question.' And the next implication is: 'Well, what the hell's wrong with you if you're *not* doing this?'"

Peterson's concern is well-founded. The virality of suicide and self-harm among adolescents is extremely well-established.[28] Study after study[29] has shown that media reports of suicide can increase incidence among teens. In the 1980s, a concerted effort in Vienna, Austria, to limit media coverage of subway suicides had a stunning effect: the number of suicides by subway dropped by 75 percent.[30]

According to a CDC report, risk of copycat suicide behavior is particularly high where the subject of the suicide is valorized; where talk of suicide is *repetitive or excessive* and can become a preoccupation among at-risk youth; where suicide is *presented as a means of coping* with life's problems, and where *details of methods* are provided.[31]

It's almost as if the school survey authors read this list and decided, deliberately, to *include* each: *advertising* suicide as something adolescents do; *talking about it* repeatedly and excessively; *presenting it as a means of coping with personal problems*; offering *details as to methods*.

Consider one survey, authored by the CDC and given to middle schoolers in Delaware. "The next 3 questions ask about attempted suicide," it informs kids as young as twelve. "Sometimes people feel so depressed about the future that they may consider attempting suicide or killing themselves."[32] That sounds a whole lot like presenting suicide as a *means of coping with personal problems*.

Jam-packed are the surveys with "details of methods." The 2021 Florida Middle School Health Behavior Survey, remember, asked: "During the past year, did you do something to purposely hurt yourself without wanting to die, such as cutting or burning yourself on purpose?"[33]

As we've seen, the famous D.A.R.E. campaign led to increased teen drug use, perhaps for this very reason: it may have created curiosity about the very activity it hoped to disparage.[34]

And this is what so many adolescents I interviewed confirmed: they get the sense that almost everyone around them is on the verge of a breakdown.

Under the banner of "whole child" education and "trauma-informed care," educators greet every child with the emotional analogue of a gurney, all but begging kids to hop in. They never wait to see who might be injured because every child is encouraged to see herself as overtaxed and worn out. They encourage every child, constantly, to think about herself and her struggles.

Hell Is Thinking about Yourself

"Self-consciousness," or what Peterson calls "self-reflection on the feeling state," and neurotic suffering are virtually indistinguishable, clinically and psychometrically. "Insofar as you're thinking about yourself, you're depressed and anxious," Peterson said. "There's no difference between thinking about yourself and being depressed and anxious. *They are the same thing.*"[35]

Since anxiety and depression are highly comorbid (tend to go together) and are often treated with the same medication, this is less far-fetched than it might seem. Anxiety and depression may be different aspects of the same habits of mind: excessive thinking about yourself. That doesn't mean that anxiety and depression are your fault or that every anxious or depressed person can simply cure themselves. But it does suggest that for those visited by milder versions, there is the chance to reclaim the reins of mood by turning your focus away from yourself.

Here is a trick Peterson often used in his clinical practice. To his socially anxious patients, he recommended the following: When you go to a party, think about putting others at ease. Focus entirely on how *others* might be feeling. *Do* something nice for someone else. Stop thinking about yourself.[36]

"By making our children obsessively focused on their autonomous selves, all we do is pull them out of their social context, isolate them, and make them neurotic," Peterson said. "And so any clinician that tells you that there's no connection between constantly harassing people about their mental health, and making them miserable ... they're *clueless*. They have no idea what they're talking about."

It's our social context that keeps us sane, Peterson said. Mental health professionals typically assume that sanity is somehow inside your head. But it isn't—at least not entirely. "Sanity is the harmony that emerges as a consequence of being embedded in multiple social institutions," he said.

If we left kids alone to play and exist, relatively unfettered, in their social worlds—without our monitoring, advice-giving, and interruption—they would generally learn to get along with others, and they would tend to feel less despondent. We might need to interrupt rare cases of bullying. But otherwise, being part of a softball team or Girl Scouts, telling secrets to your best friend that you don't also share with your mom—that's the stuff that helps keep adolescents in balance, and kickstarts the freewheeling process of discovery and manufacture that ultimately produces a stable identity.

Instead, schools regularly insert themselves between parent and child and between kids and their peers. Schools prompt kids to consider their existences and identities in total isolation. Schools push kids to mull on their failures and disappointments—to feel ever more desperately alone.

That's very different from asking a kid the sorts of things adults have always asked kids: "How is school going?" "How do you like your teachers?" "How's the baseball team?" "How is the seventh grade?" "How's your family?" "What are you learning in school?" "What's your favorite class?" All great questions that may prompt personal reflection on a child's life. But in every instance, the conceit is the same: *You are part of a social fabric, a society, a community, a family, a team. What do you think about our broader world?*

But ask a kid: "How are *you* feeling today?" as our schools now do on a routine basis, and you tear kids from that social fabric. You ask them to conceive of themselves as free radicals, hurtling through the universe without a tether. This sort of contemplation is inherently destabilizing. It may even be indistinguishable from unhappiness itself.

Chapter 8

•

Full of Empathy
and Mean as Hell

C hloe[1] had a trick for surviving her Kafkaesque tenth-grade
year. Each day, before she entered the century-old hallways
of the Spence School, alma mater to the nabob daughters of
knickerbocker, Chloe shoved fully charged AirPods into her ear canals.
They gave her a small pocket of comfort as she proceeded, friendless,
through the halls and sat at lunch each day, alone.

"Not one person would talk to her," her mother told me. Not even the
girls she'd known since kindergarten. "She would go out to lunch alone,
she would be alone every weekend, every single night. There was an understanding that everyone knew what was going on."

In October of 2018, the fifteen-year-old advanced math student had
committed the cardinal sin of joking with two camp friends about the
worst possible costumes for an upcoming Halloween party. What should
the three of them *definitely not* go as this year? "George Washington,
Thomas Jefferson, and James Madison." Lame. Other definite noes: "Pro-

ton, neutron, and electron." Too geeky. "Isotope, ion, and unstable atom." They were cracking up. "Sine, cosine, and tangent."

Chloe was clever, and she knew it. A member of Spence's varsity tennis team and an academic star, she thought up clever triads the way other kids perform tricks with their skateboards. Chloe and the two other girls took turns contributing to the list of hypothetical nixed costumes, sure to be among the worst-received of all time.

"Ablative, accusative, nominative," Chloe ticked off. "Subjunctive, infinitive, imperative"; "Moses, Jesus, Mohammed"; "Slaves, indigenous people, white settlers." It was funny! Relief for a girl who spent an unreasonable portion of her life bent over books. She kept going: "free trade, partial government intervention, and communism"; "Hitler, Mussolini, Stalin"; "racism, sexism, antisemitism."[2]

The beaten horse was quite dead by then, but she and her friends laughed, enjoying their own cleverness. They were young and smart and, without boys around, free to let their nerd flags fly. Chloe posted the goofy exchange to her private Instagram account. With that, she knocked over the card table on which her careful life was set.

The next day at school, two of Chloe's Spence classmates confronted her at school, claiming that they were offended by her post. Chloe immediately apologized to the girls and took it down. But it was too late; and the confrontation, pro forma. The girls had already taken screenshots of the transgressive post and run to the administration. They claimed they had been victimized by the post's racism and antisemitism.

Other Spence girls registered the metallic tang of blood in the water. They ran to the administration to lodge their own complaints. They falsely claimed Chloe had joked online about dressing up with her friends as "slaves and slaveholders" and "Jews and Hitler." Chloe had made them feel "scared and unsafe."

Spence's director of institutional equity and a small group of administrators called Chloe to account for herself. She broke down, crying hysterically, according to a complaint later filed by her parents. She had never been in trouble before.

Spence administrators convened two full-grade assemblies—without Chloe present—to discuss the "incident," which had begun to take on a life of its own. At the assemblies, administrators publicly accused Chloe of having engaged in racist conduct, though they never specified what that racist conduct was.

Several of the accusers admitted they had not seen the offending post and no administrator had bothered to read its text, according to the complaint. The hurt feelings of Chloe's accusers sufficed. Their pain, proof positive of harm.

Throughout the discussions of Chloe's alleged antisemitism, no school official noted that none of the offended students was Jewish. Neither were Spence's administrators. But Chloe *is* Jewish. Two years earlier, many of her accusers had attended her bat mitzvah.

Chloe apologized to the offended students several times. One school administrator insisted that Chloe provide a "racialized" apology to one of her accusers, meaning she had to apologize "as a white girl." Chloe did as she was asked. It was never enough.

One might have assumed that at Spence, where "emotional and social competencies" are explicit educational priorities, such calculated interpersonal cruelty would be a rarity.[3] Shouldn't having "empathy" as a core value mean that a school can see things from the perspective of an unfairly accused teen? How could a school that trumpets "empathy" as one of the "key skills of civic engagement" have had so little to spare for Chloe?[4]

Brittle Monsters

By the time I talked to Chloe's mother, I knew that schools' therapeutic interventions weren't likely to produce healthier, more emotionally resilient kids. But I assumed, at a bare minimum, that the empathy focus ought at least to have fostered a more caring environment. Teaching "empathy" has been a stated purpose of social-emotional learning since the program's inception.[5] CASEL, the standard-bearer of social-emotional learning curricula, defines SEL as the process through which young people learn to "feel and show empathy for others."[6] Teaching kids to *empathize* with others is part of "social awareness," one of the "five core competencies" SEL promises to teach.[7] So why would social-emotional learning coincide with the startling eruption of interpersonal cruelty?

"It creates unbelievable narcissists," Parisa, an Iranian-born mother who sends her son to one of New York's most prestigious prep schools, told me. All of this self-focus invariably leads kids to the realization that someone in the class is making them unhappy, she says. "Which then requires policing the classroom so people with the wrong opinion have to either not speak or say the wrong thing and take the consequence."

Caitlin is a Korean American who sends her kids to a posh school in California. She told me that, at today's tony prep schools, all of which emphasize social-emotional skills, "only what you believe and what you feel matters. You don't have to treat grownups with trust or respect," she said. "They don't know more than you. Only what you feel is what you know. And then you're just letting loose a bunch of tiny little narcissists and giving them reasons to attack each other."

In the contemporary therapeutic school environment, students are not merely tyrannized by their own feelings. They live under the tyranny of each other's. And unlike the strict schools of bygone eras, the contemporary rule of feelings is endlessly capricious, vague in its dictates, unconcerned with facts or evidence. Punishments escalate until the aggrieved are satisfied, at last bored by the riot they caused. Not knowing who might accuse you next is a little like reaching into a garbage disposal to retrieve a bottle cap. The spidery worry that someone might flip a switch lingers long after you've safely retracted your fingers from the grinding plates.

The Problem with Empathy

One might mistakenly assume that there's some sort of empathy paradox. Perhaps schools are teaching "empathy" all wrong, and if they fixed their methods, great social harmony would result? Not so. As academic psychologists who study empathy know, injustice and cruelty may even be the *predictable* result of placing a precedence on empathy.

"Empathy is a spotlight focusing on certain people in the here and now," Yale professor of psychology Paul Bloom writes in his important book, *Against Empathy*. "This makes us care more about them, but it leaves us insensitive to the long-term consequences of our acts and blind as well to the suffering of those we do not or cannot empathize with. Empathy is biased, pushing us in the direction of parochialism and racism."

Intellectually, we can value the lives of billions of people across the globe. "But what we can't do is empathize with all of them," he writes. "Indeed, you cannot empathize with more than one or two people at a time. Try it."[8]

The inability to empathize with more than two people at once is not anyone's fault. It's simply a feature of empathy's natural limitations. "It's a spotlight that has a narrow focus, one that shines most brightly on those we love and gets dim for those who are strange or different or frightening," Bloom writes. It strikes me that we know this rather instinctively: nepotism bans are based on the recognition that our natural empathy for kin sacrifices fairness and, ultimately, the welfare of the group.

Make fairness your guide and you lay the groundwork for treating everyone equally. But put empathy in charge—feel the pain of the "victims" in front of you—and you're not only likely to treat the "out group" much worse.[9] You may even treat *everyone* worse. A police captain who empathizes with an incompetent officer leaves the public less safe as a result (and the officer less safe, too).

The most selfless acts a mammal commits she does on behalf of her children. The most violent, in their defense. Where empathy rules human interactions, we see a remarkable nurturing of insiders alongside cruelty and indifference to interlopers.

This may explain why therapists sometimes inadvertently encourage a client to divorce by making relationship-undermining statements and portraying the absent spouse unfavorably.[10] It's not that these therapists are necessarily callous; they may simply be *empathic.*

Therapists readily empathize with the paying clients in front of them over those who have no opportunity to testify in their own defense. How natural to suggest cooling off the relationship with Mom, dispatching a "friendship breakup" text, or hatching the "amicable divorce." It's awfully hard to think about a child you've never met—say, the little girl whose life is about to be sliced in two—when her tearful mom is perched on your couch.

Empathy invariably involves a choice of *whose feelings to coronate* and *whose to disregard.* Overreliance on empathy as a guide to mediating human affairs leads to precisely the injustices we see today in schools: phony show trials allegedly in defense of marginalized students, alongside breathtaking cruelty to undesirables. Empathy supplies a narrow aperture of intense caring. Those outside it blur into nothing.

Schools often preach empathy on the theory that those who feel the pain of their fellow students will be more likely to treat them better, but there is simply no proof of this. "It's not true that those who do evil are necessarily low in empathy or that those who refrain from evil are high in empathy," Bloom writes.[11]

People who are motivated by fairness or a keen sense of right and wrong will often treat people humanely, despite feeling no particular empathy with the beneficiaries. Someone who returns a lost wallet is probably not motivated by empathy; she typically doesn't know the owner. She does this because she believes it is right.

Conversely, psychopaths utilize empathy to exploit their victims.[12] Conmen, seducers of elderly widows, and the worst kind of mean girls have perfected this "dark empathy."

In a therapeutic, empathy-based system, the first and loudest to cry foul can capture a school administration's full support and commandeer its punitive arsenal. In this light, it is unsurprising that our most emotionally attuned schools would be scenes of ethical bedlam.

The Tattletale Generation

Consider the messages therapeutic education broadcasts to students: *You can't manage your own conflicts. You are filled with trauma and need our "trauma-informed care." You are constantly contemplating suicide or engaging in self-harm. You are breaking or broken. You cannot possibly survive a bad grade or a firm deadline—challenges kids have met since the invention of school.*

Like the disempowered masses of a totalitarian regime, kids reach for the remaining implement in an otherwise empty toolbox: tattling. Virtually every parent I talked to mentioned with alarm the profusion of tattling at their kids' schools—even at the high school level.

One mom, Ellen, who consults to private school parents, apprised me of a bizarre and chilling trend among the rising generation. Many teens maintain a cache of screenshots to incriminate their friends *just in case* they should need to retaliate against an accuser.

A major part of Ellen's national consulting business involves advising families whose kids have been accused by another student. And the moment a parent contacts her for help in such a crisis, that parent also typically sends along an incriminating cache on the student accuser. At first,

Ellen was stunned. *How did you come across these old pictures?* she would ask. The answer was always the same: *Oh, my kid saved these screenshots of her friends saying something racist or doing something stupid—just in case.*

Call it insurance. Call it blackmail. Call it what it is: utterly bananas.

"The whole reason why we have juvenile laws that allow for sealing of records before the age of eighteen is because society recognizes the importance of these young kids who have made mistakes getting a fresh start with a clean record," Ellen said. But racism or the endless fill-in-the-phobia allegations made by young people rarely require substantiation to inflict real damage. Nor do they ever occur in the court of law, where they would be sealed. They exist on kids' phones. In the worst instances, they threaten to trail a child for decades—maybe for the rest of her life.

As I listened to Ellen, I wondered if this was a local phenomenon. But in July of 2020, the *New York Times* reported on dozens of instances in which universities had rescinded admissions of students after having received screenshots of racist or inappropriate Snapchat communications, Instagram posts, or texts—all of it sent to the universities by other students.[13] Some of the videos and screenshots were of incidents that had occurred years earlier—meaning, students had been maintaining the caches for years, just as Ellen had told me.

This is a consequence of the life we have made for the rising generation. Monitored like babies in cribs, treated like patients in a psychiatric ward, they disbelieve they can trust each other or handle conflicts themselves. They slide into the habits of "grudge informants," pitiable citizens of Stalin's Russia, Mao's China, and today's high school. Resolving mundane conflicts with peers seems above their paygrade. Better to inform their superiors. They do not behave like teammates in a great society. They behave like the survivors of the remnants of one, after all order has broken down.

Consider the corruption of character that would lead a student to store screenshots for use against her classmates and friends—the sustained flirtation with evil. The rising generation tattles on their professors for failing to incorporate the newest update to the ever-expanding concordance of problematic phrases. They complain about their bosses to HR with the elan of vindictive prosecutors. They do so without embarrassment or self-reflection.

The obvious next question: Who raised these kids?

Chapter 9

•

The Road Paved
by Gentle Parents

My little brother and I were "latchkey kids," which meant the school bus dropped us off at 3:45 p.m. each day, one block from our suburban Maryland home. We let ourselves into an empty house, quiet and dark in the late afternoon, and turned on the TV for company. At four p.m., *Batman: The Animated Series* arrived, then *Saved by the Bell*. If we were hungry, we fed a Healthy Choice meal into the microwave or heated up Chef Boyardee ravioli from a can. Occasionally, we started our homework. More often, we didn't. (No one checked.)

None of our neighbors or friends considered us ignored or deprived. Our parents were attorneys. Mom was stuck at work until at least five p.m., occasionally much later. We had a working phone in case of emergency. Loneliness and boredom tugged at our hearts and minds. Most of the kids on the block were in the same boat. A few of them got into trouble: experimenting sexually, smoking cigarettes, punching holes in the insulation of a house under construction. (Okay, the last one included me.)

My generation's parents divorced in larger numbers than America had ever seen.[1] Adults often acted as if that was the best outcome for everyone. They said it made kids happy to see their parents fulfilled by new relationships. But the kids who turned up to math class without a textbook because they'd left it at their dad's house and wouldn't see him again until Saturday didn't seem happier because their father was starting a new, better life. They were just kids without the right textbook.

For many members of my generation, adolescence was a trial. We reached adulthood and millions of us entered therapy.[2] We had kids of our own, purchased stacks of parenting books, most of them written by shrinks, and began to reevaluate our childhoods.

Shouldn't Flowers Bloom in Powdered Sugar?

We'd all been spanked as kids, but suddenly, that made us feel ashamed; it came to seem like abuse. We'd all been yelled at and punished when we talked back or acted out, but that now seemed off-limits with our own. Most of us came home after school to empty houses. But in retrospect, that level of neglect seemed to warrant a visit from Child Services. Our parents attended few of our soccer games; but if we skipped even our kids' practices, we felt like we'd abandoned them at Port Authority.

That the vast majority of us ended up in pretty good shape—that we married, made and kept friends, held down jobs, and created lives that required others to depend on us because they could—carried a whiff of dumb luck. We assumed it was *despite* our parents' terribly uncool manner of child-rearing that we turned out okay. We would have been so much better off, we decided, if only we'd had gentler and more involved parents.

With our own kids, we used soft voices, met them at eye level, and asked them constantly how they felt about things. It seemed obvious: How do you produce gentle, calm kids? With gentle, calm parenting. We constantly invited our kids to weigh in on all of the choices we made for them. We asked our kids for feedback on the job *we* were doing.

The fevered insecurity of contemporary parenting first announced itself to me when I signed my twin four-year-old boys up for piano lessons. Once a week, a Soviet Jewish émigré redolent of Russian stoicism and expensive perfume clicked into our West Los Angeles home. For a single half-hour session, she taught my boys to sit up straight and find middle C.

The boys learned to repeat "Every Good Boy Does Fine" and "All Cows Eat Grass" while their fingers traced the lines and spaces on an enlarged version of the grand staff. Gradually, they learned to plink out very simple and satisfying tunes. She was pleased. I was a mess.

"Was it *your* decision to start the boys on piano or *theirs*?" other mothers wanted to know.

"Both," I lied.

The question didn't deter me, but it rattled me. I began checking in regularly with my boys to make sure they were "still enjoying piano." Then I reassured the Russian piano teacher that they remained game for her instruction.

Finally, she leveled with me. "You must stop this. Sometimes they will like the piano; sometimes they won't. This is normal. Stop asking."

Where had I gotten the idea that at every moment of their lives, my boys were supposed to be gleefully engaged? Why was I so insecure? I had endured all sorts of lessons and sports teams as a kid; some I stuck with—most, I dropped. Neither of my parents lost sleep fretting over the optimal age to start me in tap dance. No one monitored my ongoing yen to become the next Bojangles.

By my generation decided that the ideal parent was never stern or disengaged or even particularly natural. The ideal parent emerged through training and constant practice. All parents became amateur shrinks, and every shrink—even a childless one—was a parenting expert. Parents began to sound less like parents—in the traditional, American vein—and more like therapists. "Sammy, I see that you're feeling frustrated. Is there a way you could express your frustration *without* biting your sister?"

It never occurred to us that "unconditional positive regard" and deep listening may be feasible from a shrink for a single fifty-minute session per week but that it's a little less practicable for parents interacting with kids for tens of thousands of hours, in endlessly varied circumstances, over the course of years.

Dear God, we were tired. That's how we knew we were great parents: we'd reached Level 5 exhaustion. Moms were putting in 50 percent more time with their kids than parents did in the 1960s; dads—twice as much.[3] We *must* be doing a better job.

And yet by objective measures, we weren't. We had replaced one set of problems for another. Everything we were doing felt so virtuous. Everything we were producing seemed so broken.

When asked, our kids said they were miserable. Our kids didn't want to leave their rooms. Our kids didn't date. Our kids moved home and stayed. They didn't want to get married or have kids.[4] Our kids were on four or six different psychotropic drugs. None of it seemed to make them feel better. None of it seemed to make them feel anything at all.

We assumed with perfect faith (and wholly without evidence) that gentler parenting could only produce thriving children. Shouldn't flowers bloom in powdered sugar?

Turns out, they grow best in dirt.

"Knock It Off, Shake It Off"

America once had a more masculine style of parenting. It's a style traditionally occupied by Dad (though, really, I've seen women employ it to great effect). This is the style I've called "knock it off, shake it off" parenting.[5] The sort that met kids' interpersonal conflict with "Work it out yourselves," and greeted kids' mishaps with "You'll live." A loving but stolid insistence that young children get back on the horse and carry on.

"Knock it off" didn't suffice in the face of all misbehavior. But in the main, it put the onus on kids to figure out what was wrong with their conduct and desist. "Knock it off" didn't overexplain: It credited kids with common sense or nudged them to develop it. Rules had exceptions and workarounds, but "knock it off" signaled a parent's disinclination to become entangled in them. Every kid who hopes to hold down a job without making himself a terrible (and disposable) burden to an employer needed to master this art of following simple instruction—without seven hundred time-consuming follow-up questions. "Knock it off" meant: *You're a smart kid, figure it out.* But also: *You can.*

"Shake it off" didn't solve the worst injuries, of course, but that was never its purpose. (No one except a sadist ever thought a child could run on a broken leg.) And it rarely operated alone: the other parent, the gentler one, often cushioned its impact. But "shake it off" did a helluva job playing triage nurse to kids' minor heartaches and injuries, proving to kids that the hurt or fear or possibility of failure need not overwhelm them. "Shake it off" provided its own kind of tough love and emotional nourishment. It taught kids to soldier into a world with the hopeful disregard of danger that a cynic might term naivete. Others call it courage.[6]

In the last generation, all traces of tough love and rule-bound parenting have been supplanted by a more empathetic style, the one once associated with moms. Most dads have been told explicitly—or made to feel—that the approach their own fathers took was wrong and their native instincts no guide.

But even Mom isn't in charge today—not really. The proof is how many books she must read to establish her competence as a mother. She may not trust her husband's instincts with the kids, but she regards her own as only marginally better. And her parents' methods? Obsolete as the Yellow Pages. Unlike most of the experts, her parents raised a few kids who managed to become self-supporting, capable, and dependable citizens. But her parents corrected and punished their way through child-rearing, so Mom discards most of their example off the bat. In its place, she deploys phrases borrowed from her shrink. ("Why don't we try taking a few breaths together now, Harper?")

Mom's therapist may not have had any stable romantic relationship to speak of, and she raised no more than one child of her own. (The outcome of that effort, anyone's guess.) But her therapist knows all about mental health. She therefore must know more about parenting than the people who've actually done it. Which is a little like soliciting the advice of a biologist on how to make love.

For at least a generation, Mom hasn't provided her children escape from the quackery of wellness culture, and she certainly is no bulwark against it. She is an *ersatz* therapist, practicing bad therapy on kids whose emotions grow increasingly unruly, whose behavior eludes the traps set by her affected questioning. When she has no patience left to offer, she turns a gimlet eye on her offspring and downgrades her assessment: *Maddie has significant challenges and needs a great deal of additional support.*

Battered Mommy Syndrome

In September of 2021, I attended a dinner of five couples, all young and upper middle class, denizens of an affluent West LA neighborhood. One father, I'll call him "Alan," excitedly relayed a parenting fail his wife had witnessed at the playground. A young, well-heeled mother was struggling with a recalcitrant six-year-old son. "Please be a good boy," the woman had said to her son. "If you're good for just five minutes, when we get home, I'll let you do anything you want. What do you want?"

The little boy looked his mother straight in the eye. "I want to punch you in the face," he said.

We dinner guests laughed uproariously, shrill with worry that we, too, might be raising little Pol Pots.

But then Alan said, "I don't care how many experts we have to consult or how much we have to pay, I don't want to end up with *that*."

Here, finally lucid, was the dastardly trap of modern parenting. The woman at the park, straining to be gentler than her parents likely ever were with her, met by her son's contempt; Alan, believing that there must be some expert who can assert the necessary authority to control his own child.

Moms like the one at the park are everywhere practicing expert techniques of positive incentives, devising the proper consequences, pleading with kids to behave, afraid of the kids they are raising.

Life Hacks for Abused Parents

A friend's wife became a parenting coach, and one of the popular videos she posted begins with this: "Have you ever been at a loss for what to do when your kid hits, kicks, bites, or scratches you? If so, I have a tool for you!"

Can you imagine your own parents asking that question? Can you imagine thinking, as a four- or five-year-old, that you would kick, hit, or bite your parents—*more than once*?

You may be thinking: *Well, my parents spanked me.* Or, *But I was afraid of my parents. I don't want my kids to be afraid of me.* You have nothing to worry about. This generation of kids is absolutely *not* afraid of their parents. They think their parents are nice people. And they are frequently contemptuous of them.

The mom coach suggested the following script: "Sweetie, I know you are so upset because I gave you the blue cup instead of the green cup—or because I told you it was time to take your fort down. But next time you're upset, we can clench our fists or stomp our feet or tell Mommy what's wrong and I might be able to help."

This is precisely the playbook propounded by a raft of therapeutic parenting books, from the iconic *How to Talk So Kids Will Listen and Listen So Kids Will Talk* to *Raising Your Spirited Child*. The approach to bad behavior is always *therapeutic*—meaning it is nonjudgmental. It's the parent's job to understand a child's frustration—never the child's job to learn to control his impulses.

Such parents typically eschew all punishment. At most, they might allow a child to live with the result of what she has done. If a child throws a toy at the wall and it breaks, the parent points out that now the toy is broken and isn't that sad? A kid writes on the wall, and you tell her it makes you unhappy when people write on the wall and you ask her to help repaint the wall. Those are *consequences*.

Where things get a little murky is when the "consequences" aren't actually consequences. They're punishments in dress-up. "Since you threw your food on the floor, I cannot take you to the park. I cannot take anyone to the park who throws their food on the floor, because now I have to spend the time I would have spent at the park cleaning this up. Would you like to help clean it up?" This is supposed to impress the child because after all, the parent has avoided appealing to her own authority. She merely offers *description* of what happened, *non-hierarchical* invitation to "connect" over the new task, and so much *shrugging of shoulders*: "I don't make the rules here! I just follow them."

But of course, it's also bollocks. A parent *can* take a kid to the park who has thrown his food on the floor. She just doesn't want to. And she *does* make the rules—or, at least, she's chosen to adopt the rules, supplied by the parenting experts. But here is the parent straining to act as therapist, divesting herself of moral judgment, refusing to chide bad behavior, pretending her hands are tied.

"Anyone Have Advice about How to Get a Three-Year-Old to Accept the Consequences?"

If someone wanted to kill all human desire to reproduce—to achieve, at last, this thing environmentalists call "population control"—steering readers to the *Slate* Parenting Facebook group might be a promising way to start.

Home to an educated, conscientious, liberal-leaning readership of eighteen thousand regular members, the *Slate* Parenting Facebook group provides a worthy terrarium in which to observe highly educated, progressive, therapist-directed parents as they air dilemmas and seek advice from their equally flummoxed counterparts. These preppy parents have read stacks of parenting books and listened to thousands of hours of parenting podcasts. Many adhere to "gentle parenting," a therapy-infused model that requires parents to give choices instead of orders.[7] (Parents get plenty of orders; children get none.)

These parents are "intentional" about everything. Even before they had kids, they adopted a parenting philosophy. So does it work?

The short answer is no. The longer answer is noooooooooooooo.

Believing their kids may have "sensory" issues, they hunt for cumulous fabrics, snip the tags from every undershirt. When their kids express aural discomfort at the roar of a toilet, the parents search for a school with a quieter flush. They avoid shampooing the hair of kids who don't like water poured over their heads, while their kids grow *more* determined in their refusal to bathe.

"Anyone have advice about how to get a three-year-old to accept the consequences?" writes Airin, one frustrated parent. "When he hits, kicks, or yells (no provocation), how do I get him to calm down? I've tried addressing his feelings and time-outs. But when he goes into time-out, he gets very destructive and violent (throwing anything he can lift) or attacks me if I'm there."

Another parent volunteers: We have a dedicated "'calming corner' with pillows, feelings posters, and cards, in her bedroom and in the living room." Another recommends: "We use apology chores," so that the violent child never has to face the pain of being "isolated or forced to hold still."

A parent identified as "Rico" offers: "With our kid, we use an 'I don't like it when you hit me so I'm gonna stand up and stop playing for a while' approach."

These parents proudly declare that they avoid ever saying "no" to their children. They regard time-outs as cruel and "triggering." Isolating a child in his room? Emotionally hurtful—and out of the question.

Even in response to violence, they offer almost no correction and absolutely no judgment. Instead, they announce their preferences: "I don't like it when you hit, so I'm gonna stand up." *De gustibus non est disputandum. I don't prefer to be hit; others may differ.*

But does this sort of announcement end the disruption? "He often throws himself down and cries after that, but that's just part of the learning process," Rico writes.

I have never interviewed the man who bought a Siberian-Bengal tiger and tried to raise him in a Harlem apartment.[8] But the parents of *Slate* often sound like I imagine he must have felt: lowering raw chickens on a pole through an open window so as not to displease the feral creature he'd long since lost the ability to control.

"Have you tried any sensory items to help him regulate, like a weighted Stuffie or a blanket?" asks another parent. "I would gently tackle him into his room and stay with him, wrapped around him, until he started to come down the other side of his tantrum." It's easy, really. Just tackle him and hold him down for twenty minutes or so. (Here's hoping you've got nothing cooking on the stove, and no other kids who need tackling!)

The *Slate* parents are rich in kids who lash out like Sonny Corleone when a kid at preschool chooses a toy they wanted—or does nothing at all. "What do you do for a 3.5 yr old who doesn't seem to care about any consequences? He is super bright and has some mild sensory issues. I have always tried to be a gentle parent (absolutely no physical punishment) though I know I yell way too much," a parent named Hollie writes, a little abjectly. "He is super strong. I've tried time-outs but I end up having to hold him the whole time and generally end up getting punched in the face (usually accidentally)," she says, oblivious to her own battered mommy syndrome.

"I take away things like screen time. He just doesn't seem to care. For instance he jumps on our couch, super unsafe. He also will get mad and throw things at his sister like matchbox cars. Am I raising a sociopath? Help!"

She intends this as a joke. One hopes the next kid to get beaned by a metal matchbox car finds it funny. As melee weapons, they work well—as projectiles, even better. But don't imagine mom ever takes away the matchbox car or sends Junior to his room. (At most, she takes away the expensive gaming screen she supplies.)

Notice, too, the only grounds the mom believes she has for objection to her son's bad behavior is that it's "unsafe" for the monster himself. She can't possibly say, "Don't jump on our furniture; you'll break it." Or even, "Don't jump on things that don't belong to you."

That this child will one day break someone else's sofa without regret—having never been told that it is wrong, that he can and must stifle the urge to destroy—feels like the inevitable next act of the psychodrama.

Could Mom benefit from the guidance of an expert? Of course not. She already has one. "Please note that I have worked with an OT for the stuff," she writes. "He sleeps with a compression sheet and we do lots of activities for his sensory stuff. The quarantine has completely changed his schedule, but I had these issues before. I'd love any advice on how to

get his attention and let him know I mean business." Yes, preferably before he maims his sister.

But siblings or bystanders are rarely considered. Their rights never
cross mom's mind. Empathy is nothing if not monogamous, everybody
else—sister, Grandma, other kids at school—be damned. That's just
Levi's inner turmoil spilling out!

"Anger can often be anxiety or shame in young children," opines
another mom in response. Indeed. You can't correct a presumptively
trauma-filled tot. And if you send him to the isolation of a (toy-packed)
room? That may be enough to inflict childhood trauma.

Gabor Maté claimed this explicitly, during his appearance on Joe
Rogan's podcast. Appalled by the idea that a parent would compel an
angry child who lashes out to sit by himself until he calms down, Maté
offers a perfect encapsulation of therapeutic parenting's view of discipline: "Notice the assumption: anger in a young child is neither normal
nor acceptable. . . . [The child] is not to be accepted for who she is, only
for how she is. Here's the problem: even if the parent wins the behavior-
modification game, the child loses. We have instilled in her the anxiety of
being rejected if her emotional self were to surface."[9]

Maté then catastrophizes the consequence to the child of even this
mild imposition of discipline. "When you repress healthy anger because
you're programmed to do so because some parenting expert told your
parents that an angry child should be banished from your presence . . .
then they learn to suppress their anger all their lives. That represses the
immune system. Now, the immune system turns against you or it cannot
fight off malignancy."[10] Send a kid to his room, wreck his immune system for life.

When one *Slate* mom, Liz, writes to complain that her "emotional
roller coaster" of a five-year-old daughter often collapsed in screaming
fits in the weeks after she broke her arm, *Slate* parents rush in with diagnoses. "It sounds like she is having a trauma response," opines Brian.

"Remember, Post Traumatic Stress is a normal reaction to an abnormal traumatic event." (No, actually, it isn't; *resilience* is the normal response.)

"This may be a sensory issue for her, combined with difficulty regulating emotions," suggests Maggie. She suggests the likely culprit is "ADHD or another neurodivergence." It's not just her arm that's broken. She has a psychological problem, of that *Slate* parents are sure; they just haven't decided what diagnostic code to offer insurance.

Occasionally, it dawns on a *Slate* parent that the therapeutic approach might be part of the problem. A self-described "gentle parent," Heather writes that every morning her six-year-old daughter refuses to get dressed, complaining that her clothes are too rough, demanding others. And yet Heather writes: "I was out of town part of last week and she got dressed with no issues for my husband on school days so I think it's all related to me."

Dad levels with the kid, issues a direct order, expects the kid to comply, and—voila!—she can. Where is the Enigma cryptology team when we need it?

In the end, Mom dislikes being with her daughter. "I hate every morning," Mom writes in a moment of honesty.

It's inevitable, isn't it? The people who make parenting look exhausting aren't all that fond of the kids they've raised. If it's any consolation— the rising generation's employers and colleagues aren't smitten with them, either.

Pity the Gentle Dada

There's a charming and admirably honest book that encapsulates the miserable predicament of the expert-directed parent: *Raising Raffi*, by Keith Gessen. Gessen is a Harvard-educated writer and editor who tears his hair out for over two hundred pages, while consulting every possible book on how to coax his toddler, Raffi, to behave.

Gessen approaches the project of his son with so much trepidation, haplessness, and apology, you would think he was trying to build a seaworthy canoe out of Ikea pressboard and a fistful of cabinet pegs. "I wrote this book out of desperation," he writes.

Gessen is equipped with a superlative education, a devoted wife and partner in child-rearing, helpful parents and in-laws, and a network of generous friends. And yet every chapter is threaded with a live wire of paternal anguish at how many critical mistakes Gessen believes he is making. Each purported misstep sends him back to the parenting books, bloated with grief and self-reproach. His three-year-old son kicks and punches and headbutts Gessen and hurls a plastic cup at his nose.

In exasperation, Gessen finds himself yelling and reproving Raffi because he just can't take the boy's bad behavior anymore; each time, Gessen is sickened with just how much like an old-fashioned parent he sounds. The one thing he knows is that he doesn't want to be the sort of parent of the generation that raised him. They are the bad kind of parents, the ones who yell, punish, and lay down firm rules.

Gessen knows he's supposed to be endlessly patient, thoroughly gentle, while constantly urging Raffi to see the light. But it's distressing to watch your son nearly end the fragile life of his newborn brother by attempting to twist off the baby's head like a bottle cap. It stings when a plastic cup hits your nose. It apparently really hurts to get kicked in the nuts.

Fed up with Raffi's penchant for hitting his parents and other kids, and throwing his food on the floor, Gessen and his wife make a "sticker chart" to reward Raffi for the times when he does *not* hit others. But this kid was not born yesterday. Raffi insists that Gessen and his wife also make a sticker chart for themselves, and they dutifully comply—one for each of them, on the fridge, as if there are three errant children in the family, not one. Raffi's violence toward other children does not abate.

"We'd done everything right, had been totally consistent from one situation to the next—and it hadn't mattered,"[11] Gessen writes, sounding defeated.

Once—just once—when Raffi is attempting to wrench the head off his newborn brother, ignoring Gessen's command to stop, Gessen gives the boy's hand a smack. This launches Gessen into a maelstrom of guilt and self-doubt. The clever boy runs straight to Mom, who leaps to Raffi's defense and demands to know if Gessen in fact hit their son.

"Dada's not nice," the little boy declares.

"The words cut me to the quick," Gessen writes. "If there was one thing I aspired to be, it was nice. I wanted to be nice. I wanted my son to feel that I was a warm presence in his life."[12]

Miserable, Gessen apologizes desperately to the little boy, who openly reproaches him. Gessen's wife implores Raffi to forgive his father; nothin' doin'.

When Raffi can't sleep, Gessen lies down in the bed next to the boy. Raffi repays him by pinching and kicking him as soon as Gessen dozes off. Gessen yells because it hurts, only to find himself down the now-familiar oubliette of apology and self-reproach.

When Raffi tells him, "You're a bad dada and I'm never going to listen to you again!" Gessen despairs: "I felt he was right. I was not a good dada. But I didn't know what else to do."

You almost want to shake Gessen and tell him what no parenting book will: Raffi wants someone to take charge—someone other than the three-year-old boy himself. It makes him angry to see his father debase himself with so much therapeutic arabesque and high-minded flummox. It makes Raffi want to punch his father in the nose. Because that little boy needs a father—most importantly for his own sake, but also for the sake of the kids he slugs at the park.

These parents aren't succeeding, and they aren't happy. They're dug in, like soldiers planning to see the battle through because they can't un-enlist. Their lives, objectively, seem very bad.

They may mock parents of previous eras as emotionally distant disciplinarians. But is it *less* cruel to set your kid up for so much interpersonal failure? Kinder to send a child with a taste for clocking adults off to school, where such behavior is likely to be greeted by a quick referral to a mental health expert and the recommendation that he begin psychiatric medications?

My Child Is So Sensitive!

Whenever parents become "educated" in the therapeutic method, they invariably conclude that they have a "sensitive child." Nearly every recent parenting book I've read prompts readers toward that notion.

Gessen writes, about Raffi: "He was a sensitive baby, and he grew into a sensitive toddler, and now he is a sensitive boy. The world is not something he can ignore; it impinges on him; he sees it and hears it and feels it deeply."[13] How do you punish a child who's constantly "impinged on" by the world?

You can't. You coddle, you forgive, you beg. You treat him as you would a child with an *actual* disorder. Except that, most of the time, these children didn't start out with actual disorders. They were simply treated as if they had them.

The notion that you have a "sensitive child" flatters the parent—who, presumably, was sensitive enough to have recognized it. As neuropsychologist Rita Eichenstein told me, parents who accommodate kids' sensitivities often inadvertently help create sensitive children. The environment they curate is so frictionless, it offers the child no preparation for the normal chaos of the world.

Sensitive children, it turns out, make other people fairly miserable.

Brittle Darlings

I've had my kids' friends come to my home and attempt to order me around in the same vein as they do their parents: "This chicken is terrible. I want noodles!" Or, "This cookie looks like poo. I want something else." (The child was six, and the cookie, chocolate.) They issue orders with gusto, like Veruca Salt egged on by her father's servility. They have no idea they have done anything wrong.

One parenting coach, Rebecah Freeling, observed to me that when entitlement is nurtured in a child, what's normal at three becomes unbearable in a child of seven, eight, or nine. "And in teenagers, that entitlement is dangerous," she said.

I found my way to Freeling by way of parenting groups that raved about the levelheaded advice she offered—and how crucial her wisdom had been to them. And one of the things she impresses upon parents is the need to "hold the line"—i.e., stick to the rules and consequences you set, and stop endlessly accommodating.

I asked her to describe for me the sort of entitlement she believed parents were nurturing. "'*I don't want macaroni and cheese, make me a grilled cheese sandwich!*' Then you make a grilled cheese sandwich. '*I don't want a grilled cheese sandwich! Make chicken nuggets.*' There's that," she said. "And then there's just also four-, five-, or six-year-olds going like, '*Water, Mommy. Water now! Mommy, you forgot the salt! You didn't bring me my snack from school! . . . Now I'm going to scream all the way home.*'"

Parents Are Morons, Say Experts

We parents are by now so accustomed to being called our schools' "partners" in raising our children, we hardly notice the demotion. Pediatricians *tell us* what our kids need from us emotionally (and not only medically); school psychologists *inform us* how to talk to our kids about hard things, or send home prompts for important "social emotional discussions." No one solicits parents' advice because our advice is nonexpert and, therefore, presumably without worth.

"Parents are often experts about their children's bodies. They know that a temperature above 98.6 degrees is a fever," concedes child psychiatrist and parenting guru Daniel J. Siegel in his bestselling book, *The Whole-Brain Child*. "They know to clean out a cut so it doesn't get infected. They know which foods are most likely to leave their child wired before bedtime."[14]

Isn't that darling? Parents know something about their own children. In Siegel's estimation, about as much as a middle school babysitter.

The problem with parents, according to Siegel, is that they don't know enough neuroscience. "Even the most caring, best-educated parents often lack basic information about their child's brain."[15]

Funny, you know who also lacks "basic information" about a child's brain? Neuroscientists. Every one of the neuroscientists and psychiatrists I spoke to impressed upon me how little we know about what goes on in the brain, or the relationship between neurological events and human emotion and behavior. The brain is astonishingly, endlessly complex, they all told me—full of feedback mechanisms about which we know little to nothing at all.

It's not actually possible to know much about what's going on in our kids' brains—and thank goodness, it also isn't necessary. We know it isn't necessary because the human race wasn't blessed with entrepreneurial child psychiatrists like Daniel J. Siegel until quite recently. And yet, for thousands of years, parents have raised good and even wonderful people.

Parental authority, however, turns out to be indispensable as far as children's welfare is concerned. Historically, it is "the one source of authority that every society takes seriously from way back in biblical times until very recently," the great British sociologist Frank Furedi told me.

For thousands of years, until the therapeutic turn in parenting, societies took it for granted that parents' primary job was to transmit their values to their children. And, of course, parents are the ultimate experts on their own values. Once parents decided the goal of child-rearing was emotional wellness, they effectively conceded that the actual authorities were therapists.

"Instead of saying, 'I'll be on his case, I'll guide that child, I'll try to understand that child, I'll take charge of his moral and intellectual development,' they kind of outsource parental authority to a bunch of schmucks who come in with all these latest rubbish ideas that make matters worse," Furedi said. Experts have completely ignored good evidence about what actually works with kids because it didn't grant them the centrality they crave.

The Birth of "Parenting Styles"

Investigation into "parenting styles" began with a brilliant psychologist of the 1960s named Diana Baumrind. After studying the ways parents attempt to control the behavior of children, Baumrind discerned three general approaches: permissive, authoritative, and authoritarian.[16]

The "permissive parent" assiduously avoids punishment. She affirms the child's impulses, desires, and actions, and consults the child about family decisions. She makes few demands on the child with regard to responsibilities and orderly behavior. "She presents herself to the child as a resource for him to use as he wishes, not as an ideal for him to emulate, nor as an active agent responsible for shaping or altering his future behavior,"[17] Baumrind explains.

The "authoritarian parent" values a child's obedience as a virtue, holds a child's behavior to an absolute standard, works to keep the child in his place, restricts his autonomy, and does not ever encourage a give-and-take discussion about her rules.[18]

Neither approach produced particularly happy or successful adults.

The "authoritative parent," however, is loving and rule based. She attempts to direct the child's activities in a rational manner, encourages a give-and-take with her child, but "exerts firm control at points of parent-child divergence." Where her point of view on a household rule ultimately conflicts with that of her child, she wins. She maintains high standards for her child's behavior "and does not base her decisions on group consensus or the individual child's desires."[19]

In studies that still manage to chagrin therapists, Baumrind found that authoritative parenting styles produced the most successful, independent, self-reliant, and best emotionally regulated kids; it also produced the happiest kids—those less likely to report suffering from anxiety and depression.[20]

This is a remarkably sturdy research finding: kids are happiest when raised in a loving environment that holds their behavior to high standards, expects them to contribute meaningfully to the household, and is *willing to punish* when behavior falls short. And it flies in the face of virtually everything therapists and parenting books now exhort.

Few parents today, even those who believe they are "authoritative," are willing to punish their children with any degree of consistency or seriousness. They may claim the mantle of "authoritative parenting," but watch what they do and how they talk to their kids: it lacks any sense of parental authority. If anything, it shares much in common with the permissive style Baumrind found produced such unfortunate results.

But today's expert-led parents are not simply "permissive"; they are arguably much worse. Not only do they ape the *affirmation* and refusal-to-punish impulses that led to mediocre outcomes generations ago, they fail to achieve the one virtue of "permissive" parents of yore: granting their kids a generous ambit of autonomy and independence. Therapeutic parents are permissive parents who also smother and micromanage.

And while the "authoritarian" parents fare no better—today, that term describes a null set. There is hardly a parent in the West today who will inculcate obedience as the highest virtue. Therapists who decry the excesses of "authoritarian parenting" are often pulling a bait-and-switch: pretending that the *authoritative* methods lead to disappointing results.

Vanishingly few American-born parents are willing to be "authoritative" with their kids, in the Baumrind sense. Even when they think they are being "authoritative," they cajole and plead and explain. They absorb violence from first graders they would never tolerate from a puppy.

There's an intriguing book that tidily makes this point: *Hunt, Gather, Parent*, by Michaeleen Doucleff. Western parents, Doucleff decides, have no idea what they're doing.

After the gentle parenting methods let her down, Doucleff attempts what she thinks is the "authoritative" style—and claims that it, too, failed her. But for her, "authoritative" parenting somehow involves mutely absorbing physical abuse from her three-year-old daughter, Rosy: "Eventually, her tantrums turned nuclear. She'd bite, flail her arms, and start running around the house upturning furniture."[21] When Doucleff tries to pick Rosy up during her tantrums, "she had the habit of slapping me across the face. Some mornings, I left the house with a red handprint across my cheek."

(Reading that, I could only hope that one day, Rosy and Raffi fall in love and give us the Netflix special we deserve.)

Doucleff reaches rock bottom when she realizes she's dreading her time with the daughter she struggled for years to conceive. "I feared that Rosy and I were becoming enemies."

Doucleff tromps around the globe in search of happy parents with well-adjusted, orderly kids. Mayan parents on the Yucatan Peninsula; Inuit in northern Canada; and hunter gatherers in Tanzania. These parents invite their toddlers to help them with the housework; do not overly praise their kids; exert a calm, steady authority; and let their kids take risks and fail, so that they become strong. Doucleff even reluctantly admits that in nearly every culture around the world—including those she admires—parents give the errant child a brisk spanking.[22] Doucleff envies these cultures—their confident closeness with their children; the happy, competent, generous, chore-doing kids they are raising. She wishes Americans had these parenting traditions. She rarely seems to notice that until very recently, we *did*.

This is the "authoritative" parenting today's parents cannot bring themselves to commit to. And here, I must cop to something: it isn't *only* the mental health establishment's fault that we parents veered so desperately off course. The experts took advantage. But we Gen Xers were an easy mark.

Having surrendered our own friendships and adult life for the sake of attending every soccer game, we wanted a small something in return: that our kids tell us everything and make us their best friends. And when you punish—for the duration of the punishment—kids don't give you that. If we acted like actual authorities in our own houses—those who didn't need to grovel and endlessly explain—we worried we would lose their affection and constant access to everything transpiring in their hearts and minds.

Take away their smartphones? We never really considered it. They couldn't bear it, but neither could we. How could we find out how they did on that math test, seconds after its completion? We couldn't wait until the end of the school day to check in on our besties!

But no one respects a needy friend. They might tolerate her, but she's kind of a drag. The moment our support and affirmation were made explicitly unconditional and entirely indestructible, our kids knew they didn't have to do anything to sustain our permanent high regard.

The saddest part? Not only do we rarely motivate our kids to better behavior, many of our children don't like us very much. There is *more* parental estrangement today than in generations past. And the young adults who are cutting off their parents in record numbers are often those raised by the most indulgent and devoted parents.

They Don't Like Us All That Much

I asked clinical psychologist and expert in family estrangement Joshua Coleman about the recent rise in adult children cutting off their parents. Did these parents typically abuse the children who cut them out of their lives?

Most often, Coleman says, "they cut off the parents because they're trying to have an experience of independence and strength that the parents couldn't provide them." The problem is, most often, not too little love but too much—of the contemporary, smothering sort.

The young adults who cut off their parents often say they feel crushed by the burden of serving as the buttress for their parents' emotional lives. This isn't tiger mom–style high expectations, which may place pressure on a child to achieve, but where the ultimate success accrues to the kid herself. The contemporary American style is the needier, plaintive sort: *Text me and tell me that you're having fun, so I don't worry.* When young adults can't excise mom's anxious and needy voice from their heads— they may feel the need to banish her from their lives.

But wait a minute, I asked Coleman. I have a father to whom I am still very close, who installed his voice in my head. And yet I couldn't imagine cutting him off or telling him he needed to "fix himself," as so many of today's young people apparently inform their parents, at the encouragement of their therapists.

I describe one signal memory for Coleman. A little more than a decade ago, I was in Germany, watching men bungee jump off a very tall building. Then—and every time I considered participating in any activity I regarded as similarly insane—I heard my father's voice, bright as the morning sun: "She died doing *what*?"

I can't do it, was the resulting resolution I'd made on various such occasions in my twenties. *It is too unforgivably stupid.*

But, Coleman explained, that was different. In ridiculing me, my father's voice acknowledged that I was my own, independent person. His voice said, in effect: *If you're going to do something that dumb, it's on you.* As opposed to today's parents who communicate something very different: *"'Oh, my God, don't do that. Because if you did, it would ruin my life with sorrow.'* That might be a different kind of a message," Coleman said.

For the sake of a good relationship with our kids, we are failing them miserably. We are raising far more self-involved, undisciplined, and unlikeable children. Perhaps unhappiest of all: All of our sucking up to them doesn't even guarantee the relationship. They are willing to tolerate it as long as we pay the bills; after that, they're often just not that into us.

Angela: "He Told Me He's Having Some Really Big Breakthroughs"

Remember Angela, the member of the television production crew? Her bright son Jayden had received a 504 accommodation so that he could take untimed tests while in high school. Jayden had since graduated, and Angela and her husband could not seem to motivate Jayden to finish his college applications or seek work; they could barely get him to leave the house. Angela hired a therapist to help Jayden with his anxiety and depression.

I asked Angela if she'd seen improvements in her son after he had been in therapy for three months.

"He told me that he's having some really big breakthroughs, that therapy is really helping him, but I don't know what that means," she said. The therapist assured Angela that the therapy is working. "It's just going to take a little time."

Once a state-champion athlete, Jayden had decided in the tenth grade, with the help of his high school counselor, that he was transgender and really a girl. Since then he'd been threatening to begin a course of hormone treatments. Now eighteen, he no longer required parental consent to commence medical transformation. Insurance would pay for it. He could legally change his name any time he wanted to. But he hadn't made any moves toward completing those, either.

Angela hoped the therapist would nudge Jayden toward his future. "'He's just so riddled with anxiety,'" the therapist informed Angela. Be patient, the therapist advised her. Apply no pressure, hope for the best. The therapist said she was "trying to work with him to get him to the place" where he could move forward with his life. "She thinks that an autism diagnosis can help," said Angela. Come again?

Jayden had been receiving mental health care since the third grade, when a neuropsychological evaluation first turned up a "sensory processing disorder" diagnosis (not recognized by the major diagnostic manuals of psychiatry). Not even Jayden's high school counselor thought he had autism. If Jayden met *some* of the criteria for autism, certainly he must be far from a clear case? The therapist was still mulling diagnoses.

Angela firmly believes the therapy is working. "I totally trust her," Angela said about the woman she'd hired. Jayden had assured her he was having a lot of "breakthroughs" in therapy (probably while grabbing another Monster Energy drink from the fridge en route to a humming Xbox).

Had the months of therapy improved Angela's relationship with Jayden? "A week ago, he said we were narcissistic, abusive parents. And he said that as soon as he moves out, he's never going to see us again."

So that would be a "No."

But Angela's friends told her that, with teenagers, "this is totally normal behavior. When they're trying to move on, they're angry with you." She clings to that.

Desperate that our kids always, at every moment, feel our love, we came to equate punishment with cruelty. And besides, the experts assured us: punishment doesn't work. "Instead of the child feeling sorry for what he has done and thinking about how he can make amends," the child "becomes preoccupied with revenge fantasies," write the authors of *How to Talk So Kids Will Listen*, quoting child psychologist Haim Ginott. "In other words, by punishing a child, we actually deprive him of the very important inner process of facing his own misbehavior."[23]

Ginott may well be right that punishment very often does not occasion soul-searching in the child sent to his room. But of course, soul-searching was never the point of punishment. Self-reflection is the therapeutic quest.

Parents' objectives were different and four fold: We wanted kids to knock it off when their bad behavior involved mistreating others or their property. We wanted to let our kids know who was in charge—us, not them. We wanted them to feel bad that their behavior crossed a line and to internalize that boundary. And we wanted to give their poor sister, who'd just been clocked in the head with a Magna-Tile, a little justice.

A kid sent to her room may use the time to self-reflect, but she may not. And she may choose to overstep the boundary again. *But at least she knows it's there.* She knows there is something beyond her feelings— respect for others. And that no matter how she may feel, she must find a way to stay within the bounds of tolerable behavior. Her parents have sent her to her room because they believe she can learn to control herself.

The au courant idea that even humane punishments "don't work" is something Baumrind calls a "myth." Baumrind also found that demands for neatness in children is associated with *less* hostile and *less* delinquent kids and that it was incorrect to assume that high expectations would result in passive-aggressive rebellion.[24]

And while Baumrind did not advocate spanking, she found that "occasional, mild spanking" did not traumatize children.[25] Cue the outrage. But it's true: studies have been unable to support supposed links between spanking and externalizing disorders.[26]

What actually makes for miserable kids? Placing them in charge. Failing to hold their behavior to high standards and not punishing them when they deliberately allow it to fall short. And, yes—according to Baumrind—what else makes for an unhappy kid? Parents behaving in a consistently "affirmative manner toward the child's impulses, desires and actions."[27]

Want to know why the rising generation of kids doesn't want to have children of their own? It's because we made parenting look so damn miserable. It's because we listened to all the experts and convinced ourselves we couldn't possibly appeal to life experience, judgment, knowledge gleaned over decades—tens of thousands of hours with our kids—or what our parents had done, and figure this thing out for ourselves. It's because forty-year-old parents—accomplished, brilliant, and blessed with a spouse—treat the raising of kids like a calculus problem that was put to them in the dead of night, gun to the head: *Get it right or I pull this trigger.*

We played a part with our kids: the therapeutic parent. We let them throw food on the floor and kick us and hit us—and each time extended them more understanding. We offered them an endless array of choices. And we absolutely renounced our own authority.

And it scared them. It scared these kids so badly. Look at them. They know there's no one running the place. They know they're far too young to be exercising the amount of power we've handed them. They know that if they've brought their towering father, an accomplished man in his forties, to his knees, clueless and despairing—then something has gone desperately wrong.

The kids believed us when we treated their hurt feelings as deadly serious. More than their father's financial worries—more serious than their grandmother's poor health. They trusted us that their feelings and worries were the most important things on earth. They are collapsing under the weight of all that worry.

Worst of all, they don't believe we can help them. We don't make them feel secure because we've told them—over and over, in so many ways— we're scared out of our minds, and we aren't actually in charge. We are just following what the pediatrician, or the therapist, or the teacher, or school counselor, or the occupational therapist told us to do. He's in charge, she's in charge, our kids are in charge. *We* aren't in charge.

How can you comfort a child whom you've assured, *I don't have the power here.* You can't. And so . . . they aren't.

There Are Planets Where Parents Are Admired

Here's where I admit: it isn't easy. Raising good kids in a culture that undermines parental authority at every turn—where parents are the dupes and morons and bigots on every television show—is damn near impossible. This point was made to me by pediatrician and author Leonard Sax. And it was reinforced by a parenting coach who told me about an Indian American client I'll call "Tanvi."

Tanvi was constantly astonished and dismayed that her daughter treated her so much more disrespectfully in America than Tanvi would ever have treated her own parents back in India. "My kid's mouthing off to me in public," Tanvi told her coach, hurt and confounded.

At last, she figured out why: "If you're in India, if you're a little kid and you mouth off to your parents in public, all the other adults around glare at you. Here [in America], if a kid mouths off to a parent in public, all the parents now glare at the *parent*."

In India, the culture supports the idea that a child should treat her parent respectfully—and other parents will enforce that with their stares. In America, the onus is entirely on the parent. And we wonder: "What have you done wrong to deserve a tongue-lashing from your child?"

I decided to talk to parents who'd raised healthy, productive adults. Many of those who were willing to provide straight talk turned out to be immigrants.

My friend Julia is the sort who leaves other women aching with envy: a Harvard-trained economist and navy reservist in her spare time, she is married to a husband she loves and is raising three great kids. She's not only *impressive* in the career sense, she is the sort of friend who will pick up your kids if can't get to them, who shows up at a kid's birthday party ready to help out in the kitchen, engage the kids in activity, or chat with your mom. She manages to juggle all of a working mom's demands without ever seeming frazzled or shrill or batty. She is, in other words, precisely the sort of adult any of us would be proud to have raised.

So, of course, I needed to talk to her mother. Her *single* mother.

Rhoda—who died last year of cancer—was lively and charming. A thinker, avid reader, and outspoken feminist. She was also a real crack-up, full of sharp insight and a balls-to-the-wall manner of delivery that gave you the rare gift of someone who was letting you see her true self. Almost immediately, I adored her.

So when Rhoda called me out of the blue two years ago to discuss something I'd written, I took the opportunity to steer her to what I wanted to know: How did you do it? How did you raise this wonderful adult, on a professor's income, *all by yourself*?

A black South African, Rhoda married Julia's father, a white German, who hit Rhoda when Julia was little.[28] Rhoda divorced him, and then carried on a successful career as an academic and human rights activist, building community wherever she went, applying what money she had to cello lessons and tuition for her daughter. She didn't believe in spanking, she told me, but she established clear rules for Julia, who is, to this day, one of the most unfailingly polite, principled, and charming women I know.

What were we Americans doing so wrong? "In third world countries," Rhoda said, "parenting is very authoritarian because the leaders are very authoritarian. America is on the other side—completely lack boundaries and authority." We needed something in between.

I heard this from other immigrants: the problem with American parenting is that we do not assert our authority with our own children. We do not make it a priority to pass down *our* values to our own kids; we seem to expect the culture to do this for us. It's okay to allow for some give-and-take with children, but in the end, it must be *our* judgment that carries the day.

Kids need adult authority, they know they need it, Rhoda insisted to me. And then she said something that stopped me in my tracks: "That's why they all go off and join BLM. They're looking for daddy."

True, the rising generation *is* more politically radical than previous generations—attracted especially to far-left political movements. But it had never occurred to me that this might have anything to do with the parenting style with which they were raised.[29] Was she right? Was the child and adolescent yearning for authority so great that they would go searching for it from other adults, like underfed kids eating paint chips off the walls?

Liberal Parents, Radical Children

Myrieme Nadri-Churchill is a psychotherapist and executive director of the Boston-based nonprofit Parents for Peace, which helps families recover their adult children from the clutches of extremist groups:

Neo-Nazis, Proud Boys, the Taliban. Born in Casablanca to an African Muslim father and a white Christian mother, Nadri-Churchill's first lessons in extremism landed in the 1970s, with rocks hurled at her by the bullies at school.

Nadri-Churchill is a waterfall of insight, but so mistrustful of American journalists' tendency to twist her words, I knew I had to meet her in person. I flew to Boston to sit with her at the home of a mutual friend.

Now middle-aged, she carries herself with the invisible epaulets of natural leadership. Her hair falls in a shoulder-length fountain of black ringlets. Her speech, full of fire. English is her third language, and she wrestles impatiently against it, bristling with the need to be understood.

Nadri-Churchill says she has helped hundreds of American families extract their young-adult children from extremist cults, often coordinating with US government agencies in the rescue effort. And she told me, in effect, that Rhoda was right: "The majority of the kids that are sucked into supremacy, they are from families that are liberal. It's really astonishing to see how many kids that are in white supremacy, Neo-Nazi groups, Antifa, and even Islamism come from nice liberal families."

In so many liberal American families today, she said, parents disavow their authority, give children endless choices, and constantly solicit kids' opinions on major life decisions. But the hunger for authority and boundaries is profoundly connected to a child's sense of self and well-being. It does not dissipate simply because parents fail to supply it.

"Extremist groups give children a script, they give them a sense of direction. They tell them you eat this, you don't eat that. You go in this direction, you do this, they give them a script," she said again, repeating the word "script." "It's almost like extremist groups have replaced parenting."

This point was famously made by public intellectual Midge Decter in the 1970s, to explain why so many kids with doting parents and capacious freedom had turned into adults who inclined toward extremist movements.

Decter faulted her generation of parents, the first to praise children lavishly and expect far less contribution to the household. They overlooked outright disrespect and catered to their children's feelings. "We refused to assume, partly on ideological grounds but also, I think, on esthetic grounds, the central obligations of parenthood: to make ourselves the final authority on good and bad, right and wrong, and to take the consequences of what might turn out to be a lifelong battle," she wrote.

Despite the unprecedented number of hours they had lavished on their kids, Decter argued, parents her age were fundamentally neglectful.[30] "We pronounced you strong when you were still weak in order to avoid the struggles with you that would have fed your strength. We proclaimed you sound when you were foolish in order to avoid taking part in the long, slow, slogging effort that is the only route to genuine maturity of mind and feeling."[31]

If Decter's generation of permissive parents got this ball rolling, boy did we run with it. We showered kids with trivial freedoms (*What color would you like to dye your hair? You look so cool!*) and appointed middle school kids co-arbiters of the family's values—what high school to attend, whether to attend church or synagogue, or even whether they needed to hug elderly relatives or give Grandma a call. We explained away misbehavior as a matter of human psychology. (*Aiden loved your gift! He didn't say "thank you" because he was feeling intimidated.*) We believed if we controlled and monitored every square inch of their environments, we would never need to demand that kids govern themselves.

Parenting without Authority: the Consequence

Today, as more than one parenting coach and pediatrician told me, kids arrive at school having never heard the word "no." They don't know how to conform to the expectations set by their teachers—they've had no practice. No one asked them to sit at the table through dinner, employ basic table manners. No one forced them to wait on a snack or an activity that they wanted *right now*. No one made them wait until a sibling or parent finished speaking before announcing their own desires to the household.

And now, the teacher is upset. She needs to teach a whole class of kids how to read. She needs to introduce subtraction to twenty first graders. She can't reasonably deal with kids who wander off, refuse to listen to directions, make it impossible to teach the others.

At the psychologist's behest, with the principal's encouragement, the teacher delivers a now familiar ultimatum: If you want your kid to remain in this class, maybe take him for an evaluation? Just to check. The implication: *It might make everybody happier if we got him on some medication.*

Chapter 10

•

Spare the Rod,
Drug the Child

Maayan would not sit quietly, his preschool teacher said. He was disruptive, messy, curious, but also dreamy. At the teacher's insistence, Maayan's parents took him to a doctor who immediately agreed: The boy had "severe" ADHD.

Maayan "wasn't born. He came out like from a cannon," his father, Yaakov Ophir, told me. Highly energetic, inattentive at school, spacey, disorganized, messy, tending to lose his belongings, Maayan met all the diagnostic criteria. The doctor advised that the four-year-old boy immediately start on Ritalin.

That was precisely the sort of advice that Ophir had offered parents in his clinical therapy practice outside of Jerusalem. "Ritalin will help your son stop feeling dumb," Ophir recalls telling one mother. "His self-esteem is continuously under attack. If he is not treated with medications, he will grow up feeling excessive guilt for all his misbehaviors."[1] At the time, Ophir believed this was good advice.

But faced with the prospect of medicating his own child, he found himself suddenly caught in a hailstorm of doubt. What was ADHD, really? He realized he didn't know.

An academic psychologist at the Technion, Israel's premier research institution, Ophir began reading. He wanted to know the nature of a disorder that afflicted over *15 percent* of boys in America.[2] Precaution gave way to preoccupation. The more he read, the more convinced he became of two things: ADHD—characterized by overstimulation and distractibility—didn't meet the standard definition of a "disorder." And Ritalin was no solution at all.

There are "4Ds" of abnormal psychology, Ophir reasoned: deviance, distress, dysfunction, and danger. ADHD doesn't meet any of them. With an incidence of over 10 percent of in the United States, and an astounding 20 percent of Israeli children and young adults,[3] ADHD isn't rare or "deviant."[4]

ADHD also doesn't cause distress in the child. These kids pose no real danger, Ophir pointed out to me—neither to others nor to themselves. As for dysfunction, "Yes, children with ADHD-like traits will probably have a hard time in school," he allowed. "They will have a reduced ability in school, at least the way that schools are built today—sitting in for long hours in the classroom, listening to sometimes boring lectures. That does not fit any child, maybe, but it does not fit children who are more energetic and more distracted."

A real disorder interferes with the ability to lead a normal life, Ophir said. But a trait that makes it harder to sit still for long hours? Well, there are plenty of jobs in which broad awareness of opportunity and danger may even be an asset. Like venture capital or the military, for example.[5]

"Can these children dress themselves? Can they learn to take a shower? Can they do the basic missions, the basic tasks of the day? Of course, they can," Ophir said. "In depression, for example, a person may be confined to his bed. He finds it so hard to get out of bed, he doesn't go to work. So you see the impairment of the function. In ADHD, it does not exist." Stimulant medications are powerful, psychoactive drugs that cross the blood-brain barrier, Ophir pointed out to me, referring to the class of drugs that includes Ritalin, Adderall, Concerta, and Strattera. Studies show that stimulants pose high risk of dependency and addiction.[6] Stimulants may also become less effective over time—meaning a child may need to take increasing doses to equal the original effect. Worst of all, and unlike techniques that modify behavior, discontinuing stimulants transports a child back to square one, with the added burden of withdrawal symptoms. Based on his research, Ophir wrote an op-ed for the left-wing newspaper *Haaretz* titled "ADHD Is Not an Illness and Ritalin Is Not a Cure." Virality ensued. One of the top ADHD researchers in Israel wrote a letter to the Ministry of Health, Ophir says, threatening his license.

But Ophir did not back down. He found his way to the work of Thomas Armstrong, an American academic psychologist who, skeptical of prescribing stimulants to children, developed nondrug strategies for managing hyperactivity in kids.[7] In 2022, Ophir published his own book with the same title as his controversial article.

By then, Maayan was ten. Ophir says he and his wife have successfully treated Maayan's ADHD with a series of behavioral modifications: chores, discipline, and structure. Ophir says these have helped Maayan thrive. Maayan makes his own lunch every day, unloads the dishwasher after every cycle, and gets his little sister to the school bus. Maayan may never be exactly like other kids, Ophir says; he may always be full of energy, distractable, and fall deeply into thought. That is more than fine with the Ophirs.

Medicating Away Bad Feelings

Ophir successfully avoided treating his son's ADHD with medication by pursuing a program of behavioral modification. What about anxiety and depression? Is there ever reason to resist banishing those with meds?

I asked Notre Dame psychology professor Scott Monroe, an expert on depressive disorders, what he thinks about putting adolescents on antidepressants. "My personal opinion is, I would be very hesitant to do that."

Why?

"Because they're powerful drugs, and the brain systems haven't solidified in adolescence. Male forebrains don't really come together until almost the mid-twenties and there's individual variation there. I'm not a biologist—I don't know how badly it can impair brain development. But it seems like those are prime years. I'd want to find alternatives before implementing that."

What about antianxiety drugs? Are they effective? I asked Steve Hollon, a professor of psychology at Vanderbilt University and an expert in the treatment of depression. "They're about as effective as alcohol and only slightly more addictive," he said. They blunt pain; they do not fix or cure—meaning, if you ever discontinue them, look out.

Unlike adults who choose to begin a course of psychotropic pharmaceuticals, medicated adolescents may never discover whether they *can* handle life at full strength. If we don't allow teens to face the slings and arrows of outrageous fortune, they may never learn to weather them. They might look a lot like the young adults arriving on our college campuses—the ones careering toward nervous breakdown.

I began to wonder if teens placed on antidepressants might also lose something of the fullness of socialization—navigating peers, winning affection and testing it, suffering a hurt and muddling through. Would years in which their mental hardware was commandeered by meds amount to years they did not fully inhabit? And if so, wouldn't many seem much younger than they are?

I asked Hollon what we'd expect to see in a society that indiscriminately placed moody teenagers on antidepressants and nervous teens on antianxiety medication.

"Oh, they wouldn't learn to cope," he said.

Anxiety and Even Depression
Can Be Good for Us

There are costs to extirpating anxiety and depression, beyond side effects. Beyond even the loss of socialization and of learning to cope with social stressors. There is also the loss of the *benefits* anxiety and depression provide. You read that right: anxiety and depression exist for a reason.

Anxiety is anticipatory fear—worry about the threat of danger yet to come. Every anxiety expert I spoke to agreed: anxiety is not all bad.

Evolutionary psychologists think anxiety evolved to make us more alert to situations in which a tiger might be lurking behind the bush. "Arousal in the face of danger increases the chances of escape, and thus gives us an obvious selective advantage," evolutionary psychiatrist Randolph Nesse explains in his fascinating book *Good Reasons for Bad Feelings*.[8] Anticipating danger buys us time and grants us additional options for evading harm.

Depression is not all bad, either, and it, too, has a purpose: to protectively shut down the system, often after we've been overpowered, allowing us to retool and contemplate a different approach. So that we withdraw from the thing that caused us harm and take stock.[9]

When depression occurs after a significant failure or loss, it suppresses our inclination to act before we can do something rash: chase after the boy who dumped us; scream at the boss who fired us; throw good money after bad; or perform idiotic acts of high dudgeon in the face of rejection. Evolutionary psychologists often claim that "a depressive episode is one way of withdrawing from what they call an 'unpropitious situation,'" Monroe said. When you've failed or lost, sometimes the best thing for you to do is sit tight and lick your wounds.

Would any of us ever perform at our best without fear of failure? Anxiety has been linked to creativity, intelligence, and getting us out of a bad situation quickly. It might also help us make clearer memories; pre-Christmas jitters help create a lifetime of Christmas memories.[10] The memory of your first kiss may stay with you forever *because* of the anxiety that precipitated it.

When either of these closely related responses to danger becomes excessive—when anxiety or depression interferes with your ability to function—it may rise to the level of disorder. If your internal "smoke alarm," as Nesse has called it, is always blaring when there is no fire, it's not helping anything. This is a "dysregulation of a normal defense," Nesse said.

But in the main, anxiety and depression are healthy responses to life's threats and debacles. Either can be uncomfortable and, if they preclude normal functioning, disordered. But anxiety and depression themselves aren't a dysfunction. It's only if you're experiencing chronic anxiety or depression *that you cannot otherwise resolve* that you might begin to consider pharmaceutical intervention.

If, however, your depression is occasioned by an unhappy relationship, a job you feel trapped in, a breakup, or the death of someone you love, that may qualify as "depression," but it isn't necessarily pathological. Taking drugs to combat sadness may sabotage your resolve to set your life on a better course or do those things that might help you not just to plod through, but to heal. On antidepressants, you may feel at peace with your sad circumstances—but you may also be less likely to remediate them.

Andy Thomson, a psychiatrist at the University of Virginia, made this point to the *New York Times* with an anecdote taken from his own clinical practice. "I remember one patient who came in and said she needed to reduce her dosage. I asked her if the antidepressants were working, and she said something I'll never forget," Thomson said. "'Yes, they're working great,' she told me. 'I feel so much better. But I'm still married to the same alcoholic son of a bitch. It's just now he's tolerable.'"[11]

Put another way, antidepressants sometimes transform a short-term, acute pain into a low-grade chronic one. "If you give [adolescents] medication for anxiety—and I would say, you could extend it to depression—if you palliate those symptoms, you are messing with the natural adaptive resources of the human being that has evolved over centuries," Monroe said.

Not all anxiety amounts to anxiety disorder. Not all bouts of depression constitute depressive disorder. Some amount of each, however painful, may do us good, helping us react faster, remember more clearly, or even think more deeply about our lives.

In a controversial but highly intriguing hypothesis, Thomson and evolutionary psychologist Paul Andrews argue that depression may even spur a deeper form of analytical thinking, known as Type 2 thinking. Depression's well-known symptom—stopping you from engaging in social activity—may be evolution's way of curtailing distraction so that you can reflect unimpeded on your problem.[12] It is no accident that Churchill's and Lincoln's deep moral insights were preceded by periods of depression, Andrews told me. "The function of the depressed mood is to employ this Type 2 thinking to try and help you analyze and hopefully solve your problems," he said.

If young people view their bad feelings as intrinsically pathological, they will look to drugs to provide the relief, Nesse pointed out to me. If, instead, they view the bad feelings as a natural outgrowth of their situation, they might be more inspired to make changes. After they exit a destructive relationship or put feelers out for a new job, they may not only feel relief but justifiable pride. And they will have a basis for believing that the next time things go south, they can turn things around again, too.

Melanie: The Doctor Put Our Eleven-Year-Old on Antidepressants (He Was Out of Ideas)

Melanie has spent years worrying over her "really sensitive child," Dylan. She liked taking him to the park with the other kids from his preschool class, but when he threw tantrums and refused to go, she abandoned that activity. When he complained that the other boys in his class were too rough, she held him back so he could hang with a gentler cohort. When he complained that the car ride to visit his cousins was too long, the visits ended.

Melanie took her preschooler to a therapist to figure out why he didn't like school. The therapist decided there was nothing wrong with Dylan but continued to see the child for as long as insurance would pay for it. Dylan enjoyed the extra attention.

Dylan's ups and downs tormented Melanie. He would suddenly be very interested in a sport, lose interest, then regain it without warning. "He goes through these phases where he's up. And that's why I always wondered if he had some type of chemical imbalance,[13] you know, with depression. Because sometimes he was up and happy and willing to try things and go for it. And then other times, he was like 'No, no, whatever.'"

When Dylan complained that being called on in class by the teacher made him nervous, Melanie asked the teacher to stop calling on him. The teacher agreed.

In fourth grade, Dylan began to have panic attacks in class. If he struggled with a math problem, he would cry. "He doesn't like to do anything if he's not really good at it," Melanie told me. "He can't seem to tolerate feeling like he hasn't done well or failed. Even though nobody else really cares."

Thanksgiving of 2021, when Dylan was eleven, he woke his parents up at daybreak, screaming bloody murder, complaining of a terrible stomachache. "His whole face—you know, so much pain. He'd have like diarrhea and vomiting at the same time and, we were pretty freaked out." For a period of four months, they took him to a series of doctors. Melanie didn't just cancel Thanksgiving—she stopped leaving him alone at all. Melanie and her husband stopped going on dates.

But no gastroenterologist could find anything wrong with him. Finally, not knowing what else to do, one of his doctors put Dylan on Lexapro, an antidepressant. Was it helping? Melanie wasn't sure.

"I'd have to say, this motherhood thing is kicking my ass," Melanie told me.

This became a typical story I heard from parents: Their kid was inattentive in class, restless, weird, recalcitrant, or generally unhappy. A first trip to the neuropsychologist indicates he's "within normal range." The neuropsychologist reviews the child's symptoms, observes the child, consults his vast diagnostic toolkit, and declines to peg the child as disordered.

But then the child gets into a fight with another kid at school, or the teacher complains he's distracting in class, or he's just not doing what she asked. But what's *wrong* with him? That part remains vague. A pediatrician saves the day by prescribing psychiatric medication.

These parents seemed like they'd been forced to drive the highway in a car with no windshield, random debris constantly hitting them in the face. New diagnoses, new explanations, new medications, new therapies. They were miserable, and not just *until* they started their kids on psychiatric medications—after that, too. They were white-knuckling parenting, awaiting the conveyance of the medication's fresh side effects: sleeplessness, mood swings, weight gain, shallow hugs.

A question arrived nightly to their bedside, like a child who refuses sleep: *Why can't anyone fix this?*

Meds as an Alternative to Discipline

We didn't *want* to place our kids in a chemical straitjacket. We didn't plan to spend our days dreaming up manipulative ways to cover for them when they failed (begging their teachers over email to forgive missed assignments; pleading with coaches to let them on to teams they didn't make; firing off a vaguely litigious email to the principal if the coach wasn't immediately solicitous). We aren't proud of the times we sneaked an AirTag into their backpacks or tracked their movements on an app on our phones; we simply had no faith in the judgment of those we'd raised. We *know* kids do best when they're given some independence. We just couldn't trust them with it. Our guaranteed high regard, never withheld, could not inspire them to better behavior.

Therapeutic parenting seemed gentler in the moment and kinder to the individual kid. But when you took a step back, the picture changed, new characters swam into view. A child who hit other kids and never faced punishment—he went on doing that until he was medicated. A child who couldn't pay attention because she spent each morning glued to an interactive screen—she became a distraction to other students in class. We medicated her as well.

"Relief" is the word gentle parents use most often when a pediatrician at last hands them a diagnosis and prescription: *We were so relieved to know what was wrong with him*, many parents have told me.

But then the meds needed adjusting. There are unintended side effects. Adding a second drug lessened the side effect of the first. The next thing we knew, we were raising teens on two, four—*ten* different psychiatric drugs.[14]

The Smile

Halfway through my very long night interviewing Ophir over Zoom, I caught a flutter of something: a smile. Whenever he recalled something Maayan had said or done that seemed ADHD-like, there it was, flashing across my monitor like a bird taking wing.

Ophir told me all the things that made Maayan different: the way Maayan likes to mix his ice cream with soft cheese, how roughly he loads plates into the dishwasher. Ophir urged me to watch videos of Maayan being creative or quirky or cute. He was so obviously *tickled* by the kid. And that's when I realized: I hadn't observed this from a single American parent I interviewed whose children had been variously diagnosed and medicated. *Not one.*

Each had the harried, exhausted feel of someone who'd been up for days. They stated their love for the child many times, but it was a heavy, wearied sort of love. They mentioned the shallow hugs and listlessness, the constant adjustment of meds and agonizing wait for the appearance of new side effects. Their voices fell flat. If you listened only to their tone, the feeling they gave off most distinctly was of defeat.

Here was Yaakov Ophir, ignoring the advice of established experts in his own profession, loving his kid as he was. Giving the kid far *more* rules and structure—and chores!—than so many of today's experts deem advisable.

Ophir listed the chores, from laundry to gardening, that he and his wife had assigned to Maayan as a way of combating the carelessness that comes from being a certain type of boy. The kid wasn't exactly neat, Ophir wanted me to know. "He's not the most organized. He's not organized at all. And only last week, he lost his new sandals that we just bought him. And do you know how many shirts and sandals? It's very expensive to raise such a child."

Funny he should mention that.

My twin sons, at the same age, had lost *eight* sweatshirts at school over the previous year. *Eight.* And since this was 2021, while the pandemic raged and any adult could be Typhoid Mary, I wasn't allowed into the school to dig through the lost and found in the hopes of finding them.

But while Ophir clearly saw plenty of room for improvement, he didn't regard his son as disabled. He wasn't about to lower his standards for Maayan, either. "He only walks with shoes, not with sandals, although it's very hot here," Ophir told me. "Until we get these sandals back, we'll not buy a new one."

It struck me that so many of the parents I met who had turned their kids' lives over to psychiatry, didn't seem to enjoy their kids anymore. Ophir not only loved, but *enjoyed* his kid madly. He didn't care what Maayan's teachers had to say. (And really, truly, why should he?) This was *his son*, and Ophir was wild about him just as he was.

We lost this somewhere along the way: the sense that these kids we raise, they're ours. Our responsibility and our privilege. We are not the subordinates of the school psychologist or the pediatrician or our kids' teachers. We are more important than all of them combined—as far as our kids are concerned. We gave our kids life, we sustained it, and we are the ones who bear the direct emotional consequences of how those lives turn out. It's time we acted like it.

I don't know how to raise your kid. I don't know your values. And I distrust, instinctively, most who would claim to know these things. I certainly don't believe that any mental health expert *does*. They've already cocked up this child-rearing thing so badly.

Mental health experts have earned a hearty dose of skepticism that they know how to help a child thrive. They are famously slow to acknowledge even their disastrous errors.[15] If anything, the past two decades suggest that today's mental health experts ought to take a hard look at all of their advice and consider the possibility that much of it is dead wrong.

They have presided over a disaster. They convinced a generation of parents who wanted to give their kids everything—who devoted more time and energy to their children than any prior—that we didn't know what we were doing. They convinced us that parenting involved skills and expertise, things we needed them to provide us.

But parenting is not a skill. It's a relationship—or, it was. Before the experts professionalized it, turning time with our kids into a loathsome chore. We aped and practiced their stilted way of speaking, disavowed our instincts, wiped out our histories, and landed here: pleading with miserable kids to perk up and behave. A lousy trick to play on people who'd wanted kids so badly. Lousier for the kids whose parents view them as a grim obligation.

The experts trained us to see our own children as they did: objectively. We began measuring our kids against an ideal the experts set for attention or agreeableness or pliability to a teacher's wishes. As if conformity to a teacher's wishes were the best measure of our little girl or boy.

I don't know how to raise your kid. But you do.

Part III

Maybe There's Nothing Wrong with Our Kids

But life without meaning is the torture
Of restlessness and vague desire—
It is a boat longing for the sea and yet afraid.

—Edgar Lee Masters

Chapter 11

●

This Will Be Our
Final Session

There's a story my father likes to tell about his mother, a Jew of German extraction who was bright and imperious and cutting. Her manicure, flawless. Her hair, neatly set. She excelled at every card game from bridge to blackjack and made quick work of the *New York Times* crossword (in pen).

More comfortable with silence than blather, she had little patience for prudery and favored the honesty of a dirty joke. Family was her truest religion. But she rarely doted on or embraced any of her four children. Even by the standard of the 1960s, she was cold.

Motherhood was a role she performed diligently and with dispatch. When my father showed early promise as an artist at the age of six, she enrolled her dreamy second son in a drafting class. One day, when she arrived to pick him up after the session, the art teacher asked to speak with her.

"Your son spends a lot of time staring out the window," the artist said to my grandmother. "I think there might be something wrong with him."

My grandmother decided then and there that the art teacher was an imbecile. "I pay you to teach him art, not to psychoanalyze my son." The snap of her will, decisive as the shiny clasp on her handbag.

For my father, the memory of that exchange always provided proof, rarely paid out in compliments or hugs, of her deep maternal love. But I offer it here for what it is: pure anachronism.

Today, the story would likely proceed differently. The mother would panic and invite the art teacher to tell her more. The rest of the snowball's descent is predictable. At the parents' invitation, a now-familiar phalanx of professionals would blunder in, lodging themselves between parent and child: therapists, teachers, educational and parenting experts, psychiatrists, and even activists—anyone with an opinion about a child they may have just met and for whom they have neither love nor responsibility. None of whom bears the slightest consequence of their bad advice.

Love Means Occasionally Telling an Expert to Get Lost

"One of the unfortunate things about Anglo-American culture is that it's become extremely wary of what I call 'informal relationships,' the relationships between men and women, between adults and children," British sociologist Frank Furedi told me.

We mistrust spontaneous and unregulated interactions, which are seen as dangerous and full of unacceptable risk (giving offense, experiencing shame or rejection, exerting undue "power"). So we regulate and sanitize them with "education" and interventions.

But as a brilliant academic psychologist pointed out to me,[1] this process of regulating our relationships also drains interactions of their vitality and meaning, rendering them uninteresting or awkward. The response, then, is even more intervention. More training workshops for parents. More lessons for fourth-grade girls on "How to Be a Good

Friend." There is no end to it—no point at which the so-called experts say: *Maybe we shouldn't push our snouts into this area of their lives—the giggly inner sanctum of girl friendship? Maybe we should leave these kids alone.*

The great African American poet Robert Hayden felt his father's devotion not through any declaration, which his father may never have made, but paid out in steady acts of sacrifice. "Sundays too my father got up early and put his clothes on in the blueblack cold," Hayden wrote.[2] "Then with cracked hands that ached from labor in the weekday weather made banked fires blaze. No one ever thanked him." Warmed by the fire, bolstered by his father's durable love, Hayden asks: "What did I know, what did I know of love's austere and lonely offices?"

It may not have been perfect, but given the laconic, stoical man his father seems to have been—maybe it was. Anything else from such a man might have felt like artifice.

For years, therapeutic experts have attempted to iron out the idiosyncrasies of parent-child interaction—and in the last two decades, all but succeeded. They injected ideology and faux perfectionism into the parent-child relationship, and subjected every aspect to their examination and judgment.

Parent-child relationships have always varied according to values, family culture, and the variegations of personality. Our friendships and marriages and sibling and parent relationships aren't precious because they conform to an approved pattern. They are precious because they are *ours*.

Parents, Subtract Yourselves

Experts are not the only ones getting in the way of our kids' normal maturation; parents' epidemic of overinvolvement in kids' lives is by now the stuff of legend. We ask teachers to seat our elementary kids next to others we've chosen, demand to speak to high school teachers and even college professors who dare give our children a bad grade, and intervene with our young adults' bosses (all stories people have told me).

WhatsApp has become a nightmarish blizzard of parental anxiety: *Does anyone know what's on tomorrow's social studies test? Did Mrs. Tyler assign science homework?* This, even for fourteen-year-olds.

And yet we know—not only because the best psychological research indicates it, but also from years of inherited wisdom—that kids need space from adult oversight. They thrive with independence, a certain level of responsibility and autonomy and, yes, failure. They never learn to do for themselves if we do everything for them. Risky play—rough-and-tumble, or involving heights, sharp tools, and some actual danger—not only rewards kids with joy and social competence, it may make them less phobic and better able to navigate and assess risks in the future.[3] Small failures and injuries *help* rather than hurt kids.

But the advice "give them autonomy" or "assign them tasks that maximize independence" gets things backward. It only ends up participating in the problem of ruining our kids through overtreatment. You don't *give* a child independence any more than you *give* a child confidence, however much it flatters us to think we do. In most circumstances, you simply get out of their way—stop interfering—and independence takes its course.

In our cluttered lives, buffeted by trivial communication and pointless alerts, the way to a calmer, healthier existence must begin with *subtraction.*[4] Take all the stuff you're doing for your kids—all the tech and entertainment you supply and activities you schedule—and toss about a third of it out. Our kids were doing so much better when they had less—less distraction, less stimulation, less supervision, less intervention, less interference, less accommodation, less parenting. The weight of psychological research demonstrates what kids need most is for their parents (and technology) to stop interrupting, monitoring, curating—diverting them from the organic miracle of growing up.

They Aren't Weak—Unless We Make Them That Way

Stop acting as if your child will die if she doesn't get her snack; that she'll fall apart if she's made to sit next to an obnoxious child in class. If she's not in the same reading group as her friends, don't call the teacher and insist that the groups be reorganized because your daughter can't possibly discuss *Wonder* seated next to anyone but Kennedy.

Stop implanting your outsized worries in their heads. Stop flinging the word "bullying" around just because another girl said something mean to your daughter; that's an unpleasantness she's destined to face again and must learn to handle. Stop monitoring and evaluating everything your kids do and stop overpraising them for doing things that aren't hard. You're not spurring them to adulthood, you're insisting that they always regard themselves as little children.

Stop telling them they're weak, in so many ways; if you could do something at their age, let them give it a whirl. They aren't weak—unless you make them that way. They're remarkably sturdy and naturally very strong.

Somewhere along the line, we forgot all this. We abjured authority and lost all perspective. Any evidence of a mental health "symptom" became a command that we immediately hand the kid over to an expert. We forgot that with adolescents, some things are a phase. Many episodes of teen sadness will resolve on their own.

Cognitive behavioral psychologist Roger McFillin told me he believes even minor cutting isn't necessarily a dire crisis in every instance. "We are aware that when self-harm serves the purpose of seeking nurturing, attention, or evading responsibility, responding to such behavior in this manner will only reinforce its occurrence. Regrettably, some adolescents have acquired the skill of weaponizing self-injury."

He tells parents they shouldn't immediately feed their daughters into the mental health pipeline the second their daughters experiment with it. How does he advise parents to respond to minor cutting? In some contexts, parents should just ignore it.[5]

In other words, when your teen acts out: Keep your head. Remain in charge. Don't immediately hand off your kid to a mental health expert. *You* decide whether she is in crisis or not.

I am no perfect parent. I have yelled at my kids too much and for the wrong things, criticized needlessly, and gotten angrier than I should have over minor provocations. I write late into the night, wake up tired, push through the morning in a cranky haze, and once sent my son off to school with an empty container in place of a lunch. I have forgotten to fill out permission slips, failed to keep abreast of parental chatter over the best teachers and sports teams, and declined to volunteer for all manner of school endeavor that struck me as an intolerable waste of time.

But after I began researching for this book, I made a few adjustments. For one, I informed my kids: I would no longer be reading the school's daily homework reminder emails. Anything related to homework assignments or tests, I told my kids, they were responsible to know. If this meant they missed an assignment, better it happened in elementary or middle school, where the academic consequences are miniscule. I resolved to opt out of turning disorganized elementary school kids into dependent high schoolers.

When my then nine-year-old daughter begged to be able to walk home from the bus stop by herself, I began letting her. I did this not because *I* was ready. (I so obviously was not: the cars are so big; she was so small.) Worries assailed me from the moment of drop off until the second she knocked on the door. I opened the front door three, four times to see if I could spot her down the road. She loved her walks; I hated them.

I allowed this primarily because when I talked to parents, I learned something. When kids miss their "window" of independence—of wanting to hazard a risk and venture something new on their own—they stop asking for it. I talked to mothers who had forbidden their kids to walk around the neighborhoods when they were little. By the time the kids turned thirteen, they couldn't be dislodged from the house.

A nine-year-old who walks home by herself enters the house full of triumph. A twelve-year-old who accomplishes the same task feels nothing. *He* knows this is hardly a great achievement. Having been trained to accept the cramped confines of a cage, by the time the door is flung open—when he's eligible to get his driver's license, say—he may have surrendered to his captivity.

After I spoke with Yaakov Ophir, I pressed my sons into household errands. Every Friday, before the start of the Sabbath, I sent them on scooters to the market with an empty backpack, a list, and a credit card. Every time they returned home in one piece, I heaved a sigh of relief.

No amount of pleading and hectoring had persuaded them to talk to adults on their own, keep track of their belongings, write things down. But under the pressure of this errand, they looked for cars before they crossed the street, kept track of my credit card, carefully scanned my list, and asked clerks where to find packs of yeast. (If they forgot an item, I sent them back.)

For the first time in his life, one my sons—far from my best organized child—implored me to look through my recipes and *make sure* the list covered everything I needed. Not because he had been taught executive functioning or organizational skills. Exigency taught him these, coupled with a profound distaste for being sent to the store *twice*.

My sons got to know the people who worked at our market. They learned their way around the neighborhood. They began, for the first time, to take note of their surroundings—not because I'd hectored them to pay attention (though I had). But because I had gotten *out of the way*.

No single activity has been better for my kids—their spiritedness, their maturity, their sense of responsibility or sense of self—than sleepaway camp. No amount of badgering from me about picking up after themselves made any dent in their behavior at all; not until their high school–aged counselors insisted upon it. No amount of pleading got them to flush a toilet or put up the seat. Not until they'd been assigned latrine duty.

Again, all I did was subtract my hovering, nervous, neurotic self and let older kids inspire them. If you can scrape together the money for a no-technology sleepaway camp that will reinforce your values, do it. There is no easier way to subtract yourselves and allow independence, risk-taking, autonomy, and true friendship to take its course.

What We Can Learn from a Three-Year-Old Japanese Kid

At just shy of three years old, Hiroki is excited to execute his first errand. Armed with a yellow flag, three items committed to memory, cash in a vinyl purse, and the world's squeakiest sandals, he heads off to the market a half-mile from his home in Kagoshima Prefecture. When he must cross a busy street, Hiroki holds his yellow flag high, so that drivers can spot him.

At the store, he purchases packages of meat and fishcakes and a cone of flowers, which he drags the whole way home. But arrive, he does, full of triumph to his mother's praise and open arms. *Old Enough!* is the title of this Netflix reality show, which each week features a new Japanese toddler sent on a first errand, in a culture that actively fosters independence in very young kids.

According to Yulia Chentsova Dutton, the comparative cultural psychologist who heads the Culture and Emotions Lab at Georgetown University, the Netflix show may lead viewers to exaggerate the age at which Japanese kids are typically pressed into service. (They are more likely to be five.) But it is more or less accurate. "They're walking to school, they're navigating the environment that they're in very early—starting at around the age of five," she told me. "A seven, eight-year-old Japanese child might get on the Metro, might get on the bus independently, go to school, come back, so they have plentiful, frequent independence. Oftentimes, they do it together, so you see whole groups of Japanese children navigating the city together, going to school, and so they're building peer relationships meanwhile."

This isn't merely an accidental cultural artifact. Like other high-income countries that are relatively low in disorders of anxiety and depression—Israel being another—Japan has an ideological commitment to giving children freedom to work out conflict and navigate their world without monitoring and adult oversight. In Japan, Chentsova Dutton told me, preschools often include hiding spaces on the playground, deliberately designed for kids to play without the burden of adult surveillance.

"When they're at school, the teachers have this sense that some amount of less supervised time and peer interactions without adults meddling is very developmentally appropriate and important," she said. Their playgrounds often feature little boulders and streams. Aren't Japanese teachers worried a preschooler will get hurt? That's the point. They want minor mishaps—scraped knees, wet socks, "so children learn to better regulate when they're feeling those signals of 'this may be risky'— they know how to react to that."

I thought, with embarrassment, of my daughter's school and the assistant principal's flush of pride as she told me she had just created new playground rules for handball "so that the girls would stop arguing when one of the girls got out." Thanks to the new rules our assistant principal introduced, no kid ever got "out," the stakes for the game collapsed, and so did the fun; the kids stopped playing it. And they lost another opportunity to work out conflicts on their own.

Eight is the official age at which schoolchildren in Israel are expected to get themselves to school—on the bus, if necessary. I mentioned this to Chentsova Dutton, who already knew, based on her time studying cultural attitudes toward child independence in Israel.

In American discussions of child development, we tend to talk about kids building life "skills," as if such things were acquired in isolation: like a good golf swing. But making your way home from school isn't like that, Chentsova Dutton discovered when she followed Israeli kids on their walks. "They are interacting with peers, they are giving direction to some tourists, they're stopping by the bakery, they're buying bread, they're sitting there, having a snack. And with that, it's sort of a sense of competency. Like, 'I know how to navigate this environment.'"

What she sees—and studies—on American college campuses is precisely the opposite. Students tell her: "Look, by the time my parents felt it was safe for me to play outside, I was like thirteen and had no interest in playing outside. That period was completely missed. It never happened."

Treating Adolescent Anxiety with Doses of Independence

Lenore Skenazy, author of *Free Range Kids*, has spearheaded the Let Grow movement, based on a simple intuition: kids don't know what they *can* do if we don't give them the freedom and risk to try. Kids who feel like they can't do are unhappy, fearful kids. A growing body of research supports her.[6]

Disorders of anxiety and depression are both associated with neuroticism—negative hyper-reactivity to one's environment. Independent activity may promote well-being in children through short-term joy and long-term habituation to the routine stressors of life.[7]

One of America's leading academic psychologists, Peter Gray, a cofounder of Let Grow, thinks that the decline in independent activity by school-aged children and teens over the past five or six decades is a "primary cause" in the decline of their mental health.[8] In a brand-new academic paper reviewing a voluminous body of research, Gray concludes that unsupervised play, risky play, and independent activity in which a young person contributes to the welfare of a group all produce immediate happiness and foster long-term psychological resilience.[9] None of those benefits come from monitored play, which, as far as psychological resilience or immediate joy is concerned, isn't really "play" at all.

In a related recent study, Chentsova Dutton and her team interviewed students from Turkey, Russia, Canada, and America and asked them to describe "risky" or dangerous experiences they had had in the previous month.[10] She found that American students were far more likely to exaggerate the risks posed by quotidian events—being alone outside or riding in an Uber—and less able to discriminate between actual dangers and imagined ones. "Both Turkish and Russian students described witnessing events that involved actual risk: violent fights on public transportation; hazardous driving conditions caused by drunk drivers; women being aggressively followed on the street,"[11] according to a journalist who reviewed the study. Having never learned to manage social risk or harm, American students were more likely to be made anxious by routine incidents of normal life.

American parents will balk. They will insist that they extend their kids all sorts of independence. But as Chentsova Dutton points out, none of the choices American parents typically afford their children involve any actual danger or risk—and, therefore, none offers the satisfaction of agency spent and achievement realized. "Americans are offering children ridiculous number of choices, completely safe choices—none of them are influential choices. *What are you going to drink? What are you going to eat? Is it the red shirt or the white shirt?* Giving children the sense of '*I am calling the shots, I am in charge. I am deciding, I am influencing.*'" But all are safe, controlled, and trivial options.

This describes, to a T, the sorts of questions parents toss at children all the time, like a half dozen tennis balls lobbed to distract them. And it is precisely what so many therapeutic parenting books advise: *To avoid conflict with your child who doesn't want to do what you're asking, present him with a choice: "You have to go to school today, but you can choose what music we listen to in the car."* Last year, my sons' math teacher routinely assigned ten problems of homework from a sheet that included twenty: The students could *choose* which ten problems to complete. *A new era of choice and freedom! Do you hear the people sing?* No? Me neither.

According to Chentsova Dutton, such manipulations may momentarily distract kids into compliance, but eventually, the subterfuge runs out. Kids know they're being patronized. "And I think when they're hitting college, or hitting high school, maybe even a little earlier, that actually, [they know] all of those were fake choices; that they haven't been given any influential choices in their life."

"What would be an influential choice?"

"Something they'll decide without participation of their parents that can actually result in something really good or really bad happening to them."

Here are some decisions we once (but no longer) extended to teens in America: Whether to go to college. (Nope, everyone goes.) Whom to date. (Moot; no one does.) Whom to befriend. (Mom chooses.) What activities to do. (Mom chooses.) What route to take to school. (Mom gets you there.) Even *how to be* a friend. (Counselors and teachers now inquire into this and offer correction.)

In his clinical practice, based on a similar intuition, psychology professor and cognitive behavioral therapist Camilo Ortiz has begun treating anxious adolescents with independence. "When parents hover and prevent children from independently exploring the world around them, they foster many of the processes that scientists have identified as causes of anxiety," he has written.[12] "Kids who don't practice independence (yes, it is a skill that withers without practice) are less self-confident, have worse social skills, are less tolerant of uncertainty, have worse problem-solving skills, and are less resilient."

Ortiz believes acts of independence can help alleviate even unrelated fears. Of his method with kids, he has joked, "So you're scared of the dark? Go to the deli and buy me a half a pound of salami." The child's feeling of efficacy that results from completion of this sort of task, he says, makes kids stronger in every sense: braver, less anxious, more willing to try things that are hard, and, remarkably, less of a constant burden to their stricken parents. So far, he says, the results are promising.[13]

What Real Independence Looks Like

Like Japan, Israel takes as its obligation the fostering of independence in children. Parent-teacher conferences are routinely held *with the child present*, so that the child can hear what is said about her. When new immigrant parents attempt to drive kids age eight and up to school or commandeer tasks that—in Israelis' view—are meant to be handled by children, Israeli teachers upbraid the parents for effectively putting braces on a healthy leg.

I know this, not only from Chentsova Dutton, but also my sister-in-law, who recently moved her family to Israel. When she tried to a hire a driving instructor for her sixteen-year-old son, she was told: no dice. "Sorry, but your son needs to hire me. He is my client," the man said.

She learned from other parents that on the day that her son, my nephew, would be called to report for army duty, one of the first questions he would be asked is: "How did you get here?" If the answer is "My mom drove me," elite units would toss his application. They have no use for the mollycoddled.

Sometimes, my sister-in-law told me, the Israel Defense Forces will provide young recruits a mistaken address to test the young person's ability to handle adversity. The army—and Israeli society more generally—believes it has a responsibility to force young people to handle the unexpected. They consider this essential preparation for a life full of unpleasant surprises.

When middle school youth groups put on plays in Israel, the productions are entirely student run. Which also means they're fairly awful. But they aren't designed for the benefit of the parent audience. They're designed for the benefit of the kids.

Imagine if we ran schools this way: let kids get a bad grade, get cut from a team, or put on an amateurish play so that *they* could learn from it and do better next time. (Actually, until very recently, we *did*. The 1940s-era *Seventeen* magazine proves it. The activities and plays are all entirely student run.) In contrast, at one of our local private schools here in Los Angeles, there is a school rock band; the headmaster sings in it. *Gee, that sounds like fun.*

But more importantly, it's just not very good for kids. Nature "loves small errors," as Nassim Nicholas Taleb writes in *Antifragile*. Errors, in fact, beat the path to human greatness. All of education depends upon it, the scientific method assumes it, growth and evolution require it. That does *not mean* the elimination of standards: error means keep standards high, and let some attempts sink; let scores reflect actual ability. Moderate stress improves performance.[14]

Catastrophic errors are just that—catastrophic. You don't send a child into a knife fight as a way of toughening him up.

And perhaps this is why social media is so bad for our young: It is the knife fight of human status competition. It offers risk none of us is equipped to handle, especially our necessarily socially sensitive adolescents. We—and they—are built to handle minor social errors that result in fifteen other kids, even the whole class, laughing at us. But none of us is prepared to have Seth Rogan (9.3 million followers) make fun of our name on Twitter. None of us is prepared to have our humiliations shared with thousands *or millions*. None of us is built for it, and it is too devastating to be beneficial.[15]

Chentsova Dutton grew up in Russia, another country that builds independence in children. Each year, as a birthday present, her parents increased the permitted ambit of her tramping about on her own. Each year, they allowed a little more risk, a little more chance for danger—and, necessarily, for learning and growing. Each year, they tantalized her with a slightly greater peek at the joys of the adult world.

We've known that a sense of personal efficacy in the world is intimately connected to a sense of what we now call wellness—we've known it for a very long time. How could it not improve a child's overall fitness to feel *competent* in the world?

When we made a point of inducting children into the adult world— through the gradual assignment of chores, after-school jobs, and an allowance of hours of unsupervised time with peers—they were eager for more. More freedom, more responsibility. But today, instead, we alter the adult world around them to make it more amenable to a child.

To take just one recent example, food and beverage companies are now remaking products to turn all cuisine into finger foods to accommodate a generation that doesn't want to develop adult tastes, prefers sweeter drinks in bright colors, and still wants to consume like toddlers. "Older beer drinkers boast of putting in work to get to liking the bitter taste of beer, much as they would challenge themselves to like the tastes of coffee, olives or dark chocolate," one marketing chief told the *Wall Street Journal*. But the younger generations don't, he said.[16]

The Winners of the Great Depression

Want to know which kids fared best in the Great Depression? It wasn't the poorest kids, who were sometimes abandoned by parents who couldn't feed them. Nor was it the richest, whose lives were relatively unaffected by the Depression. According to a wonderful longitudinal study of 167 elementary school kids from Oakland, California,[17] the kids who fared best belonged to a third group: middle-class kids who took jobs, wore hand-me-downs, took in piecework or picked up a paper route, saved their money, did extra chores.

"Men and women from the deprived middle class were *more* likely to be judged relatively free of symptoms than the nondeprived, and were also rated higher on ego strength, integration of impulses and strivings, utilization of personal resources, and capacity for growth. They were characterized as more resilient, more self-confident, and less defensive."[18]

The kids who'd had to sacrifice during this period ended up with a greater work ethic and accelerated entry into the adult world.[19] Moderate deprivation and sacrifice, challenge, independence, risk that comes with autonomy—all of those turned out to be very good for these kids.

And yet my generation's style of parenting has been characterized by the opposite: *accommodation.* Parents working overtime to create a noiseless, sanitized, pain-free terrarium for kids who then cannot bear the world outside it.

"I consider it a dangerous misconception of mental hygiene to assume that what man needs in the first place is equilibrium . . . a tensionless state," wrote the great Austrian psychiatrist and Holocaust survivor Viktor Frankl. "If architects want to strengthen a decrepit arch, they increase the load which is laid upon it, for thereby the parts are joined more firmly together."[20]

If you want to strengthen a person's muscles, you force her to exercise. You don't strengthen a kid by running to the doctor for a diagnosis and pressing your kid's school for an accommodation. And here's the most important point of all: you don't need to *do* anything in order to accomplish this. You obviously don't need to *hurt* your kid's feelings in order to strengthen her. You just need to stop running interference. Stop micromanaging her relationships in the hopes that no one and nothing in the vicinity will ever make her feel the slightest bit bad. The project is doomed to backfiring. Pathogens always worm their way in, even to the most sterilized environments. Better to develop an immune system.

A Horse Walks into a Bar

Parents today might be forgiven for not remembering what humor is. Of all the rotten traits of our parenting books, they are almost uniformly dour and humorless. Sweet Lord Above, these lousy books made every moment with our kids heavy and serious. Techniques to practice, situations to monitor, problems to recognize, apologies to offer when we failed to do all the above. They paint a world of severity, where the stakes are high and dourness reigns.

But if you want to allow your child one of the soul's best defenses in an unpredictable world, drop your guard, just this once, and let things be funny again.

"Humor was another of the soul's weapons in the fight for self-preservation," Frankl observed of his time surviving Auschwitz. "It is well known that humor, more than anything else in the human make-up, can afford an aloofness and ability to rise above any situation, even only for a few seconds."[21]

I try to avoid offering positive advice, seeing as we're all so adrift in it. "Laugh with your kids" sounds like positive advice. But it isn't. Humor is among the psyche's most natural defenses. It's *censorship* that requires policing. If you want to stifle humor, you must create rules and enforce them. Otherwise, we humans laugh and poke fun at just about everything.

Humor is the embrace of the unexpected. And it's among our best psychological tools for transforming life's endless conveyor of minor disappointments into uproarious diversion.

You Are Not Alone
on This Passenger Flight

About a year ago, I was on a flight, seated behind an American family of four—two parents and two little girls. Midair, the girl who was about eight let out a protracted scream so shrill, my eardrums felt like they'd been pierced by a sharp object.

Her father, red-headed and bearded, a gentle giant, attempted to calm her down. He asked her what was wrong. He inquired about the reason for her anger toward her younger sister. He told the younger one not to pinch or whatever she had done. He urged them to reconcile.

He never once mentioned the other passengers on the plane. He didn't tell either of those girls that when they cried out, they might be disturbing ninety other people. He never mentioned that we were all sharing this space in the air, and we all had a job to do: be good neighbors for the length of the trip. He never troubled his daughters with thoughts of us.

I mentioned this to Chentsova Dutton, to find out what a Japanese parent would think of that. "To anyone from a more collectivistic culture, this is just insane," she said.

Our kids don't know that they're connected to others—because we don't tell them. We tell them they're such perfect little individuals, they can scream their pretty heads off on a plane as if they are alone. Here is the ontological problem, compounding the moral one: the solipsism it teaches, inculcating the idea that kids are free radicals, unattached to a social world. When things are good, when they are happy, that may be fine. But when things are hard, they have no one to turn to—no sense, even, that there's anyone out there who really cares about them beyond their parents.

We don't permit kids a web of stable relationships. We choose for them the very best, hand-picked friends, based on our preferences, at different locations, as if we were collecting rocks on the beach. But when you look at societies with very high rates of pathological depression, Chentsova Dutton says, two things stand out: a high value placed on individualism and high relational mobility (meaning, lots of turnover in the characters that inhabit your life).

Think, for a moment, about our kids' lives today: they don't hang out with neighborhood kids, or cousins, or many siblings, or even a bevy of classmates who follow them all through school. They have kids they see at chess club; kids on the baseball team; friends from first grade; friends from second grade—none of whom know each other. We shuffle the composition of their classes each year, on the theory that this will help make them *new* friends.

"What they end up with is this highly fragmented set of relationships," Chentsova Dutton told me. "Instead of an integrated, stable group of friends, where you get to know each other, you connect over longer periods of time, you anticipate stability, and you develop relationships that are qualitatively different in terms of what they can offer to scaffold you when things don't go so well. And so when these children hit adolescence, with their normal stressors, they're lacking in a stable support network."

Mexican immigrants to America, who do much better in terms of mental health than Americans of similar socioeconomic backgrounds, also do worse the more acculturated to American life they become. And one of the ways researchers account for this "Latino mental health paradox" is the culture they bring with them, which leads them to form relatively stable and strong social webs.[22]

I live in the City of Los Angeles, home to over half a million Central American immigrants. And one of the things you notice when, for example, two Salvadorans or Guatemalans greet each other is that they immediately inquire where, exactly, each one's family is from. They figure out who they know in common, which church each attends. If they've spoken before, even just once, they inquire after each other's families—and they really listen to the answers.

When they meet again, they check up on the progress of each other's lives; their cultures encourage this humanity and decency. It teaches them to invest in each other. If you came upon them without knowing better, you'd suspect those who'd just met had been friends for years.

All this, families and neighborhoods once provided. Our kids don't have that. They don't have a stable web of connections who care about them or really know them. Our constant emphasis on our kids' uniqueness reinforces this sense that they need be preoccupied only with themselves. That they are their own entirely bespoke individuals. That they are very much alone.

Extended Family (Yes, Those People)

My father-in-law, who grew up on a California cattle ranch, has a ludicrous, hair-raising tradition with the grandkids. Many years before his grandkids turn sixteen—when they are eleven or twelve—he takes each one to a remote area and teaches them to drive. From the moment my twin sons turned nine, I began dreading their turn at the wheel.

I love my sons, and I trust them with all kinds of things. They regularly fix all manner of computer problems in the home, and when I need someone to follow directions and put together an end table, there is no one better. But I've also known them, well, forever. They routinely slam buttons before finding out what those buttons do. They knock over every kind of glass and, if they saw a pedal, I had doubted very much they could be trusted not to stomp it.

They could get hurt. They could hurt others. The risk was great. The benefit doubtful. The activity illegal.

I was in charge of ensuring their safety. Letting them drive a two-ton vehicle with Grandpa seemed the opposite of that. No way they were driving.

But then, one day, as I was beginning to think about this book, I had a minor epiphany: What if this wasn't about *me*? What if my comfort wasn't the only consideration at play? Was it possible that, in forbidding the activity with their grandfather, I was depriving them of something more?

I thought about a conversation I had with Harvard psychiatrist Harold Bursztajn, whose parents survived the Holocaust and escaped the Lodz Ghetto by hiding in sewer pipes. Bursztajn told me that throughout the Holocaust, at the lowest ebbs of his father's life—what kept him going were the rich memories he had of his family, playing like a film reel in his mind.

Many of the young patients Bursztajn sees at Harvard know very little about their families. This renders them uniquely vulnerable, Bursztajn says, as they face life's challenges. "There's a huge amount of insecurity about 'Who am I?'" he said, of the young adult patients he's seen in the last decade. "A good deal of it is not being able to connect up with the past, not being able to have a sense of continuity. Feeling that somehow the future is a great unknown, the present is a challenge. And the past is a mystery."

When we overly restrict Grandpa's conversation or activity with our kids—much less when we banish them entirely—we interfere with our kids' sense that they are the newest stems of Pando, the aspen colony with a single root system webbing the earth. We interrupt the natural sense that: *I'm not just me. I go way back. People in my line have faced much worse and survived. I can, too.*

When you affirm kids' natural inclination to regard their challenges as sui generis and all important, when you fail to tell them that their own grandparents survived hardship, you strip them of the ability to place their own suffering in context. You divest them of the one bit of empirical proof they have that their genetic material is resilient. You cut them loose of the familial web, one of humanity's greatest sources of meaning. You force them to see their problems in isolation and to face hardship, alone.

One of the worst consequences of our hyperfocus on present feelings, our willful divorce from historical perspective, and the professionalization of our child-rearing is that we've devalued everything grandparents had to offer. We came to see them as backward, racist, crude—too playful, not playful enough, and far too likely to appeal to things their own parents had done as a guide. We corrected their interactions with our children, strictly limited them, or barred them entirely.

Grandparents weren't perfect. Grandpa said all the wrong things, showed the wrong movies, and taught the kids inappropriate jokes. He pressed them into work with tools that were dangerous, and he offered too little in the way of instruction. Grandma made all the wrong foods (*You know Aiden doesn't do well with dairy!*) and corrected the kids' poor table manners in ways that struck us as excessive.

But kids *survived* all of that, and they came away tougher, knowing they could handle adults who didn't follow the script handed to them by Mom. Kids came away with something whose sum was not easy to imagine from so many particularized parts: connection.

I let my sons go on the drive with Grandpa, in the end, not because I thought it was a good idea. I didn't "give permission," exactly. I simply let it happen. And so my sons have this riotous, hair-raising memory with a grandfather who will not be around forever.

Maybe the shared experience with their cousins of this wacky rite of passage—which none of the parents would have provided—will make them feel less alone as they head out into an uncertain future. Maybe that will be enough to prompt them to call a cousin when they need someone to talk to, or offer help when the cousin is in need. Maybe all the haphazard family holidays and rowdy family birthday parties impress upon kids the need to show up for others, to find humor in the ridiculous, to suppress irritation at the minor inconvenience of insensitive people abrading each other with intrusive questions. Maybe it helps them learn to put that irritation to productive use (like helping to load the trays of lasagna into the car or push Grandma's wheelchair) and to better calibrate realistic expectations for what each day will hold. Perhaps the absurd, touching theater of extended family also offers herd immunity against despair in the face of inevitable hardship. Extended family is worth suffering for that reason alone.

But don't take my word for it. The world's longest-running and most comprehensive psychological review of adult well-being, the Harvard Grant Study, found that the five most effective traits associated with higher life satisfaction were: altruism (focus on others); humor; sublimation ("finding gratifying alternatives to frustration and anger"); anticipation ("being realistic about future challenges"); and suppression (yes, keeping a stiff upper lip in the face of unpleasant thoughts and events).[23] Every one of the five involves taking your own feelings less seriously. Life with uncles, aunts, cousins, and grandparents helps with all of them.

"The secret to life is good and enduring intimate relationships and friendships," summarized Yale psychiatry professor Charles Barber, reviewing the study. A bunch of people you love and who love you back over a lifetime.

Chapter 12

•

Spoons Out

If you are a teenager today, you hang out with friends far less in-person—up to an hour less *per day*—than the previous generation.[1] You've heard less in-person laughter, fewer in-person jokes; seen fewer in-person tears, but also had far fewer occasions to touch—far fewer kisses and hugs than any teenager since researchers started recording these things. Far fewer in-person opportunities to make a mistake, feel bad, apologize, grow.

Your parents observe every aspect of your life unfolding on social media and—if anything happens to you or your friends—they know about it as soon as you do. There is no private kids' world of low stakes: your parents, plugged in always to WhatsApp, know about every kid caught vaping on the school overnight, hours after it occurs. They guide you through every squabble, every conflict with a teacher, every misunderstanding with a friend. By default, your parents are your best friends.

Your parents attend every practice and game and communicate regularly with your coaches and teachers. Outside of the internet, there is no place for you to mess around or experiment without their knowledge, encouragement, cheerleading, and feedback.

Your grandparents live far away. You don't know them very well, and chitchat, never practiced, isn't easy. Your parents obviously prefer you to get your direction from the adults they've hired, who report to them.

Each day is activity-jammed, presided over by a series of adults who judge your progress. They tell you when you are improving and also when you are not. They communicate the delta to your parents: "Her handsprings are crisper, but we still need to work on the balance beam." You are always, in everything you do, monitored by anxious adults.

You get less sleep than any previous generation of teens—far less than you need.[2] You are so tired some days, it feels as though you are missing a layer of skin. Worries invade unresisted.

Many of your friends have tried cutting or some other creative form of self-harm. Whenever you're down, self-harm surfaces as an option. It's part of the vernacular: a way of saying, *Ask me how I'm doing.* Suicide hotlines are advertised more conspicuously around your school than prom. It's painfully obvious that the school counselor is always sniffing kids for suicide like a German shepherd on the hunt for plastic explosives.

For good reason, your parents and teachers are frantic over your mental health. Half of your friends are seeing shrinks or on psychiatric drugs or both. Your parents are concerned enough to hire a therapist to talk to you each week. "There are no wrong answers," the woman in stretchy black pants and plastic glasses assures you over the soft tinkling of a prefab indoor water fountain. But, it turns out, there are lots of wrong answers—some of which trigger a diagnosis. No matter how good of a week you've had, or how well you followed the therapist's advice, she never says: "You're fixed! No need to return."

You've had a diagnosis for at least a year; it's begun to feel as much a part of you as your own name. Your parents are obviously relieved to have a label for what's wrong with you. Most of your friends have a diagnosis, too. It functions as an amulet; you begin to suspect it may be the most important thing about you. But also, it makes you feel like a glass with a starburst crack—damaged in a permanent way. You'll never be a load-bearing object, strong enough to carry others.

Your therapist suggests medication might help, and the pediatrician is happy to oblige. The drugs make you calmer and keep you from crashing, but sometimes you wish the training wheels weren't welded on. Who knows what you might be able to do without them? You've been on SSRIs for so long, it's hard to know.

You've packed on pounds. You can't help it; the drugs make you less inhibited around food. They've killed your sex drive. You're not even sure if that matters. You spend a lot more time on the sofa. You no longer feel bad about that, but you're also far less inclined to budge.

Whenever you have to wait for anything—food to arrive, a show to start, your friend to speak—your skin starts to itch. You've been conditioned all your life to find waiting unbearable. You carry an accommodation machine in your pocket, which might as well be called a rumination device. It drives you deeper into the forest of your own mind to be haunted by shadows: the ex-boyfriend who didn't want you, the party you missed, the numberless ways you don't stack up.

Your smartphone caters to your every whim, which seems great, but then it's made it so much harder to adjust to the unclickable world. Everything real is also disappointing. No friend is as funny as a video you can pull up on your phone. No girl as hot as the endless catwalk in your pocket. You could meet someone for pizza, but with a swipe it arrives at your door; "contact-free delivery" means you don't even need to talk to the pizza guy.

Sometimes with a classmate you let your guard down and trade messages you shouldn't. It was only a joke, but it's never only a joke. Friends preserve everything you say in screenshots. You do the same, so that the deterrence of mutual assured destruction applies, enforced by teachers and administrators and college admissions committees.

You've rarely spent a whole afternoon with a friend who lent you her full attention. You don't know most of her secrets, and she doesn't know yours; she's already divulged her most intimate worries to a therapist. Rehashing it all again seems so pointless.

You don't really have time for friends, anyway. Your full-time, unpaid internship consumes every extra minute: five, six, eight hours a day—the settings don't lie—staring at your phone.

"My mental health sucks," you tell the group chat. The others say theirs does, too. You can't believe your dad had an actual job at your age. You don't feel ready for anything like that.

You've only ever known this overmanaged, veal-calf life. Occasionally it occurs to you to wonder: *What if taking the risk is the only way to feel ready? What if the solution to adolescent mental health problems is to outgrow adolescence?* That may explain why the unending parade of accommodation and intervention, which stretch childhood out like taffy, has only prolonged your torture.

For Parents: A Thought on the Purpose of Childhood

When you have a child, everything changes. Not just your daily routine, your household economy, the sorts of friends you make, or the places you vacation. You achieve a toehold in human society: you are someone's mother or father.

You are the one the kid cries out for when she is hurt or sick. You, clutching the armrest and stifling shrieks as she learns to drive. The one going to bed every night with a phone beside you, turned up to full volume, as you wait for news that she made it safely to her destination, got the job she wanted so much, or had a child of her own.

You are somebody in this world because you are *everything* to your kid. When she considers how an adult should conduct herself, her mind invariably turns to you. Even if she wishes to depart from your example, yours will forever be the blueprint from which she fashions a life.

You don't need sophisticated knowledge of the human brain and its infinitely complex systems to discover what's troubling your own kids. You likely don't need mind-altering meds to cure them. You simply need a willingness to improve your kid's life by removing the bad stuff and making space for the good.

It's like the old joke: *A man walks into a doctor's office with a complaint: "Whenever I drink coffee, I get this sharp pain in my eye."*

The doctor replies: "Try removing the spoon."

The solution doesn't require a doctor. It requires only a change in a person's life: that he stop doing the things that are obviously hurting him. The climate alarmism, the we're-descending-into-fascism talk, the hunt for repressed trauma, the iPhone, the therapy they don't need. The crisis is not organic. It's something we ushered in the door.

There is nothing scarier to a child than the sight of her parents overmatched and afraid. Cognitive behavioral therapists have effectively treated children's anxiety by treating the anxiety in their parents because parents often transmit worries to kids. But we can transmit calm, too. We can be brave for them because that is what every life, if it is well-lived, requires: that we face the things that frighten us, that we *try* and try and try again—whether we feel up to it each time or not.

When you mute the expert advice, when you log off *Slate* Parenting, when you lay down rules according to your values, and insist your kids abide by them—you will be surprised by just how much you like your kids. Because the truth is, you should. There is nothing in life that comes close to the remarkable adventure of raising them.

Have you ever watched a young mother loading groceries into her car, with a toddler in one arm? There is no sight lovelier or more arresting. She is tired and busy and has so much on her mind—her whole world, braced in the steel hinge of her arm.

A colt is born nearly ready to run the Preakness. Our children enter the world, howling incompetents. Why do human children take so long to grow up? Why did nature create a period of prolonged childhood?

As far as I can tell, the *purpose* of childhood is to allow kids to take risks—things that involve getting all kinds of hurt—and to practice the skills they will need as adults while they are still safely under their parents' roofs. Childhood exists to allow kids to hazard an unpredictable friend, lose a ball game, stand up to a bully, pick themselves up, offer another kid a hand. We want them to venture out and get their hearts broken, try and fail, and at last succeed—all while we're still in the next bedroom.

That's what a happy childhood *is*: experiencing all of the pains of adulthood, in smaller doses, so that they build up immunity to the poison of heartache and loss. And when they stumble, most of the time they don't need a session with a school counselor. They need to be told: shake it off. They need to see in our eyes not worry but faith that they're going to be just fine. We want all of this to happen when they're young. If they find themselves facing disappointment or rejection for the first time as adults, something has gone terribly wrong.

Parents know this. It's why—before the experts got involved—we were always beta testing our kids: teasing, hectoring, hugging. Letting them feel the pain of ignoring our warnings but then helping them up, brushing them off, sending them on their way.

It's the reason fathers clamp the chubby ankles of a toddler, flip him upside down, toss him high into the air, to the tune of the child's shrieking laughter. They are girding the kid for the future: deliberately inducing excitement and fear when they can manage the risk, ready to catch him in their arms.

Try removing the spoon. If the doctor in the joke had been a little less ethical, or had just an ounce less sense, he would have prescribed painkillers, ordered an MRI, and charged for a full eye exam. What was necessary was simply a negative: the elimination of the obvious thing introducing the harm.

We've allowed our kids to drink from mugs full of such spoons: the iPad when they were little, then the iPhone, which was worse. Each began the process of vitiating their attention, leaching away their joy in the world around them, which could only pale in comparison. When they stayed inside, alone, they hardly even knew what they were missing.

So much technology brought endless accommodation. We habituated our kids to a life in which nearly all of their desires were immediately met—to order up any particular show, to stop it the second it bored them, then order up the next; or some food; or new shoes; or even a friend's face. The slower pace of richer, more meaningful life, the moments that tee up conversation—an elevator ride, a waiting room, a checkout line, a bike ride—became all but intolerable.

Schools stocked their faculties with mental health staff and rushed to play therapist—prompting our kids to think endlessly about their feelings—routinely, formally, before waiting to see if they had a problem. Counselors were so eager to talk about our kids' pain. They explored and aggrandized every worry because they are in the worry business.

I spoke recently to the mother of a seventeen-year-old boy who, briefly, in middle school, had been diagnosed with ADHD, placed on Ritalin, and made to see a therapist. When he didn't like how the Ritalin made him feel, his parents reluctantly let him give it up. But years later, having at last found areas at which he excelled and subjects that captured his sustained interest, he came to resent the time he spent in therapy. He told his mother: "Going to therapy is like learning to ski by focusing on the trees."

If school mental health experts actually wanted to repair our kids' mental health, the first thing they would do is ban smartphones during the school day.[3] The evidence that social media harms kids' sense of well-being is all but incontrovertible. But I would go further: smartphones are an accommodation, a gizmo of avoidance and rumination—the last thing our kids need while they are reaching for adulthood. Smartphones are not the only force luring teens into a vicious cycle of negative self-focus, but they are perhaps the most ubiquitous and most persuasive.[4]

Counselors worth their salt would say: "We cannot work in this environment. If you want us to help your kids, the first thing we must insist is that all phones are collected at the start of school and not returned until day's end." What could be easier? It's a little like a school nurse insisting, "The first thing I must insist is that we ban smoking on campus. Smoking makes all health problems worse. If you want me to help kids, let's start by creating the preconditions for good health."

But school mental health staff only very rarely, if ever, insist their schools ban smartphones, even during the day.[5] Instead, they arrogate to themselves hefty portions of school curricula and dispense "wellness" tips: *Try meditation, try mindfulness, try gratitude journaling. Tell us your problems; we'll make you better.* They behave as if they were motivated not by the desire to banish kids' emotional distress but to expand their own influence.

Therapists of every kind dispense diagnoses without any thought to the trouble this causes: to kids' sense of efficacy, to kids' definition of self. Doctors ply kids with psychotropic medication that limits their ability to feel things, to cope and to grow. Never warning them of the powerful withdrawal symptoms they may feel should they ever wish to see what it's like to exist in the world without the emotional snowsuit.

The drugs we give still-developing minds—two, three, even ten at a time[6]—stymie the intellect, dampen the sex drive, cap the emotions, maybe even dull the conscience. We send kids off to school this way—tetchy one minute, zombie the next. Numb to pain and worry, dimmed in intellect and motivation, sensing, dimly, that there's a whole life they're missing: their own.

For too long, we parents let this happen. We began to anchor ourselves to the diagnoses slapped on our kids by someone who doesn't know them one one-millionth as well as we do. It's no wonder our kids began to identify with their diagnoses. *We* began to identify them this way, too.

We downgraded our own children without even realizing it. The things we had grown up doing—we decided they couldn't possibly handle. "Well, she can't go on a flight without an iPad." Or, "I can't take away her iPhone; every girl in her class has one." Or, "I know I stayed home by myself when I was her age, but things are different now." On and on. Risks we managed without a thought, we decided they never could.

We began to look at our own kids as if they came bearing a Nutrition Facts label: a taxonomy of disorder. While writing this book, I listened closely to the way parents talked about their kids. "Well, she's my ADHD kid," I heard more than one mom say. "He's actually really smart and sensitive, but he has sensory processing issues," I heard over and over in response to mundane questions about how their kids were doing.

One friend announced his son's admission to state college on Facebook this way: "It's quite something that this dyslexic kid who had trouble early on in school, got to high school and really exceeded everyone's expectations, including, I dare say, his own."

I thought of a few dyslexic people I have known: one of them, a math whiz. She went to Wharton, studied finance, and then headed to Wall Street before starting a series of ventures of her own. To us, she was the friend who organized ski trips, wheedling and negotiating a series of fantastic adventures, each innovative and surprising.

When we refer to our own children by the labels the interlopers give us, we allow these experts to corrode our relationship with our children. We permit experts to downgrade how we see our daughters and sons.

Did Thomas Jefferson's mom think of him as "my dyslexic son"? Or John F. Kennedy's? Would either have become president if they had? It's unnatural for parents to see their children this way. The tags and labels are occasionally useful for experts, but for us, they just get in the way. They are reductive and demeaning, and they have absolutely no business polluting a parent's love.

We think of our kids according to our own categories: the softness of their cheeks, the fluttering of their hands in ours, the smell of their hair when we kiss them good night. I know one of my sons by his operettas of outrage followed, minutes later, by sheepish apology. My view of him, partially etched by the time he suddenly cursed out his twin brother at the Passover Seder. After we sent him to his room, we laughed until we cried.

He is the child who never fails to ask me how my day went and really listen to the answer. He makes a daily devotional of Dodgers stats and Packers scores, and also those of their rivals, ready to help his teams with timely reconnaissance. At night, he sings quietly to himself as he heads off to sleep.

My daughter still holds my hand just to walk around the house. She needles, she jokes, she intrudes. She screams when she laughs. She is our family mascot, and at the kids' school, each of us is known principally by our relation to her.

My other son is always the most protective of me, for reasons I cannot fathom and could not deserve. Quickest to lift anything heavy for me and to worry for my safety. His mind occupies itself with a farrago of puns, puzzles, and connective thoughts. He must recount the day's events to me before collapsing in sleep.

I could identify my kids by challenges they face, but it feels like a betrayal even to set them down. Who am I to decide what's a challenge anyway? These kids are really mine only for the earliest stage of what they will become. Some of the traits I might record as a flaw will turn out, in unexpected contexts, to prove a strength. Or the reason that another person, one day, comes to love them very much. Many people love their spouses for their quirks. I've never heard of anyone loving another for her diagnosis.

And I know my kids will face hardship and pain—a thought that pierces my heart like a hot needle. I read obituaries. *The Wall Street Journal* is filled with dot-inked images of great men and women whose gangbuster lives were stippled with poverty and pain. Men and women who wrote great books, founded important companies, invented extraordinary things, married and formed wonderful friendships, filled their homes with children and grandchildren.

Even the very best lives contain some measure of pain. That much is unavoidable.

But if we want kids to register the endless bounty of life's pleasures, we must get out of their way, and get the tech out of their way, too. Screens do not offer companionship—not the sort that fills us up, anyway. Your kids don't require an iPad to survive a dinner or car trip any more than you did. Teens manage fine with flip phones. They aren't weaker than you—unless you make them so.

Proceed by subtraction. Clean the dirt out of the cut and the body heals itself. Until you've subtracted environmental contaminants that may be hampering your kids—expert, tech, monitoring, meddling, medicinal, or otherwise—you may not know how happy she is or could be.

How do you know whether to put your thirteen-year-old in therapy? Simple: don't take your kid to a shrink unless you've exhausted all other options. If you must sign your adolescent up for therapy, research the therapist as you would any surgeon. In all but the most serious cases, your child is much better off without them. In all but the direst circumstances, your child will benefit immeasurably from knowing *you* are in charge—and that you don't think there's something wrong with her.

Stop allowing interlopers to insert themselves between you and your kids. Adolescents who are suffering with anxiety and depression are obviously not being helped by the current and pervasive mental health treatments. Healthy adolescence can be mercurial and maddening; we know this because we lived it. Today, normal teens are being made ill by the unnecessary treatments our mental health experts dispense indiscriminately. Perhaps most insidiously, the experts insist on habituating our kids into a never-ending confrontation with the one question no therapist can resist: *And how did that make you feel?* When looped in a young mind, it's a question that increases dysregulation, inhibits growth, turns teens into toddlers and young adults into the never-quite-ready.

Preventive mental health intervention—by definition, unnecessary—stultifies maturation, trapping young people in a punishing loop of rumination on feelings, treatment dependency, powerful risk aversion. It inhibits the normal process of adolescing out of youth and casting off the angst of adolescence. We interpret young people's stultification as mental illness. But very often, it isn't. It's the malaise that sets in when they realize they're the age their grandfather was when he married their grandmother, and they're too scared to ask a girl out.

That isn't a mental health crisis. It's closer to an emotional hypochondriasis and iatrogenesis crisis. It trucks not in neuroanatomy but a weakening of the soul—fear and disappointment and lack of capacity, the coiled horror of their own passivity. The unmissable verdict that they have failed to grow up.

As for the therapist who's always supplying candidate diagnoses: more than likely, she isn't discovering bona fide pathology. She may simply be leading your child to think of herself as sick and to behave as if she were.

The Few, the Proud

Iian was a senior associate at the fancy law firm where I was, briefly, a mediocre new hire. Brilliant and ferociously hardworking, Iian was liked by everyone. His one failing? He drove a fifteen-year-old[7] Ford Taurus.

When Iian made partner, the firm conditioned the offer on his buying a new car. The partners wanted him to think that his car embarrassed them—that it would make them look bad to the firm's fancy clients. But I suspected they weren't actually embarrassed by his car. They were *afraid* of him.

Iian's car represented a metallic beige provocation, proving beyond all doubt that Iian didn't care about the baubles. He simply liked the work. He couldn't be bought, and he couldn't be distracted. This filled his competitors with unholy terror.

And so it is with parents. The culture devises ways to denigrate us: for being out of shape and harried and exhausted. We wear "mom jeans" and tell "dad jokes" or have a "dad bod." An unending parade of *New York Times* articles purporting to document the misery of parents does its level best to portray us as sad, useless, pitiable.[8]

Everyone nursing a private agenda for the next generation knows we are the obstacle. They cannot match our stake in what these kids become. They cannot begin to imagine the depth of our love.

I often hear parenting experts talk about the "decision to have children" as if having kids were a bit of consumerism, akin to opting for a moonroof or heated steering wheel. It isn't like that at all. It's a calling, the shedding of an old skin, the forming of a new one. You don't have kids because you think it'll be fun or because you're looking for a new hobby. You don't become a Navy SEAL because you have nothing better to do.

You have kids because you feel that, for you, a full life requires it. That level of self-sacrifice and continuity with the future, the tumbling joy and punch-drunk love, are not even on the menu anywhere else.

Parents know this. We avoid saying so out of respect for those who don't have kids and as a courtesy to those who can't. But the truth is, if you're thinking that having kids is a decision like any other, there probably is no good *reason*. Either your whole being inclines toward it or it might not.

But the desire to have kids can be inculcated, and we should try. Tell your kids: *I brought you into this world to play a part in something far bigger than yourself. An indispensable strand in the cord of our family. Don't be the cord's frayed edge.*

We want people in a society to have kids not because it necessarily makes them better people. Not because having kids is the only way to contribute to the world. (Very obviously, it isn't.) We want people to have kids because parents are the keystone in any civilization—the only cohort that cannot be compromised.

Other people may claim to care about our collective future, but only parents *need* things to turn out well. We've made the deepest, most personal of investments: we've released into the world the ultimate measure of ourselves.

Others may look at us with pity. They see the dark thumbprints under our eyes, the silvery stretch marks on our hips. Ah, but those are the battle scars.

There is no pride I've felt in any personal achievement that matches the day my shy, four-year-old son announced his name to the assembled audience of parents at his first piano recital. I have never felt so close to God as I did the day any of my kids was yanked into the world, when I first heard their cries, and felt certain only a miracle could account for it. No wave of tenderness has equaled the knee-buckling sensation of holding any of my kids in my arms.

Claims from experts that they know—or more laughably, that they care—what's best for our kids with anything comparable to the degree that we do ought to be met with derision, contempt, the creeps. The experts are out there, minting young patients faster than anyone could possibly cure them. They watch a rising tide of adolescent suffering and present themselves as its solution. Most of them ought to be fired on the spot.

Remove the spoons: the technology, the hovering, the monitoring, the constant doubt. The diagnosing of ordinary behaviors as pathological. The psychiatric medications you aren't convinced your child needs. The expert evaluations. Banish from their lives everyone with the tendency to treat your children as disordered.

You don't need them. You never needed them. And your kids are almost certainly better off without them.

Having kids is the best, most worthy thing you could possibly do. Raise them well. You're the only one who can.

Acknowledgments

Viewed from a certain perspective, ordinary life is filled with trauma. But it isn't, really. It's full of miracles.

Keith Urbahn took me on as a client when so many literary agents were afraid to go near me. I will always do my best to ensure that he and the whole Javelin team have the last laugh.

Bria Sandford of Sentinel believed in this book from the very beginning. Her editorial insight improved this work immeasurably. Her kindness and friendship were a bonus. Adrian Zackheim and the entire Sentinel and Penguin Random House crew never wavered in their support. Pablo Delcan swept in at the eleventh hour with a brilliant design for this cover.

Dorit Waldman is razor-sharp, full of insight and good humor. I could not have written this research-heavy book without her.

Jonathan Rosen is a brilliant reader. He pushed me to deepen and refine these ideas.

Bari Weiss and Nellie Bowles were with me start to finish, full of encouragement, wisdom, and love.

Noah Pollak helped at every opportunity, and placed Parents Defending Education's arsenal of documents at my disposal. With regard to school surveys, Rhyen Staley helped generously and mightily.

Jesse and Yael Sage housed me on a research trip. The incomparable Sally Satel offered insights and introduced me to so many of her wonderful colleagues. Mark Gerson, Lisa Logan, Stephanie Winn, Marco Del Guidice, Lenore Skenazy, Sophie Melamed, and Maud Maron shook the trees. Moshe Lifschitz led me through the alien landscape of mental-health apps. Paul McHugh, Leonard Sax, Larry Diller, Rita Eichenstein, Stella O'Malley, Jennie Bristow, Robert Pondiscio, James Lindsay, and Max Eden offered wisdom. R. Christopher Barden, Candace Jackson, and Mark Pendergrast improved my understanding of technical issues in psychology and law. Brian Anderson provided constant encouragement. Joshua Coleman gave me the idea for the title of this book.

My mother, father, mother-in-law, and father-in-law are unflagging in their generosity and generous in their love. I am grateful, daily, for each of them.

When our three kids head off to sleepaway camp each summer, the house aches with silence, and I remember how much joy tromps around with them, announcing itself at a holler. All three strenuously objected to my writing this book. Still, R gave me insight into his generation and top-notch hugs. J, stories and opinions and the gift of his smile. D provided snuggles and the finest research assistance ever offered by a ten-year-old.

In an important sense, my life began the day I met Zach. He read every draft and improved every idea in this book, steered me right and made me laugh. Our life so often feels like the overpacked house of the Yiddish folktale. And it comes bearing the same lesson: the overfullness is the good, and the good is the point.

Notes

Introduction: We Just Wanted Happy Kids

1. "Suicide Risk Screening Tool," National Institute of Mental Health Toolkit, accessed August 6, 2023, https://www.nimh.nih.gov/sites/default/files/documents/research/research-conducted-at-nimh/asq-toolkit-materials/asq-tool/screening_tool_asq_nimh_toolkit.pdf.
2. "Script for Nursing Staff," National Institute of Mental Health Toolkit: Youth Outpatient, accessed August 6, 2023, https://www.nimh.nih.gov/sites/default/files/documents/research/research-conducted-at-nimh/asq-toolkit-materials/youth-outpatient/nurse_script_outpatient_youth_asq_nimh_toolkit.pdf.
3. According to the American Psychological Association, 26 percent of Gen Xers received therapy or other mental health treatments in 2018 alone. "Stress in America™: Generation Z," American Psychological Association, October 2018, https://www.apa.org/news/press/releases/stress/2018/stress-gen-z.pdf.
4. See, for example, Gibson, Lindsay C., *Adult Children of Emotionally Immature Parents: How to Heal from Distant, Rejecting, or Self-Involved Parents* (New Harbinger: Oakland, 2015).
5. "[O]nly 55% of Gen Z and millennials plan to have children. One in four of those surveyed, aged between 18 and 34, has ruled out parenthood entirely, with the most common reason cited being 'wanting time for themselves.'" India, Freya, "Why Doesn't Gen Z Want Children," *UnHerd*, July 29, 2023, https://unherd.com/thepost/why-doesnt-gen-z-want-children.

6. In the years since Jonathan Haidt and Greg Lukianoff first observed the apparent oversensitivity of this generation in their landmark text, *The Coddling of the American Mind*, it has become clear that the psychological state of young people is even worse than they described. The rising generation's problems exceed "safetyism," the idea that emotional and physical safety had supplanted every other value, leading to a vast expansion in young people's understanding of harm. Young people today are intellectually and emotionally unprepared to engage with ideas with which they disagree. In greater numbers than ever recorded, young people writhe in psychic pain and are hitting all the markers of adulthood far later than previous generations.

7. See Horovitz, Bruce, "Companies Embrace Older Workers as Younger Employees Quit or Become Less Reliable," *Time*, December 20, 2021, https://time.com /6129715/age-inclusive-workplaces; Giddings, Andy, "Companies Refuse to Hire 'Unreliable' Young Workers," BBC News, July 3, 2023, https://www.bbc.com /news/uk-england-shropshire-66066246.

8. Moms told me this in interviews. See also Prince, Kate, "Study Reveals Teens Are Too Scared to Drive," Moms.com, December 13, 2018, https://www.moms.com /teens-scared-to-drive/.

9. "The Ask Suicide-Screening Questions (ASQ) toolkit is designed to screen medical patients ages 8 years and above for the risk of suicide." National Institute of Mental Health, accessed September 12, 2023, https://www.nimh.nih.gov/research/re search-conducted-at-nimh/asq-toolkit-materials.

Chapter 1: Iatrogenesis

1. Anything that happens between a child and therapist counts as therapy, in other words; see the American Academy of Child & Adolescent Psychiatry website, www .aacap.org/AACAP/Families_and_Youth/Facts_for_Families/FFF-Guide /Psychotherapies-For-Children-And-Adolescents-086.aspx. The full definition is: "Psychotherapy is a form of psychiatric treatment that involves therapeutic conversations and interactions between a therapist and a child or family. It can help children and families understand and resolve problems, modify behavior, and make positive changes in their lives. There are several types of psychotherapy that involve different approaches, techniques, and interventions. At times, a combination of different psychotherapy approaches may be helpful. In some cases, a combination of medication with psychotherapy may be more effective."

2. The American Psychological Association's definition, in full: "*psychotherapy* n. any psychological service provided by a trained professional that primarily uses forms of communication and interaction to assess, diagnose, and treat dysfunctional emotional reactions, ways of thinking, and behavior patterns. Psychotherapy may be provided to individuals, couples (see couples therapy), families (see family

therapy), or members of a group (see group therapy). There are many types of psychotherapy, but generally they fall into four major categories: psychodynamic psychotherapy, cognitive therapy or behavior therapy, humanistic therapy, and integrative psychotherapy. The psychotherapist is an individual who has been professionally trained and licensed (in the United States by a state board) to treat mental, emotional, and behavioral disorders by psychological means. He or she may be a clinical psychologist, psychiatrist, counselor, social worker, or psychiatric nurse. Also called therapy; talk therapy—psychotherapeutic adj." *APA Dictionary of Psychology*, accessed July 28, 2023, https://dictionary.apa.org/psychotherapy.

In case your head wasn't already spinning, the APA defines a therapist as "an individual who has been trained in and practices one or more types of therapy to treat mental or physical disorders or diseases."

3. The incidence of preventable medical error in hospitals is stunning and has been estimated as causing four hundred thousand injuries per year. See James, John T., "A New, Evidence-Based Estimate of Patient Harms Associated with Hospital Care," *Journal of Personal Safety* (September 2013), https://pubmed.ncbi.nlm.nih .gov/23860193.

4. Perlow, David L., "Surgeons Sometimes Operate on the Wrong Body Part. There's an Easy Fix," *Washington Post*, November 19, 2021, www.washingtonpost.com/out look/surgeons-sometimes-operate-on-the-wrong-body-part-theres-an-easy-fix /2021/11/19/c690ef94-4889-11ec-95dc-5f2a96e00fa3_story.html; see also Page, Leigh, "Doctors Doing Wrong-Site Surgery: Why Is It Still Happening," WebMD, September 30, 2021, https://www.the-hospitalist.org/hospitalist/article/246847 /mixed-topics/mds-doing-wrong-site-surgery-why-it-still-happening.

5. McHugh, Paul R., and Glenn Treisman, "PTSD: A Problematic Diagnostic Category," *Journal of Anxiety Disorders* 21, no. 2 (2006): 211–22, doi: 10.1016/j.janxdis.2006.09.003.

6. Rose, Suzanna, "Psychological Debriefing for Preventing Post-Traumatic Stress Disorder (PTSD)," *Cochrane Database of Systematic Reviews* (April 2002), www .ncbi.nlm.nih.gov/pmc/articles/PMC7032695.

7. Lilienfeld, Scott O., "Psychological Treatments That Cause Harm," *Perspectives on Psychological Science* (March 2007): 59, https://doi.org/10.1111/j.1745 -6916.2007.00029.x; Rona, Roberto J., et al., "Post-Deployment Screening for Mental Disorders and Tailored Advice about Help-Seeking in the UK Military: a Cluster Randomized Control Trial," *Lancet* 389 (April 8, 2017):1410–423, https:// doi.org/10.1016/S0140-6736(16)32398-4. See also Jonsson, Ulf, et al., "Reporting of Harms in Randomized Controlled Trials of Psychological Interventions for Mental and Behavioral Disorders," *Contemporary Clinical Trials* 38, no. 1 (2014): 1–8, https://doi.org/10.1016/j.cct.2014.02.005; McHugh and Triesman, "PTSD: A Problematic Diagnostic Category."

8. See, for example, Lilienfeld, "Psychological Treatments That Cause Harm"; Jonsson, "Reporting of Harms in Randomized Controlled Trials"; Bonnell, C., and Jamal Melendez-Torris, "'Dark Logic': Theorizing the Harmful Consequences of Public Health Interventions," *Journal of Epidemiology and Community Health* 69, no. 1 (January 2015): 95–98, https://pubmed.ncbi.nlm.nih.gov/25403381.

9. Schermuly-Haupt, Marie-Luise, et al., "Unwanted Events and Side Effects in Cognitive Behavior Therapy," *Cognitive Therapy and Research* 42, no. 3 (2018): 219–29, https://doi.org/10.1007/s10608-018-9904-y.

10. Boisvert, Charles M., and David Faust, "Iatrogenic Symptoms in Psychotherapy: A Theoretical Exploration of the Potential Impact of Labels, Language and Belief Systems," *American Journal of Psychotherapy* 56 (November 2002): 248, https://doi.org/10.1176/appi.psychotherapy.2002.56.2.244.

11. Schermuly-Haupt et al., "Unwanted Events and Side Effects in Cognitive Behavior Therapy."

12. See, for example, Boisvert and Faust, "Iatrogenic Symptoms in Psychotherapy."

13. Carlier, Ingrid V. E., et al., "Disaster-Related Post-Traumatic Stress in Police Officers: A Field Study of the Impact of Debriefing," *Stress Medicine* 14, no. 3 (1998): 143–48, https://doi.org/10.1002/(SICI)1099-1700(199807)14:3<143::AID-SMI770>3.0.CO;2-S.

14. Berk, Michael, et al., "The Elephant on the Couch: Side-Effects of Psychotherapy," *Australian and New Zealand Journal of Psychiatry* (January 2009): 789, https://doi.org/10.1080/00048670903107559.

15. Helgeson, Vicki S., et al., "Education and Peer Discussion Group Interventions and Adjustment to Breast Cancer," *Archives of General Psychiatry* 56, no. 4 (1999): 340–47, https://jamanetwork.com/journals/jamapsychiatry/article-abstract/1152701.

16. Brody, Jane E., "Often, Time Beats Therapy for Treating Grief," *New York Times*, January 27, 2004. See also Neimeyer, R.A., "Searching for the Meaning of Meaning: Grief Therapy and the Process of Reconstruction," *Death Studies* 24, no. 6 (September 2000): 541–58, https://doi.org/10.1080/07481180050121480.

17. Bonanno, George A, *The Other Side of Sadness: What the New Science of Bereavement Tells Us About Life After Loss* (New York: Basic Books, 2009). See also Pinker, Susan, "Exercise Can Be the Best Antidepressant," *Wall Street Journal*, March 23, 2023, www.wsj.com/articles/exercise-can-be-the-best-antidepressant-5101a538?mod=e2tw. ("New research finds that as little as 12 weeks of regular exercise can alleviate symptoms of depression as effectively as medication.")

18. Boardman, Samantha, "The One Question Therapists Don't Often Ask but Should," *The Dose*, October 10, 2022, https://drsamanthaboardman.bulletin.com/the-one-question-therapists-don-t-often-ask-but-should.

19. Lillienfeld, "Psychological Treatments that Cause Harm"; see also McNally, R. J., et al., "Does Early Psychological Intervention Promote Recovery from Posttraumatic

Stress?," *Psychological Science in the Public Interest* 4, no. 2 (November 2003): 45–79, https://doi.org/10.1111/1529-1006.01421.

20. See, for example, Leichsenring, Falk, et al., "The Efficacy of Psychotherapies and Pharmacotherapies for Mental Disorders in Adults: An Umbrella Review and Meta-Analytic Evaluation of Recent Meta-Analyses," *World Psychiatry* 21, no. 1 (February 2022): 133–45, https://doi.org/10.1002/wps.20941.

21. Paulson, Steven K., "Campaign Against DARE Program Launched: Drug Education: Opponents Say Psychological Technique—Letting Children Make Choices—Is Harmful," *Los Angeles Times*, June 14, 1992, www.latimes.com/archives/la-xpm-1992-06-14-me-647-story.html. According to the D.A.R.E. manual, D.A.R.E. worked with teens "to raise their self-esteem, to teach them how to make decisions on their own, and to help them identify positive alternatives to tobacco, alcohol, and drug use."

22. Paulson, "Campaign Against DARE Program Launched."

23. Werch, C.E., and D. Owen, "Iatrogenic Effects of Alcohol and Drug Prevention Programs," *Journal of Studies on Alcohol* 63, no. 5 (September 2002): 581–90, https://doi.org/10.15288/jsa.2002.63.581. See also, for example, Lynam, D. R., et al., "Project DARE: No Effects at 10-Year Follow-Up," *Journal of Consulting and Clinical Psychology* 67, no. 4 (August 1999): 590–93, https://doi.org/10.1037//0022-006x.67.4.590.

24. Lopez, German, "Why Anti-Drug Campaigns Like DARE Fail," *Vox*, September 1, 2014, www.vox.com/platform/amp/2014/9/1/5998571/why-anti-drug-campaigns-like-dare-fail; Ormel, Johan, et al., "More Treatment but No Less Depression: The Treatment-Prevalence Paradox," *Clinical Psychology Review* 91 (February 2022): 102111, https://pubmed.ncbi.nlm.nih.gov/34959153/; International Communication Association. "Parents Talking about Their Own Drug Use to Children Could Be Detrimental," *Science Daily*, February 22 2013, www.sciencedaily.com/releases/2013/02/130222083127.htm; see also Werch and Owen, "Iatrogenic Effects of Alcohol and Drug Prevention Programs."

25. See, for example, Leichsenring et al., "The Efficacy of Psychotherapies and Pharmacotherapies for Mental Disorders in Adults"; Ormel et al., "More Treatment but No Less Depression"; Berk et al., "The Elephant on the Couch."

26. See Dawes, Robyn, *House of Cards: Psychology and Psychotherapy Built on a Myth* (New York: Simon & Schuster, 1994), 42.

27. Watters, Ethan, "The Forgotten Lessons of the Recovered Memory Movement," *New York Times*, September 27, 2022, https://www.nytimes.com/2022/09/27/opinion/recovered-memory-therapy-mental-health.html.

28. Watters, "The Forgotten Lessons of the Recovered Memory Movement."

29. Rayner, Gordon, "Minister Orders Inquiry into 4,000 Per Cent Rise in Children Wanting to Change Sex," *The Telegraph* September 16, 2018, www.telegraph.co.uk

/politics/2018/09/16/minister-orders-inquiry-4000-per-cent-rise-children
-wanting. See also Shrier, Abigail, *Irreversible Damage: The Transgender Seducing Our Daughters* (Washington, DC: Regnery, 2020).

30. See, for example, Szego, Julie, "'Absolutely Devastating': Woman Sues Psychiatrist Over Gender Transition," *The Age*, August 24, 2022, www.theage.com.au/national/absolutely-devastating-woman-sues-psychiatrist-over-gender-transition-20220823-p5bbyr.html; Sanchez, Darlene McCormick, "21-Year Old Sues Doctors and Clinics for more than $1 Million Over Transgender Procedures," *Epoch Times*, July 27, 2023, www.theepochtimes.com/us/21-year-old-sues-doctors-and-clinics-for-more-than-1-million-over-transgender-procedures-5422986.

31. "Understanding Psychotherapy and How It Works," American Psychological Association, updated March 16, 2022, https://www.apa.org/topics/psychotherapy/understanding.

32. "8.8 Required Reporting of Adverse Events," AMA Code of Medical Ethics, https://code-medical-ethics.ama-assn.org/sites/default/files/2022-09/8.8%20Required%20reporting%20of%20adverse%20events%20--%20background%20reports.pdf.

33. Lilienfeld, "Psychological Treatments That Cause Harm." ("Psychology has no formal equivalent of medicine's Food and Drug Administration (FDA) to conduct Phase I or Phase II trials, both of which help to identify safety problems with novel treatments before they are disseminated to the public.")

34. Parker et al., "The Elephant on the Couch." (Citing Nutt, D.J., and Sharpe M. "Uncritical Positive Regard? Issues in the Efficacy and Safety of Psychotherapy," *Journal of Psychopharmacology* 22, no. 1 (2008): 3–6, and noting the "assumption . . . that as psychotherapy is only talking . . . no possible harm could ensue.")

35. Linden, Michael, and Marie-Luise Schermuly-Haupt, "Definition, Assessment, and Rate of Psychotherapy Side Effects," *World Psychiatry*, October 13, 2014, 306, www.ncbi.nlm.nih.gov/pmc/articles/PMC4219072.

36. See, for example, Harris, Gardiner, "Talk Doesn't Pay, So Psychiatry Turns Instead to Drug Therapy," *New York Times*, March 5, 2011, https://www.nytimes.com/2011/03/06/health/policy/06doctors.html.

37. See Jonsson et al., "Reporting of Harms in Randomized Controlled Trials."

38. Linden and Schermuly-Haupt, "Definition, Assessment, and Rate of Psychotherapy Side Effects." See also Jonsson et al., "Reporting of Harms in Randomized Controlled Trials."

Chapter 2: A Crisis in the Era of Therapy

1. All names of children and adolescents and those of their parents have been changed to protect their privacy. Names of teachers, counselors, and Beth, the psych nurse, have all been changed by request, and identified only with a pseudonymous first name so that they could speak freely without fear of repercussion at their places of employment. Those teachers and school mental health staff who were willing to go on the record are identified with a real first and last name.

2. Bethune, Sophie, "Gen Z More Likely to Report Mental Health Concerns," *Monitor on Psychology* 50, no. 1 (January 2019): 20, www.apa.org/monitor/2019/01/gen -z#:~:text=They%20are%20also%20more%20likely,15%20percent%20of% 20older%20adults.

3. Bethune, "Gen Z More Likely to Report Mental Health Concerns."

4. Fearnow, Benjamin, "42% of Gen Z Diagnosed with a Mental Health Condition, Survey Reveals," *StudyFinds*, November 7, 2022, https://studyfinds.org/gen-z -mental-health-condition; "New HHS Study in JAMA Pediatrics Shows Significant Increases in Children Diagnosed with Mental Health Conditions from 2016 to 2020," US Department of Health and Human Services, March 14, 2022, www.hhs .gov/about/news/2022/03/14/new-hhs-study-jama-pediatrics-shows-significant -increases-children-diagnosed-mental-health-conditions-2016-2020.html.

5. "Data and Statistics on Children's Mental Health," Centers for Disease Control and Prevention, March 8, 2023, www.cdc.gov/childrensmentalhealth/data.html.

6. Gussone, Felix, "10 Percent of Kids Have ADHD Now," NBC News, August 31, 2018, www.nbcnews.com/health/health-news/10-percent-kids-have-adhd-now-n90 5576.

7. American Psychiatric Association, *The Diagnostic and Statistical Manual of Mental Disorders*, 5th ed. (American Psychiatric Association: Arlington, VA, and Washington, DC, 2013), 61. ("Population surveys suggest that ADHD occurs in most cultures in about 5% of children and about 2.5% of adults.")

8. Osorio, Aubrianna, "Research Update: Children's Anxiety and Depression on the Rise," Georgetown University Health Policy Institute Center for Children and Families, March 24, 2022, https://ccf.georgetown.edu/2022/03/24/research-update -childrens-anxiety-and-depression-on-the-rise/#:~:text=By%202020%2C% 205.6%20million%20kids,had%20been%20diagnosed%20with%20depression.

9. Georgetown University, "Surge in Students Seeking Accommodations for Mental Health Disorders," *The Feed*, May 13, 2022, https://feed.georgetown.edu/access -affordability/surge-in-students-seeking-accommodations-for-mental-health -disorders.

10. Meister, Alyson, and Maude Lavanchy, "Athletes Are Shifting the Narrative around Mental Health at Work," *Harvard Business Review*, September 24, 2021, https://hbr .org/2021/09/athletes-are-shifting-the-narrative-around-mental-health-at-work.

11. Albertson-Grove, Josie, "Youth More Open about Mental Health, but Barriers Remain," *New Hampshire Union Leader*, June 18, 2022, www.unionleader.com/news /health/youth-more-open-about-mental-health-but-barriers-remain/article _1dbc955e-8c5c-574b-9755-a8a117599cba.html.

12. See Furedi, Frank, *Paranoid Parenting: Why Ignoring the Experts May Be Best for Your Child* (Chicago: Chicago Review Press, 2002), 62, 87–89.

13. Grose, Jessica, "Honey, I Shrunk the Kids," *Slate*, August 25, 2010, https://slate .com/human-interest/2010/08/are-the-offspring-of-therapists-really-more -screwed-up-than-the-children-of-non-shrinks.html. ("Childhood misbehavior is much more likely to be described in terms of therapeutic symptoms than character flaws [i.e., sensory integration, processing]. The average parent in the park can probably recite from the *DSM* [the *Diagnostic and Statistical Manual of Mental Disorders*], or at least act as an amateur child therapist.")

14. Fletcher, Jenna, "What Is Relocation Depression?," *Medical News Today*, June 1, 2023, www.medicalnewstoday.com/articles/relocation-depression.

15. Gillespie, Claire, "How to Cope with Summer Anxiety in 2022," Very Well Mind, June 27, 2022, www.verywellmind.com/how-to-cope-with-summer-anxiety -5443019.

16. Tanner, Jeremy, "AAP Issues New Guidance For Head Lice in Schools," *The Hill*, September 29, 2022, https://thehill.com/homenews/nexstar_media_wire/ 3667343 -aap-issues-new-guidance-for-head-lice-in-schools.

17. Kohli, Sahaj Kaur (@Sahajkohli), "In my recent @washingtonpost.com, a reader asks me how to handle when long-term friends & colleagues mispronounce their name. Maybe I shouldn't be surprised by the comments, but folks really don't understand how harmful this can be to a person's psyche . . . And like all microaggressions, this can take a toll on your self-esteem, making you feel devalued or unworthy or like you need to compromise parts of yourself," Twitter, September 29, 2022, https://twitter.com/sahajkohli/status/1575604715475173376.

18. Saul, Stephanie. "At N.Y.U., Students Were Failing Organic Chemistry. Who Was to Blame?," *New York Times*, October 3, 2022, www.nytimes.com/2022/10/03/us /nyu-organic-chemistry-petition.html#:~:text=But%20last%20spring%2C %20as%20the,The%20professor%20defended%20his%20standards.

19. Eva Moskowitz chronicles this in her wonderful book *In Therapy We Trust: America's Obsession with Self-Fulfillment* (Baltimore: Johns Hopkins University Press, 2001).

20. In 1946, Congress passed the National Mental Health Act.

21. Moskowitz, *In Therapy We Trust*, 151. Bored 1950s housewives required treatment for their "inferiority complexes," depression, and loneliness. Restless 1960s hippies sought "alternative consciousness," and the 1970s ushered in an era of "self-actualization." The more disposable income padding the pockets of newly prosperous Americans, the more their need for psychological treatment seemed to grow.

22. In 1946, Congress passed the National Mental Health Act. Between 1946 and 1960, membership in the American Psychological Association ballooned from 4,173 to 18,215. Moskowitz, *In Therapy We Trust*, 154.

23. Furedi, Frank, *Therapy Culture: Cultivating Vulnerability in an Uncertain Age* (New York: Routledge, 2004), 10.

24. Statista Research Department, "Total U.S. Expenditure for Mental Health Services 1986–2020," 2023, Statista, www.statista.com/statistics/252393/total-us-expenditure-for-mental-health-services.

25. Ormel, Johan, et al., "More Treatment but No Less Depression: The Treatment-Prevalence Paradox," *Clinical Psychology Review* 91 (February 2022) 102111, https://pubmed.ncbi.nlm.nih.gov/34959153.

26. Ormel et al., "More Treatment but No Less Depression."

27. See, for example, Ormel, Johan, and Michael VonKorff, "Reducing Common Mental Disorder Prevalence in Populations," *JAMA Psychiatry* 78 no. 4 (April 2021): 359–60, https://pubmed.ncbi.nlm.nih.gov/33112374.

28. It's important to note that the authors looked at *point prevalence*, not *lifetime prevalence*. Point prevalence is the signal rate in this context. After all, if someone had had a depressive episode twenty years earlier, that would count in "lifetime prevalence" but not provide an accurate marker of whether the last twenty years of psychiatric gains had made a dent in rates of depression.

29. A decade earlier, the award-winning science writer Robert Whitaker noted the same conundrum. See Whitaker, Robert, *Anatomy of an Epidemic: Magic Bullets, Psychiatric Drugs, and the Astonishing Rise of Mental Illness in America* (New York: Crown, 2010), 5. ("We should expect that the number of disabled mentally ill in the United States, on a per-capita basis, would have declined over the past fifty years," he wrote, considering the great advance in treatment of psychiatric disorders. "We should also expect the number of disabled mentally ill, on a per-capita basis, would have declined since the arrival in 1988 of Prozac and other second-generation psychiatric drugs. We should see a two-step drop in disability rates.")

    That promise never arrived. Not by a longshot: "Instead, as the psychopharmacology revolution has unfolded, the number of disabled mentally ill in the United States has *skyrocketed*.... Most disturbing of all, this modern-day plague has now spread to the nation's children."

30. "Between 1950 and 1988, the proportion of adolescents aged between fifteen and nineteen who killed themselves quadrupled," *The New Yorker* reported. Andrew Solomon, "The Mystifying Rise of Child Suicide," *The New Yorker*, April 4, 2022, www.newyorker.com/magazine/2022/04/11/the-mystifying-rise-of-child-suicide.

31. Whitaker, *Anatomy of an Epidemic*, 8.

32. Whitaker, *Anatomy of an Epidemic*, 8.

33. Vermeulen, Karla, *Generation Disaster: Coming of Age Post-9/11* (Oxford, UK: Oxford University Press, 2021), 4–5.

34. In *Generation Disaster,* Vermeulen swabs every corner of recent political history and finds eight pathogens she considers historically unique. Besides climate change (the biggie), these include: school shootings; economic recession; Donald J. Trump's presidency; social media's distortion of news events (though, interestingly, not social media itself).

  Economic recessions, panics, and crashes are so commonplace in history, and periodically of such dire severity, one almost wants to buy Vermeulen a *Wall Street Journal* subscription and a copy of *The Grapes of Wrath* to allow her to make some face-saving edits to her book's second printing. Since just the end of the Great Depression, we've had thirteen recessions in the United States.

  School shootings began in the 1990s, as Twenge pointed out to me. Though there have many more in recent years, I have talked to enough young people and those who treat them to note that not one mentioned school shootings as a primary source of kids' ongoing psychic pain. (If anything, school shootings seem to weigh most heavily on adults who dreamt up the Rube-Goldberg-meets-Terminator solutions in the form of "lockdown drills," the practice whereby schoolchildren are instructed to hide under desks while they wait to see if an imaginary intruder will murder them.) Those of us who grew up during the kidnapping hysteria and satanic ritual sex-abuse scandals of the 1980s may struggle to accept that strains of scary news will, on their own, wreck kids' mental health.

  As for Donald J. Trump having caused the adolescent mental health crisis, given that the recent spike began in the Obama era and now soars to new heights in the post-Trump years, I think we should place a low credence on that one.

35. Those who might be inclined to think that digital connection offers its own psychic benefit may simply not know the literature: loneliness can't be fooled by the simulacrum of the digital world. Time spent even with people you'd rather not be stuck with—yes, even time spent with Mom and Dad—does more to banish loneliness in teens than does virtual communication with friends. Zoom "talks" with friends—where you see their faces!—may even make loneliness worse.

36. Ortiz, Camilo, and Stephanie De Leo, "Children Are Lonelier Than Ever. Can Anything Be Done?," *Quillette*, August 16, 2021. The article discusses Twenge's research and notes, "For every increase of one standard deviation of smartphone access, loneliness increased by about .3 standard deviations. The effect for internet use was even bigger at .4 standard deviations.") www.npr.org/2017/12/17/571443683/the-call-in-teens-and-depression, reporting on a paper by Jean M. Twenge. See also Haidt, Jonathan, "The Dangerous Experiment on Teen Girls," *The Atlantic*, November 21, 2021, www.theatlantic.com/ideas/archive/2021/11/facebooks-dangerous-experiment-teen-girls/620767; Twenge, Jean M., et al., "Worldwide Increases in Adolescent Loneliness," *Journal of Adolescence* 93 (2021):

257–69, https://doi.org/10.1016/j.adolescence.2021.06.00. In an interview, Twenge said: "These trends were actually misaligned with economic factors, because they began around 2012, and that's when the U.S. economy started to improve. If you look at a time period, 2012 to 2019 were these big increases in depression and self-harm and suicide. Unemployment was going down. The stock market was going up. Things were getting better economically. So it's exactly misaligned with the time when teen depression is going up. You'd expect depression to go up when unemployment was going up, and [unemployment] goes exactly the opposite direction. It seems clear that it's not economic factors."

She rattles off all the alternative explanations she considered and discarded. "People have often asked, what about income inequality? Yes, although the biggest increases in income inequality were between 1980 and 2000, not 2012 to 2019. It's hard to think of an event that happened around 2012 and then kept going in the same direction until 2019. School shootings don't fit; that was the 1990s when those started." See Twenge, *iGen: Why Today's Super-Connected Kids Are Growing Up Less Rebellious, More Tolerant, Less Happy—and Completely Unprepared for Adulthood* (New York: Atria Books, 2018), 77–78.

37. In my last book, based on the mental health outcomes of teen girls, I begged parents not to get their teens a smartphone. Shrier, *Irreversible Damage*, 212.

38. Haidt, Jonathan, and Jean M. Twenge, "This Is Our Chance to Pull Teenagers Out of the Smartphone Trap," *New York Times*, July 31, 2021, www.nytimes.com/2021/07/31/opinion/smartphone-iphone-social-media-isolation.html.

39. Curtin, Melanie, "Bill Gates Says This Is the 'Safest' Age to Give a Child a Smartphone," *Inc*, May 10, 2017, www.inc.com/melanie-curtin/bill-gates-says-this-is-the-safest-age-to-give-a-child-a-smartphone.htm.

40. See, for example, Marshall, JoJo, "When Should You Come Between a Teenager and Their Phone? The Pros and Cons of Every Parent's Nuclear Option," *Child Mind Institute,* February 10, 2023, https://childmind.org/article/when-should-you-come-between-a-teenager-and-her-phone. See also Dennis-Tiwary, Tracy, "Taking Away the Phones Won't Solve Our Teenagers' Problems," *New York Times*, July 14, 2018, www.nytimes.com/2018/07/14/opinion/sunday/smartphone-addiction-teenagers-stress.html.

41. Kreski, Noah, et al., "Social Media Use and Depressive Symptoms Among United States Adolescents," *Journal of Adolescent Health* 68, no. 3 (March 2021): 572–79, https://doi.org/10.1016/j.jadohealth.2020.07.006. (The authors conclude: "Among US adolescents, daily social media use is not a strong or consistent risk factor for depressive symptoms.")

42. Systematic reviews of smartphone use on mental health decline of adolescents have produced mixed results, some indicating that the effect on well-being is, on average, "negative but very small." Orben, Amy, "Teenagers, Screens and Social Media: A Narrative Review of Reviews and Key Studies," *Social Psychiatry and Psychiatric*

Epidemiology 55, no. 4 (April 2020): 407–14, https://doi.org/10.1007/s00127-019-01 825-4. See also Odgers, C.L., "Annual Research Review. Adolescent Mental Health in the Digital Age: Facts, Fears, and Future Directions," *Journal of Child Psychology and Psychiatry* 61, no. 3 (March 2020): 336–84, https://doi.org/10.1111/jcpp.13190.

43. Gray, Peter, et al., "Decline in Independent Activity as a Cause of Decline in Children's Mental Well-Being: Summary of the Evidence," *The Journal of Pediatrics* 260 (September 2023): 113352, https://doi.org/10.1016/j.jpeds.2023.02.004.

44. I could find no public opposition or warnings from American Psychiatric Association, American Psychological Association, School Counselors Association, or the National Association for School Psychologists in 2020.

45. "Testimony Submitted June 10, 2020 by Arthur C. Evans, Jr., PhD, Chief Executive Officer and Executive Vice President of the American Psychological Association to the United States House of Representatives Committee on the Judiciary," American Psychological Association Services. June 10, 2020, www.apa.org/news/press /releases/police-oversight-testimony.pdf. It is unclear whether the APA is here indulging in metaphor; how else are we to understand a "racism pandemic"? But note that the APA employs the language of biology, arrogating to itself the credibility of the hard sciences without the evidentiary backing and accountability that typically attend medical claims.

46. Brief for the American Psychological Association as Amicus Curiae, *Students for Fair Admissions v. Harvard*, 600 U.S. (2023), 14–15.

47. "Psychology Stands Ready to Help Society Respond to Climate Change, APA President Says," American Psychological Association, March 1, 2022 www.apa.org /news/press/releases/2022/03/climate-change-response.

48. They did, however, find the time to pen the following op-ed, in which they recommend policymakers utilize the techniques of behavioral psychology to "nudge" the population into getting the COVID-19 vaccine. For example, passing state laws to prevent kids from coming back to school until they'd gotten the jab. Evans, Arthur C., Jr., "For a COVID-19 Vaccine to Succeed, Look to Behavioral Research," The Hill, August 17, 2020, https://thehill.com/opinion/healthcare/512316-for-a-covid -19-vaccine-to-succeed-look-to-behavioral-research.

49. Aslanian, Sasha, and Alisa Roth, "Under Pressure: Inside the College Mental Health Crisis," American Public Media Reports, August 19, 2021, www.apmre ports.org/episode/2021/08/19/under-pressure-the-college-mental-health-crisis. Those who work at universities report that the mental health services have ballooned over the past decade—and still, they cannot keep up with demand. At the University of Richmond, while enrollment has remained steady during the past fifteen years, the number of students seeking counseling services during that time has doubled. One study found that between 2009 and 2014 the number of counseling appointments made by US college students rose *six times greater than the rate of*

growth in institutional enrollment. See Lipson, Sarah Ketchen, et al., "Increased Rates of Mental Health Service Utilization by U.S. College Students: 10-Year Population-Level Trends (2007–2017)," *Psychiatric Services* (Washington, D.C.) 70, no. 1 (January 2019): 60–63, www.ncbi.nlm.nih.gov/pmc/articles/PMC6408297.

50. *Social Dilemma,* directed by Jeff Orlowski, monologue by Jonathan Haidt, Exposure Labs, 2020.

51. The number of children who killed themselves over the previous decade doubled. See chart reported in *The Sun* taken from the CDC, Allen, Felix, "Dying For Likes: Dark Truth of Social Media as US Pre-Teen Girl Suicides Soar 150% and Self-Harm TRIPLES, Netflix's *Social Dilemma* Reveals," *The Sun,* September 17, 2020, www.the-sun.com/news/1487147/social-media-suicides-self-harm-netflix-social-dilemma. In fact, the current crop of young people exhibit higher rates of suicide and depression than any generation since studies began in 1950 and far higher rates of general pessimism than any generation since the data collection began in 1960. Between 2005 and 2017—three years before the lockdowns—rates of major depression increased 52 percent in adolescents (twelve to seventeen), and 63 percent in young adults (eighteen to twenty-five). Portions of this were originally published by the author in the *Wall Street Journal.* Shrier, Abigail, "To Be Young and Pessimistic in America," *Wall Street Journal,* May 14, 2021, https://www.wsj.com/articles/to-be-young-and-pessimistic-in-america-11621019488. See also Solomon, Andrew, "The Mystifying Rise of Child Suicide," *The New Yorker,* April 4, 2020, www.newyorker.com/magazine/2022/04/11/the-mystifying-rise-of-child-suicide. Of course, the lockdowns exacerbated these trends: In 2020, nearly a quarter of eighteen- to twenty-four-year-olds reported they had seriously considered suicide in the previous thirty days, and nearly 40 percent of college students experienced depression. See "Mental Health, Substance Use, and Suicidal Ideation During the COVID-19 Pandemic," Centers for Disease Control and Prevention, August 14, 2020, www.cdc.gov/mmwr/volumes/69/wr/mm6932a1.htm. See also Zhou, Sasha, et al., "The Healthy Minds Study, Fall 2020 Data Report," https://healthymindsnetwork.org/wp-content/uploads/2021/02/HMS-Fall-2020-National-Data-Report.pdf.

52. Foer, Franklin, "Greta Thunberg Is Right to Panic," *The Atlantic,* September 20, 2019, www.theatlantic.com/ideas/archive/2019/09/greta-thunbergs-despair-is-entirely-warranted/598492.

53. See also Lomborg, Bjorn, "Climate Change Hasn't Set the World on Fire," *Wall Street Journal,* July 31, 2023, www.wsj.com/articles/climate-change-hasnt-set-the-world-on-fire-global-warming-burn-record-low-713ad3a6. With regard to wildfires, "in 2022, the last year for which there are complete data, the world hit a new record-low of 2.2% burned area."

54. Foer, "Greta Thunberg Is Right to Panic."

55. Gimbrone, Catherine, et al., "The Politics of Depression: Diverging Trends in Internalizing Symptoms among US Adolescents by Political Beliefs," *SSM-Mental Health* 2 (December 2022), https://www.sciencedirect.com/science/article/pii/S266 6560321000438. Left-leaning Bloomberg columnist Matthew Yglesias opined: "I think older progressive leaders deserve a healthy share of blame for creating institutional cultures that celebrate pessimism as a sign of political commitment while teaching young people to weaponize claims of subjective harm."

56. Ackerman, Courtney, "What Is Unconditional Positive Regard in Psychology?," *PositivePscyhology*, May 22, 2018, https://positivepsychology.com/unconditional -positive-regard.

57. Both of these create potential HIPAA violations, since college kids are no longer "kids" as far as medical privacy law is concerned.

58. See, for example, Finley, Allysia, "Climate Change Obsession Is a Real Mental Disorder," *Wall Street Journal*, July 31, 2023. The article cites a study showing that 45 percent of sixteen- to twenty-five-year-olds in ten countries "claimed they were so worried [about the climate] that they struggled to function on a daily basis, the definition of an anxiety disorder." Even a cursory consideration of the magnitude of these data suggests that wild exaggeration is afoot.

59. *See* Webster, Jamieson, "Teenagers Are Telling Us That Something Is Wrong with America," *New York Times*, October 11, 2022, www.nytimes.com/2022/10/11/opin ion/teenagers-mental-health-america.html.

60. They were clearly made fearful, upset, and anxious by the prospect of nuclear war. Nightmares were common. See Buck, Stephanie, "Fear of Nuclear Annihilation Scarred Children Growing Up in the Cold War, Studies Later Showed," *Medium*, August 29, 2017, https://timeline.com/nuclear-war-child-psychology-d1ff491b5fe0. See also Kiraly, S. J., "Psychological Effects of the Threat of Nuclear War," *Canadian Family Physician* 32 (January 1986): 170–74, www.ncbi.nlm.nih.gov/pmc/arti cles/PMC2327576.

61. See Carey, Adam, "'Generational Rupture': Anxiety and COVID Disruption Supercharge School Refusal Rates," *The Age*, February 2, 2023, www.theage.com.au/na tional/victoria/generational-rupture-anxiety-and-covid-disruption-super charge-school-refusal-rates-20230201-p5ch1u.html.

62. Soh, Debra, "What's Driving Gen Z's Aversion to Sex?," *Newsweek,* October 12, 2021, https://www.newsweek.com/whats-driving-gen-zs-aversion-sex-opinion -1638228.

63. Julian, Kate, "Why Are Young People Having So Little Sex?," *The Atlantic*, December 2018, www.theatlantic.com/magazine/archive/2018/12/the-sex-recession /573949.

64. Lasch, Christopher, *The Culture of Narcissism: American Life in an Age of Diminishing Expectations* (New York: W. W. Norton, 1979), 273.

65. Lasch, *Culture of Narcissism*, 273.

66. Pappas, Stephanie, "The Rise of Psychologists: Psychological Expertise Is in Demand Everywhere," *Monitor on Psychology* 53, no. 1 (January 2022): 44, www.apa.org/monitor/2022/01/special-rise-psychologists.

67. DeAngelis, Tori, "Mental Health, Meet Venture Capital," *Monitor on Psychology* 53, no. 1 (January 2022): 56, www.apa.org/monitor/2022/01/special-venture-capital.

68. Confidential financial deck, on file with author.

Chapter 3: Bad Therapy

1. See, for example, Weiss, Bahr, et al., "A 2-Year Follow Up of the Effectiveness of Traditional Child Psychotherapy," *Journal of Consulting and Clinical Psychology* 68 no. 6 (December 2000): 1094–1101, https://doi.org/10.1037//0022-006x.68.6.1094 (2000); Weersing, V. Robin, "Evidence Base Update of Psychosocial Treatments for Child and Adolescent Depression," *Journal of Clinical Child and Adolescent Psychology* 46, no. 1 (2017): 11–43, https://doi.org/10.1080/15374416.2016.1220310; Evans, Steven W., et al., "Evidence-Based Psychosocial Treatments for Children and Adolescents with Attention Deficit/Hyperactivity Disorder," *Journal of Clinical Child & Adolescent Psychology* 43, no. 4 (2014): 527–51, https://doi.org/10.1080/15374416.2013.850700.

2. I owe the phrase "tyranny of feelings" to behavioral and developmental pediatrician Lawrence Diller.

3. Shi, Rui, et al., "Individual Difference in Goal Motives and Goal Content: The Role of Action and State Orientation," *Journal of Pacific Rim Psychology* 12 (2018): 20, www.cambridge.org/core/services/aop-cambridge-core/content/view/AB5F6366258C5C3348FF4DE46984141F/S1834490918000089a.pdf/div-class-title-individual-difference-in-goal-motives-and-goal-content-the-role-of-action-and-state-orientation-div.pdf.

4. See Pedersen, Helene, et al., "Metacognitions and Brooding Predict Depressive Symptoms in a Community Adolescent Sample," *BMC Psychiatry* 22 (2022): 157, https://doi.org/10.1186/s12888-022-03779-5.

5. This is precisely how CBT approaches depression: by training patients to view their negative thoughts as misleading or false and encourage them to stop ruminating. To that extent, CBT is a kind of anti-therapy therapy: *Don't root endlessly around in your memory, don't constantly take your emotional pulse. Come in if you have a specific problem inhibiting daily life—phobia, obsession, insomnia. In a fixed number of sessions, we'll get you to stop your unhelpful thought patterns, so that you can get on with your life.*

6. We want to witness the best day of our kids' lives so badly, we attempt to manufacture it. This is the source of motivational dancers at bar mitzvah parties. We don't

trust our teens to feel joy on their own: we pay professional ecstatics to convince our kids they are having the time of their lives.

7. Mauss, Iris B., et al., "Can Seeking Happiness Make People Unhappy? Paradoxical Effects of Valuing Happiness," *Emotion* 11, no. 4 (August 2011): 807–15, https://pubmed.ncbi.nlm.nih.gov/21517168. See also Lauren Sharkey, "The Surprising Link between Depression and the Pursuit of Happiness," Medical News Today, January 16, 2020, www.medicalnewstoday.com/articles/327493.

8. Julian, Kate, "Childhood in an Anxious Age and the Crisis of Modern Parenting," *The Atlantic*, May 2020, 32.

9. Julian, "Childhood in an Anxious Age and the Crisis of Modern Parenting."

10. "The NACBT [National Association of Cognitive-Behavioral Therapists] was formed in response to a growing trend of mental health professionals labeling themselves 'Cognitive-Behavioral Therapists' when in fact their actual practice of counseling/psychotherapy did not resemble CBT." National Association of Cognitive-Behavioral Therapists, accessed August 1, 2023, www.nacbt.org. See also Brown, Harriet, "Looking for Evidence That Therapy Works," *New York Times*, March 25, 2013, https://archive.nytimes.com/well.blogs.nytimes.com/2013/03/25/looking-for-evidence-that-therapy-works.

    ("A survey of 200 psychologists published in 2005 found that only 17 percent of them used exposure therapy [a form of C.B.T.] with patients with post-traumatic stress disorder, despite evidence of its effectiveness." The article goes on to note: "CBT refers to a number of structured, directive types of psychotherapy that focus on the thoughts behind a patient's feelings and that often include exposure therapy and other activities. Instead, many patients are subjected to a kind of dim-sum approach—a little of this, a little of that, much of it derived more from the therapist's biases and training than from the latest research findings. And even professionals who claim to use evidence-based treatments rarely do.")

11. Julian, "Childhood in an Anxious Age and the Crisis of Modern Parenting."

12. Ravella, Shilpa, "Rethinking the Origins of Inflammatory Diseases," *Wall Street Journal*, October 8–9, 2022, C17.

13. Cleary, Belinda, "'I Had to Pick Off The Burger Bun's Sesame Seeds': Parents Share the Desperate Lengths They've Gone to in Order for Their Kids to Eat," *Daily Mail*, May 17, 2021, www.dailymail.co.uk/femail/article-9589673/Parents-share-hilarious-lengths-theyve-gone-kids-eat.html.

14. Gray, Peter, "Risky Play: Why Children Love It and Need It," *Psychology Today*, April 7, 2014, www.psychologytoday.com/us/blog/freedom-learn/201404/risky-play-why-children-love-it-and-need-it. See also Caron, Christina, "Risky Play Encourages Resilience," *New York Times*, July 21, 2020, www.nytimes.com/2020/07/21/parenting/risky-play.html.

15. See Rosenhan, David, "On Being Sane in Insane Places," *Science* 179, no. 4070 (January 1973): 250–58, https://doi.org/10.1126/science.179.4070.250.

16. As one team of researchers noted, handing someone a diagnosis "may alter their self-perceptions as they subsequently interpret most or all of their experiences as manifestations of the inherent abnormality of the 'disease process' implicated by the descriptor." Boisvert, Charles M., and David Faust, "Iatrogenic Symptoms in Psychotherapy: A Theoretical Explanation of the Potential Impact of Labels, Language, and Belief Systems," *American Journal of Psychotherapy* 56, no. 2 (2002): 244–59, https://doi.org/10.1176/appi.psychotherapy.2002.56.2.244.

17. *Prozac Nation* was a bestseller before the first Gen Z kid was born.

18. Sulkin, Maya, "America's Love Affair with Adderall," *The Free Press*, June 14, 2023, www.thefp.com/p/america-addicted-to-adderall-shortage.

19. Hetrick, Sarah, et al., "New Generation Antidepressants for Depression in Children and Adolescents: A Network Meta-Analysis," *Cochrane Library*, May 24, 2021, www.cochranelibrary.com/cdsr/doi/10.1002/14651858.CD013674.pub2/full. ("Overall, methodological shortcomings of the randomised trials make it difficult to interpret the findings with regard to the efficacy and safety of newer antidepressant medications.")

20. Hetrick, Sarah, et al., "Best Evidence Suggests Antidepressants Aren't Very Effective in Kids and Teens. What Can Be Done Instead?," *The Conversation*, May 24, 2021, https://theconversation.com/best-evidence-suggests-antidepressants-arent-very-effective-in-kids-and-teens-what-can-be-done-instead-160758. See also Cheung, Amy H., et al., "The Use of Antidepressants to Treat Depression in Children and Adolescents," *Canadian Medical Association Journal* 174, *no. 2* (January 2006): 193–200, www.cmaj.ca/content/174/2/193.full; Garland, Jane E., "Facing the Evidence: Antidepressant Treatment in Children and Adolescents," *Canadian Medical Association Journal* 170, no. 4 (February 2004): 489–91, www.ncbi.nlm.nih.gov/pmc/articles/PMC332716; Ioannidis, John P.A., "Effectiveness of Antidepressants: An Evidence Myth Constructed from a Thousand Randomized Trials?," *Philosophy, Ethics, and Humanities in Medicine* 3 (2008): 14, www.ncbi.nlm.nih.gov/pmc/articles/PMC2412901.

21. Ritalin prescribing information from the Novartis website: www.novartis.com/us-en/sites/novartis_us/files/ritalin_ritalin-sr.pdf.

22. Gabriel, Matthew, "Antidepression Discontinuation Syndrome," *Canadian Medical Association Journal* 189, no. 21 (May 2017): E747 , www.ncbi.nlm.nih.gov/pmc/articles/PMC5449237.

23. Food and Drug Administration, "Suicidality in Children and Adolescents Being Treated with Antidepressant Medications," FDA Archive, February 5, 2018, www.fda.gov/drugs/postmarket-drug-safety-information-patients-and-providers/suicidality-children-and-adolescents-being-treated-antidepressant-medications. You may have heard this familiar tale: *Some patients become suicidal after taking an antidepressant because the drug gave them motivation—motivation they used to complete the suicide.* At least one pediatrician told me this. But it's a just-so story with no

evidential backing. We simply don't know why antidepressants increase risk of suicide in some patients. See Reeves, Roy R., "Antidepressant-Induced Suicidality: An Update," *CNS Neuroscience & Therapeutics* 6, no. 4 (August 2010): 227–34, www.ncbi.nlm.nih.gov/pmc/articles/PMC6493906; Oberlander, Tim F., and Anton Miller, "Antidepressant Use in Children and Adolescents: Practice Touch Points to Guide Pediatricians," *Paediatrics & Child Health* 16, no. 9 (November 2011): 549–53, www.ncbi.nlm.nih.gov/pmc/articles/PMC3223889.

24. See Pillemer, Karl, *Fault Lines: Fractured Families and How to Mend Them* (New York: Avery, 2020). This is at least sixty-seven million Americans estranged. Pillemer believes that this may understate the problem since many are reluctant to acknowledge their family estrangement.

25. Barsky, Arthur, *Worried Sick: Our Troubled Quest for Wellness* (Boston: Little, Brown), 50–51.

Chapter 4: Social-Emotional Meddling

1. Sax, Leonard, "Who First Suggests the Diagnosis of Attention-Deficit/Hyperactivity Disorder." *Annals of Family Medicine* 1, no. 3 (September 2003): 171–74, www.ncbi.nlm.nih.gov/pmc/articles/PMC1466583.

2. The Child Mind Institute, accessed September 16, 2023, https://childmind.org/symptomchecker. ("My relationship to the child is: teacher.")

3. California calls its extensive-model program "Multi-Tiered Systems of Support," or MTSS.

4. I had to look up the YouTube video after the conference. "Brain & Amygdala Hand Model Explains How Thoughts & Emotions Fuel Anxiety," EmpowerU Education Building Resilience, YouTube, video, 1:58, May 16, 2018, www.youtube.com/watch?v=2xeDcPBD5Fk&t=4s.

5. If academic psychologists acknowledge that therapeutic interventions carry risk of iatrogenesis, why aren't they more leery of school-wide psychological interventions? A recent study noted that they should be. "The risk of iatrogenic harm and adverse effects from school-based mental interventions, even in a minority of adolescents, amounts to a potentially vast public health problem," the researchers wrote. Foulkes, Lucy, and Argyris Stringaris, "Do No Harm: Can School Mental Health Interventions Cause Iatrogenic Harm?," *BJPsych Bulletin* (February 2023): 1–3, https://doi.org/10.1192/bjb.2023.9.

6. See, for example, Birk, Max V., et al., "Just a Click Away: Action-State Orientation Moderates the Impact of Task Interruptions on Initiative," *Journal of Personality* 88, no. 2 (April 2020): 373–90, www.ncbi.nlm.nih.gov/pmc/articles/PMC7064891.

7. See, for example, Krohler, Alena, and Stefan Berti, "Taking Action or Thinking About It? State Orientation and Rumination Are Correlated in Athletes," *Frontiers*

in Psychology 10 (March 2019): 576, https://doi.org/10.3389/fpsyg.2019.00576; Gropel, Peter, et al., "Action Versus State Orientation and Self-Control Performance after Depletion," *Personality and Social Psychology Bulletin* 40, no. 4 (April 2014): 476–87, https://doi.org/10.1177/0146167213516636.

8. Modan, Naaz, "California Plans to Double School Counselors amid Shortage," K-12 Dive, August 5, 2022, https://www.k12dive.com/news/california-plans-to-double-school-counselors-amid-shortage/628991.

9. Act to amend Sections 124174, 124174.2, 124174.3, and 124174.4 of the Health and Safety Code, A.B. 912 (Cal. 2023), https://leginfo.legislature.ca.gov/faces/bill NavClient.xhtml?bill_id=202320240AB912.

10. Gottlieb, Lori, *Maybe You Should Talk to Someone: A Therapist, Her Therapist, and Our Lives Revealed* (Boston: Houghton Mifflin Harcourt, 2019), 36.

11. Hermann, Mary A., and Sharon Robinson-Kurpius, "New Guidelines on Dual Relationships," *Counseling Today*, December 9, 2006, https://ct.counseling.org/2006/12/new-guidelines-on-dual-relationships. See also Kaplan, David, "2006 Ethics Update: Allowing Dual Relationships," *Counseling Today*, March 27, 2006, https://ct.counseling.org/2006/03/ct-online-ethics-update-9; Kaplan, David, et al., "New Mandates and Imperatives in the Revised ACA Code of Ethics," *Journal of Counseling and Development* 87 (2009): 241–56, www.counseling.org/Kaplan/man dates.pdf.

12. The American School Counselor Association 2022 *ASCA Ethical Standards for School Counselors* mentions the words "advocate," "advocating," or "advocacy" thirty-seven times: www.schoolcounselor.org/getmedia/44f30280-ffe8-4b41-9ad8-f15909c3d164/EthicalStandards.pdf. "We advocate with and on behalf of students. We collaborate with every possible stakeholder, and sometimes that collaboration has to start with educating some of our stakeholders as well," school counselor and educational consultant Sandi Logan-McKibben told the assembled audience of teachers at the three-day conference.

13. See, for example, "Consent," California School-Based Health Alliance, accessed September 19, 2023, www.schoolhealthcenters.org/resources/sbhc-operations/student -records-consent-and-confidentiality/consent, which states that minors twelve and older are entitled to receive mental health services, including those provided at school, without parents' permission or knowledge; Illinois: "School-Based Health Center Consent for Mental Health Services," SHIF Healthcare, accessed September 19, 2023, https://sihf.org/media-library/documents/Behavioral_Health_Consent _Form_School-Based_.pdf; Washington: "Seattle World School Teen Health Center," Seattle Schools, accessed September 19, 2023, https://sws.seattleschools.org /wp-content/uploads/sites/89/2021/10/ParentConsentLetter-ADA.pdf; Colorado: "Colorado Lowers Age of Consent for Psychotherapy Services to 12 Years Old," *National Law Review*, July 16, 2019 www.natlawreview.com/article/colorado

-lowers-age-consent-psychotherapy-services-to-12-years-old; Florida: "Complete Information Concent Package with Principal Signature," Southeast High School, June 1, 2010, www.manateeschools.net/cms/lib/FL02202357/Centricity/Domain /1268/Complete%20information%20consent%20package%20with%20Princi pal%20signature.pdf (Consent of parent or guardian not required for outpatient mental health services.); Maryland: "Lower Age for Consent Took Effect October 1," Maryland Psychiatric Society, November 1, 2021, https://mdpsych.org/2021 /11/lower-age-for-consent-took-effect-october-1. (Parentental consent not required for minors age twelve or older to access mental health care.)

14. Glosoff, H.L., and Robert H. Pate, "Privacy and Confidentiality in School Counseling," Professional School Counseling (2002): 6, https://www.researchgate.net /publication/234700799_Privacy_and_Confidentiality_in_School_Counseling.

15. See, for example, Monger, Craig, "'Bad Things Happen Behind Closed Doors All the Time Between Kids and Adults'—Concerned Parents Address School Mental Health Counselors," *1819 News*, March 22, 2023, https://1819news.com/news /item/bad-things-happen-behind-closed-doors-all-the-time-between-kids-and -adults-concerned-parents-address-school-mental-health-counselors#:~:text= Section%2022%2D8%2D4%20of,without%20the%20child's%20parents'% 20consent. See also www.antiochschools.net/Page/13767 (stating that parent consent is not needed for school counseling in California). See also Gissen, Lillian, "Furious Washington Father Claims His Son's High School Prescribed The Teen Anti-Depressants Without Telling Him," *Daily Mail*, July 4, 2022, www.dailymail .co.uk/femail/article-10981133/Father-claims-sons-high-school-prescribed-teen -anti-depressants-without-telling-him.html; Carlson, Nancy, "To Tell or Not to Tell: The Fine Line Between Minors' Privacy and Others' Right to Know," *Counseling Today*, October 2017, www.counseling.org/docs/default-source/ethics/ethics -columns/ethics_october-2017_minor-privacy.pdf?sfvrsn=a25522c_6.

16. See, for example, Spiro, Justin (@Jusrangers), "In NY, kids can't receive 'therapy' without parental consent, but they can meet regularly with school social workers. I always push for kids to open up to parents, but why should we put another barrier to counseling for kids who aren't ready to immediately tell their parents." Twitter, March 21, 2023, 1:29 pm, https://twitter.com/jusrangers/status/1638276568 521887747?s=51&t=G7jT0d-EVW3Jp1M5AFCx_w. See also Spiro, Justin (@jus-rangers), "I think this is an important conversation. Let me give you a hypothetical: A high schooler comes to my office saying he's feeling down because of his parents' separation. I assess and there's no suicidality. He doesn't want his parents to know he's speaking to me because he thinks they'll be mad. Do I send him away immediately and leave him unsupported by both me AND his parents? Or do I meet with him a few times and help him figure out how to speak to his parents about his feelings?," Twitter, March 21, 2023, 1:41 p.m., https://twitter.com/Jusrangers/status /1638279628291821570.

17. Name changed to avoid embarrassing a teacher who was just doing precisely what her administrators directed.

18. Kahn, Jennifer, "Can Emotional Intelligence Be Taught?," *New York Times*, September 11, 2013, www.nytimes.com/2013/09/15/magazine/can-emotional-intelligence -be-taught.html.

19. As one school in Illinois put it: "SEL is more than a process, a methodology, a curriculum—it is a way of life." "Social Emotional Learning," Stevenson High School, accessed September 16, 2023, https://www.d125.org/about/sel.

20. $1.72 billion spent in social-emotional learning educational *materials alone.* "United States Social and Emotional Learning (SEL) Market Report 2022: Instructional Materials were $1.72 Billion, up 25.9% Y-o-Y and are Forecast to Increase at a Lower Rate in 2023-2024," GlobeNewswire, November 17, 2022, www.globenewswire.com/news-release/2022/11/17/2557934/0/en/United-States -Social-and-Emotional-Learning-SEL-Market-Report-2022-Instructional -Materials-were-1-72-Billion-up-25-9-Y-o-Y-and-are-Forecast-to-Increase -at-a-Lower-Rate-in-2023-2024.html; Krachman, Sara Bartolino, et al., "Accounting for the Whole Child," ASCD, February 1, 2018, https://www.ascd.org/el/articles/ac counting-for-the-whole-child.

21. Langreo, Lauraine, "How Much Time Should Schools Spend on Social-Emotional Learning?," *Education Week*, May 24, 2022, https://www.edweek.org/leadership /how-much-time-should-schools-spend-on-social-emotional-learning/2022/05.

22. "An important difference between SEL and character education is that some character education approaches are focused on developing morally responsible youth, and that is not the defining characteristic of SEL. It is important to make that distinction. Teaching morals and values can raise concerns about whether they can be changed, and whether instruction is the responsibility of families or schools." Kim Gulbrandson, "Character Education and SEL: What You Should Know," July 6, 2018, Committee for Children, www.cfchildren.org/blog/2018/07/character-edu cation-and-sel-what-you-should-know.

23. "Transformative Social-Emotional Learning (T-SEL)," Sonoma County Office of Education, accessed August 16, 2023, https://www.scoe.org/pub/htdocs/transfor mative-social-emotional-learning.html. ("Transformative SEL is a form of SEL aimed at redistributing power to promote social justice through increased engagement in school and civic life.")

24. Klein, Alyson, "Why It's So Hard to Weave Social-Emotional Learning into Academics," *Education Week*, November 7, 2022, www.edweek.org/leadership/why -its-so-hard-to-weave-social-emotional-learning-into-academics/2022/11.

25. Sadighim, Sherry, "The Big Reveal: Ethical Implications of Therapist Self-Disclosure," Society for the Advancement of Psychotherapy, 2014, https://society forpsychotherapy.org/the-big-reveal-ethical-implications-of-therapist-self -disclosure.

26. Second Step, "Empathy and Communication: Working in Groups," grade 8, lesson 6, "Additional Handout: Building Empathy," Committee for Children, 2008, 251, https://assets.ctfassets.net/wjuty07n9kzp/7v4DVtKWDduiidyzFTwilf/b0ff 74c636e6029ae57fe585f57d00f9/G8_Handout_Packet.pdf.

27. As one school in Illinois put it: "SEL is more than a process, a methodology, a curriculum—it is a way of life." "Social Emotional Learning," Stevenson High School.

28. "Friends and Friendships," PATHS Parent/Caregiver Handout, lesson 19, 2.

29. See Yang, Jing, and Li Ping, "Brain Networks of Explicit and Implicit Learning," *PLoS ONE* 7, no. 8 (August 2012): e42993, https://journals.plos.org/plosone/arti cle?id=10.1371/journal.pone.0042993.

30. See Schuchard, Julia, and Cynthia K. Thompson, "Implicit and Explicit Learning in Individuals with Agrammatic Aphasia," *Journal of Psycholinguist Research* 43, no. 3 (June 2014): 209–24, www.ncbi.nlm.nih.gov/pmc/articles/PMC3766481; Ziegler, Esther, Peter A. Edelsbrunner, and Elsbeth Stern, "The Relative Merits of Explicit and Implicit Learning of Contrasted Algebra Principles," *Educational Psychology Review* (June 2018), https://ethz.ch/content/dam/ethz/special-interest/dual/educeth -dam/documents/forschung-und-literatur/literatur-zur-lehr-und-lernforschung /Ziegler_2017.pdf.

31. Second Step, "Homework: I Spy," grade 7, lesson 1, Committee for Children, 2008, 117, https://assets.ctfassets.net/wjuty07n9kzp/5xHHFYVCVAxE1Ogc9TamlD/0c4 8c7875cba04aed33f21584f29b6f5/G7_Homework.pdf.

32. Second Step, "Homework: Life Experiences Timeline," grade 7, lesson 2, Commit- tee for Children, 2008, 143, https://assets.ctfassets.net/wjuty07n9kzp/5xHHFYV CVAxE1Ogc9TamlD/0c48c7875cba04aed33f21584f29b6f5/G7_Homework .pdf.

33. Second Step, "Recognizing Others' Perspectives," Student Handout, grade 8, unit 4, lesson 22, 2020, 1–2, https://assets.ctfassets.net/wjuty07n9kzp/3ZUNxHZDH cVCcyCMD2uzhS/5091602a8b65fe32faaab388ba51f181/ssms-g8-u4-22 -student-handout-2021.pdf.

34. Second Step, grade 4, unit 3, lesson 11.

35. Second Step, "Homework: Winning the Battle," grade 7, lesson 3, Committee for Children, 2008, 171, https://assets.ctfassets.net/wjuty07n9kzp/5xHHFYVCVAx E1Ogc9TamlD/0c48c7875cba04aed33f21584f29b6f5/G7_Homework.pdf.

36. Second Step, "Homework: The Clothing Case," grade 8, lesson 4, Committee for Children, 2008, 193.

37. Sapp, Jeff, "Why Frogs and Snakes Never Play Together: A Pourquoi of Prejudice: A Play in 3 Acts," Learning for Justice, grade level K-2, www.learningforjustice.org /classroom-resources/texts/why-frogs-and-snakes-never-play-together-a -pourquoi-of-prejudice-a-play.

38. The CASEL Guide to Schoolwide SEL: "A Supportive Classroom Environment:

Belonging and Emotional Safety" section cites: Learning for Justice, *Critical Practices for Anti-Bias Education*, Teaching Tolerance: A Project of the Southern Poverty Law Center, 2016, www.learningforjustice.org/sites/default/files/2017-06/PDA %20Critical%20Practices_0.pdf.

39. See, for example, Second Step, "Overcoming Roadblocks 1," student handout, grade 7, unit 1, lesson 5, Committee for Children, 2020, https://assets.ctfassets.net /98bcvzcrxclo/1fyRvZO01HcZFQiLfulUbf/8e8bf1e4757b050b9fb996d0a9d3f dce/handout-ms-g7-u1-05-sample.pdf.

40. "Unit 1, Lesson 5, Overcoming Roadblocks 1," Griffin Counselors, YouTube, video, 26:44, September 22, 2020, www.youtube.com/watch?v=9MsPz_iFzYE.

Chapter 5: The Schools Are Filled with Shadows

1. See "Related Service Providers & Interveners," National Resource Center for Para-educators, accessed August 9, 2023, https://nrcpara.org/resources/report/demo graphics. "There are more than 525,000 paraeducators currently employed in FTE positions nationwide. Of that number approximately 290,000 are employed in in-clusive general and special education programs, self-contained and resource rooms, transition services and early childhood settings serving children and youth with disabilities. (One critical piece of information that is very difficult to obtain are the number of paraeducators who are assigned to work one-to-one with individual learners.)"

2. "*Shadows* are on the front line of helping students with disabilities," explains the primer, *School Shadow Guidelines*. Liau, Alex, and Dr. Jed Baker, *School Shadow Guidelines* (Arlington, Texas: Future Horizons Inc., 2015) 1.

3. Graziano, P. A., A. M. Garcia, and T. D. Landis, "To Fidget or Not to Fidget, That Is the Question: A Systematic Classroom Evaluation of Fidget Spinners Among Young Children With ADHD," *Journal of Attention Disorders* 24, no. 1 (2020): 163–71, https://journals.sagepub.com/doi/full/10.1177/1087054718770009.

4. Section 504 of the Rehabilitation Act of 1973, which prohibited discrimination against students with learning disabilities, also required schools to make reasonable accommodations for such students, like allowing untimed tests for kids who needed it.

5. Algar, Selim, "Manhattan School Plagued with Violence, Parents Say Concerns Neglected," *New York Post*, February 4, 2022, https://nypost.com/2022/02/04/par ents-feel-neglected-at-middle-school-beset-by-violence.

6. "The restorative practices concept has its roots in restorative justice, a way of look-ing at criminal justice that focuses on repairing the harm done to people and rela-tionships rather than on punishing offenders (although restorative justice does not preclude incarceration of offenders or other sanctions). Originating in the 1970s as mediation between victims and offenders, by the 1990s restorative justice broadened

to include communities of care as well, with victims and offenders' families and friends participating in collaborative processes called 'conferences' and 'circles.'" Costello, Bob, Joshua Wachtel, and Ted Wachtel, *Restorative Circles in Schools: Building Community and Enhancing Learning* (Bethlehem, Pennsylvania: International Institute for Restorative Practices, 2010).

7. "Joint 'Dear Colleague' Letter," Department of Education, Office for Civil Rights, January 8, 2014, https://www2.ed.gov/about/offices/list/ocr/letters/colleague-201 401-title-vi.html.

8. Davenport, Mary, "Using Circle Practice in the Classroom," *Edutopia*, August 16, 2018, www.edutopia.org/article/using-circle-practice-classroom. (Article links to document "Setting Up a Circle: An Overview.")

9. Pollack, Andrew, and Max Eden, *Why Meadow Died* (New York: Post Hill Press, 2019), 96. See also James, Emma, "Hulking 6'6" Boy, 17, Who 'Viciously Beat His Teaching Aide Unconscious' Is Held on $1 MILLION Bond, Will Be Charged as an Adult and Faces up to 30 Years in Prison—after Being Arrested THREE Times for Battery in 2019," *Daily Mail*, February 28, 2023, www.dailymail.co.uk/news/article -11802533/Teen-knocked-teacher-arrested-THREE-times-battery-charged -adult.html. (In February 2023, a hulking high school junior in Florida named Brendan Depa—270 pounds and 6 feet 6 inches tall—launched his assigned paraprofessional ("shadow") into the air when she took away his Nintendo Switch, which he had been playing with during class. The parapro hit the ground headfirst and lost consciousness on impact. But Depa proceeded to stomp and beat her limp body anyway, until five school faculty members could pull him off.

Depa is "behaviorally disabled," and when he was arrested for the incident, mental health advocate Sue Urban said he'd been treated unfairly. Kids with behavioral disability, Urban said, "are given leeway to have these devices, so when they do lose their tempers or if they do not get into that mental space, that they can have those Switches or phones or their comfort devices, [so] that they can calm down." Depa— who'd been arrested three times on battery charges when he was thirteen—was taken into custody.)

10. Augustine, Catherine H., et al., *Can Restorative Practices Improve School Climate and Curb Suspensions? An Evaluation of the Impact of Restorative Practices in a Mid-Sized Urban School District*, (Santa Monica, CA: RAND Corporation, 2018), https://www.rand.org/pubs/research_reports/RR2840.html, 71. ("This, of course, raises the question of whether restorative practices can be effective in curbing the most violent behavior, at least within a two-year implementation period.")

11. Interestingly, the Parkland school shooter had been put through the full gamut of "restorative justice" within the Florida school system before emptying a semiautomatic rifle into its halls, murdering seventeen of the current students.

12. Henderson, Cinque, "Failing Public Schools Should Be Blamed on Out-of-Control

Kids," *New York Post*, September 14, 2018, https://nypost.com/2018/09/14/failing-public-schools-should-be-blamed-on-out-of-control-kids.

13. The notion that a child's mental health and physical health is ultimately determined (and wrecked) by the number of ACEs they accrue is based on a problematic piece of landmark psychological research: Felitti, Vincent, et al., "Relationship of Child Abuse and Household Dysfunction to Many of the Leading Causes of Death in Adults," *American Journal of Preventative Medicine* 14, no. 4 (May 1998): 245–58, www.ajpmonline.org/article/S0749-3797(98)00017-8/fulltext.

14. Felitti et al., "Relationship of Child Abuse and Household Dysfunction."

15. "Adverse Childhood Experiences Prevention Strategy," Centers for Disease Control and Prevention, September 2020, 2. www.cdc.gov/injury/pdfs/priority/ACEs-Strategic-Plan_Final_508.pdf.

16. I am grateful to the wonderful writer Robert Pondiscio for pointing me to this lecture. See Pondiscio, Robert, "Researchers Warn about Misuses of a Common Measure of Childhood Trauma," Thomas B. Fordham Institute, April 22, 2020, https://fordhaminstitute.org/national/commentary/researchers-warn-about-misuses-common-measure-childhood-trauma.

17. Henderson, Rob, "No One Expects Young Men to Do Anything and They Are Responding by Doing Nothing," Rob Henderson's Newsletter, April 24, 2022, https://robkhenderson.substack.com/p/no-one-expects-young-men-to-do-anything.

18. See Bonanno, George A., *The End of Trauma: How the New Science of Resilience Is Changing How We Think About PTSD* (New York: Basic Books, 2021).

19. See Bonnano, *End of Trauma*.

Chapter 6: Trauma Kings

1. The hospital was renamed D.C. General Hospital in 1953. In 2001, it closed. See "Gallinger Municipal Hospital Psychopathic Ward," Wikipedia, accessed September 17, 2023, https://en.wikipedia.org/wiki/Gallinger_Municipal_Hospital_Psychopathic_Ward.

2. Estrada, Louie, "Bess Lavine, Half of Mother-Daughter Judge Team, Dies at 94," *Washington Post*, October 5, 2022, www.washingtonpost.com/obituaries/2022/10/05/bess-lavine-prince-georges-judge-dead.

3. This statement and the ones that follow it are all taken from surveys reported in Vermeulen, Karla, *Generation Disaster: Coming of Age Post-9/11* (Oxford, UK: Oxford University Press, 2021).

4. "Our School's Fight," *Seventeen*, December 1947, 128.

5. While all age-groups saw a rise in suicide during the Great Depression, it largely confined itself to adults, with the most dramatic effects experienced by those

thirty-five and older. See Luo, Feijun, "Impact of Business Cycles on US Suicide Rates, 1928–2007," *American Journal of Public Health* 101, no. 6 (2011): 1139–1146, www.ncbi.nlm.nih.gov/pmc/articles/PMC3093269/#:~:text=All%20age %20groups%20experienced%20a,other%20recessions%2C%20including%20se vere%20recessions.

6. Bonnano, George, *The End of Trauma: How the New Science of Resilience Is Changing How We Think About PTSD* (New York: Basic Books, 2021), 50. ("In fact, the majority of those who had endured direct exposure to what was turning out to be the most devastating terrorist attack on record in the United States had not yet developed PTSD. It was still early, however, and many observers expected that the PTSD numbers would continue to rise. And then, to just about everyone's surprise, the rates precipitously dropped.")

7. Bonnano, George, "Resilience in the Face of Potential Trauma," *Current Directions in Psychological Science* 14, no. 3 (June 2005): 135–38.

8. Bonanno, *End of Trauma*, 43–53.

9. *See* Ngayama Hall, G. C., "Diversity in Clinical Psychology," *Clinical Psychology: Science and Practice* 13, no. 3 (2006): 258–62, https://doi.org/10.1111/j.1468-2850 .2006.00034.x. (Note the lack of diversity in the field of clinical psychology.)

10. Illouz, Eva. *Saving the Modern Soul: Therapy, Emotions, and the Culture of Self-Help* (Berkeley: University of California Press, 2008), 175.

11. Carr, Danielle, "Tell Me Why It Hurts: How Bessel van der Kolk's Once Controversial Theory of Trauma Became the Dominant Way We Make Sense of Our Lives," *New York Magazine*, July 31, 2023, https://nymag.com/intelligencer/article/trauma -bessel-van-der-kolk-the-body-keeps-the-score-profile.html.

12. I reached out to Dr. van der Kolk via email for an interview. He responded quickly and affirmatively to the request, and then abruptly ceased communication.

13. Interlandi, Jeneen, "A Revolutionary Approach to Treating PTSD," *New York Times*, May 22, 2014, www.nytimes.com/2014/05/25/magazine/a-revolutionary-approach -to-treating-ptsd.html.

14. Van der Kolk, B. A., "The Body Keeps the Score: Memory and the Evolving Psychobiology of Posttraumatic Stress," *Harvard Review Psychiatry* 1, no. 5 (1994): 253– 65, https://pubmed.ncbi.nlm.nih.gov/9384857.

15. Van der Kolk, Bessel, *The Body Keeps the Score: Brain, Mind, and Body in the Healing of Trauma* (New York: Viking, 2014), 88.

16. See van der Kolk, *Body Keeps the Score*, 293, 269. See also Maté, Gabor, *The Myth of Normal: Trauma, Illness & Healing in a Toxic Culture* (New York: Avery, 2022), 64– 66, 100–102.

17. Van der Kolk, *Body Keeps the Score*, 40–44.

18. Van der Kolk, *Body Keeps the Score*, 45.

19. Hutchinson, Tracy S., "Why Your Childhood Really Matters: The Hidden

Epidemic," *Psychology Today*, June 28, 2019, www.psychologytoday.com/us/blog/si
lencing-your-inner-bully/201906/why-your-childhood-really-matters-the
-hidden-epidemic.

20. Van der Kolk, *Body Keeps the Score*, 308.

21. Van der Kolk, *Body Keeps the Score*, 193.

22. McNally, R. J., "Debunking Myths about Trauma and Memory," *The Canadian Journal of Psychiatry* 50, no. 10 (2005): 817–22. ("There is no convincing evidence that trauma survivors exhibit implicit memories of trauma, such as psychophysiological reactivity, without also experiencing explicit memories of the horrific event as well. Thus, even when the body does 'keep the score,' so does the mind.")

23. Pendergrast, Mark, *Memory Warp* (Hinesburg, VT: Upper Access, 2021).

24. See, for example, Grey Faction, "Bessel Van der Kolk Defending Junk Science: Repressed Memory Therapy," YouTube video, 5:23, March 21, 2018, www.youtube .com/watch?v=WJd4fcXOG3w. See also Pendergrast, Mark, *The Repressed Memory Epidemic: How It Happened and What We Need to Learn from It* (Cham, Switzerland: Springer, 2017), 81–85.

25. Pendergrast, Mark, *Memory Warp: How the Myth of Repressed Memory Arose and Refuses to Die* (Hinesburg, VT: Upper Access, 2021), 106.

26. But since van der Kolk was examining adult patients who claimed earlier trauma, how did he verify their memories? After all, patients who believe they were abducted by aliens often tell researchers highly emotionally detailed and internally consistent stories, too. (See Pendergrast, *Repressed Memory Epidemic*, 82.) Van der Kolk's answer: "'There is such a thing as internal consistency, and if people tell you something with internal consistency and with appropriate affect, you tend to believe that the stories are true.'" According to Pendergrast, this suggests van der Kolk didn't believe a researcher needed independently to verify the veridicality of a subject's trauma memories. Pendergrast concludes: "For van der Kolk, *belief* trumped science." In other words, according to Pendergrast, as long as the suffering patient *believed* his own story about his traumatic experience, that seems to have been enough for van der Kolk to have regarded it as true.

27. Maté, *Myth of Normal*, 25.

28. Maté, *Myth of Normal*, 99–100.

29. Maté, *Myth of Normal*, 100.

30. Maté, *Myth of Normal*, 34.

31. Maté, *Myth of Normal*, 370–71.

32. See Furedi, Frank, *Paranoid Parenting: Why Ignoring the Experts May Be Best for Your Child* (Chicago: Chicago Review Press, 2002), discussing Emmy Werner and Ruth Smith, *Vulnerable but Invincible: A Longitudinal Study of Resilient Children and Youth* (New York: McGraw-Hill, 1982), 159.

33. Pendergrast, *Memory Warp*, 105 (quoting McNally).

34. McNally, R. J., "Debunking Myths about Trauma and Memory," *The Canadian Journal of Psychiatry* 50, no. 10 (November 2005): 817–22, https://pubmed.ncbi.nlm.nih.gov/16483114.

35. Seligman, Martin, *What You Can Change and What You Can't* (New York: Knopf, 1994), quoted in Pendergrast, *Memory Warp*, 411.

36. Van der Kolk, *Body Keeps the Score*, 354–55.

37. Van der Kolk, *Body Keeps the Score*, 355.

38. Werler, Martha M., et al., "Reporting Accuracy Among Mothers of Malformed and Nonmalformed Infants," *American Journal of Epidemiology* 129, no. 2 (February 1989): 415–21, https://doi.org/10.1093/oxfordjournals.aje.a115145.

39. Werler et al., "Reporting Accuracy Among Mothers of Malformed and Nonmalformed Infants."

40. Sufferers of peptic ulcers long fell right into this trap. For decades, doctors erroneously believed that peptic ulcers were caused by stress. Movies and TV shows promoted this view, and the public believed it. Lo and behold, when a patient showed up with an ulcer at his doctor's office, if asked, he would report: *Yes! I have been under stress!* Later, in the 1980s, research showed that a bacterium—*Helicobacter pylori*—is the root cause of ulcers.

41. Gilbertson, Mark W., et al., "Smaller Hippocampal Volume Predicts Pathologic Vulnerability to Psychological Trauma," *Nature Neuroscience* 5, no. 11 (October 2002): 1242–247, https://www.nature.com/articles/nn958.

42. Duhaime-Ross, Arielle, "Parents Who Were Physically Abused as Kids Don't Go on to Abuse Their Kids," *The Verge*, March 27, 2015, www.theverge.com/2015/3/27/8297493/child-abuse-intergenerational-transmission-violence.

43. Widom, Cathy Spatz, et al., "Intergenerational Transmission of Child Abuse and Neglect: Real or Detection Bias?," *Science*, March 27, 2015, www.science.org/doi/10.1126/science.1259917. Widom did, however, find that children who suffered abuse went on to higher rates of juvenile delinquency as well as adult criminal behavior, though an examination of the details of this finding reveals complexities and subtleties that often complicate any simple "violence begets violence" headline. Widom, Cathy Spatz, "The Cycle of Violence," *Science*, April 14, 1989, 160–66. *See also* Widom, Cathy Spatz, "An Update on the 'Cycle of Violence,'" *National Institute of Justice Research in Brief*, February 2001. ("Compared with control males, abused and neglected males were *not* at increased risk for violent offending as juveniles or adults." The study, however, did show that among males who became violent offenders, those in the Abused and Neglected Group had a "significantly larger number of arrests for violence than control males." She also found that "white abused and neglected children were no more likely to be arrested for a violent crime than their nonabused and nonneglected counterparts." Her study also showed that, among those arrested as juveniles, "childhood abuse and neglect had no apparent

effect on the continuation of juvenile offending into adulthood.") For our purposes, note that a properly conducted forward-facing study leads to results that are not only more valid, they are also more complex and nuanced than the reductive notion that "childhood trauma causes adult pathology."

44. This phrase is attributed to British psychologist and pioneering memory researcher Sir Frederic C. Bartlett (1886–1969). It has been described as the propensity of humans "to impose structure and order to understand the world around them, even when their experience does not conform neatly to their prior categories." For more on Bartlett and effort after meaning, see Roediger, Henry L., "Bartlett, Frederic Charles," Washington University, http://psychnet.wustl.edu/memory/wp-content /uploads/2018/04/Roediger-2003.pdf.

45. See, generally, Widom, "Cycle of Violence," 160–66. ("Many studies are methodologically weak and limited because of an overdependence on self-report and retrospective data, inadequate documentation of child abuse and neglect, and infrequent use of baseline data from control groups.")

46. McNally pointed out to me that these sorts of physical responses to reminders of the trauma are among the criteria for a PTSD diagnosis. "One of the goals in treating PTSD is to desensitize people to their memories of traumatic experiences—which they can remember all too well!—such that they no longer have these intense bodily reactions when they think about the trauma," he said.

47. Raphael, Karen G., et al., "Childhood Victimization and Pain in Adulthood: A Prospective Investigation," *Pain* 92, no. 1-2 (May 2001): 283–93, https://sci-hubtw .hkvisa.net/10.1016/s0304-3959(01)00270-6.

48. McNally and his colleagues have studied subjects who claim to have memories of space alien abduction. Their intensely emotional psychophysiological responses to scripts about their (highly improbable) experiences have been compared with those of PTSD patients. The authors write in the paper's conclusion: "The physiological markers of emotion that accompany recollection of a memory cannot be taken as evidence of the memory's authenticity." See McNally, R. J., et al., "Psychophysiological Responding During Script-Driven Imagery in People Reporting Abduction by Space Aliens," *Psychological Science* 15, no. 7 (July 2004): 493–97, https://pubmed .ncbi.nlm.nih.gov/15200635.

49. American Psychological Association, "Eminent Psychologists of the 20th Century," *Review of General Psychology* 6, no. 2 (July/August 2002), www.apa.org/mon itor/julaug02/eminent.

50. Loftus, Elizabeth, "How Reliable Is Your Memory?," TED Global, June 2013, www.ted.com/talks/elizabeth_loftus_how_reliable_is_your_memory?lan guage=en.

51. Elizabeth, "How Reliable Is Your Memory?"

52. See Loftus, Elizabeth, "Leading Questions and the Eyewitness Report," *Cognitive*

Psychology 7, no. 4 (1975): 560–72, https://psycnet.apa.org/record/1976-08916 -001. See also Loftus, E.F., and J.C. Palmer, "Reconstruction of Automobile Destruction: An Example of Interaction between Language and Memory," *Journal of Verbal Learning and Verbal Behavior* 13, no. 5 (1974): 585–89, https://link.springer .com/chapter/10.1007/978-1-4684-4820-7_2. See also Loftus, Elizabeth, and Zanni Guido, "Eyewitness Testimony: The Influence of the Wording of a Question," *Bulletin of the Psychonomic Society* 5 (1975): 86–88, doi: 10.3758/BF03336715.

53. Garven, Sena, et al., "More Than Suggestion: The Effect of Interviewing Techniques from the McMartin Preschool Case," *Journal of Applied Psychology* 83, no. 3 (1998): 347–59, https://psycnet.apa.org/doi/10.1037/0021-9010.83.3.347.

54. As American neurobiologist and recipient of the APA Award for Distinguished Scientific Contributions to Psychology, James McGaugh has written: "The concept of 'body memories' is nonsense, if by that you mean that memories are stored outside of the central nervous system. The notion that because there are receptors for neuropeptides located outside of the brain, there is also memory at those receptors, is at best a very strange hypothesis for which there is no evidence." Quoted in Pendergrast, *Memory Warp*, 107. For a thorough, lucid, and engaging discussion of the calamity of repressed memory, it's worth reading Mark Pendergrast's many books on the subject.

55. Maté, *Myth of Normal*, 63–66. For a critique of the idea, see Carey, Benedict, "Can We Really Inherit Trauma?," *New York Times*, December 10, 2018, www.nytimes .com/2018/12/10/health/mind-epigenetics-genes.html.

56. See, for example, Helgeson, V. S, et al., "Education and Peer Discussion Group Interventions and Adjustment to Breast Cancer," *Archives of General Psychiatry* 56, no. 4 (April 1999): 340–47, https://doi.org/10.1001/archpsyc.56.4.340. ("Bringing people together who face a common problem may have the unintended effect of increasing their anxiety about their condition [i.e., feeling fearful and anxious when seeing someone who is worse off].")

57. Nicole LePera (@Theholisticpsyc), "Do you struggle in relationships, fear abandonment, and don't like asking for help? You might have been parentified," Twitter, January 4, 2023, 8:05 a.m., https://twitter.com/Theholisticpsyc/status/161066879 3747099649.

58. Nicole LePera (@Theholisticpsyc), "CHILDREN OF IMMIGRANTS: parents who sacrifice and bring their child to another country for a better life are forced to rely on their children for help with language, paying bills, or understanding cultural norms. Children play adult roles out of necessity," Twitter, January 4, 2023, 11:05 a.m., https://twitter.com/Theholisticpsyc/status/1610668808875954178.

59. Van der Kolk, *The Body Keeps the Score*, 145.

60. Nicole LePera (@Theholisticpsyc), "C-PTSD symptoms: issues regulating your emotions, feelings of unworthiness, distrust towards people and the world around you, hypervigilance, strong inner critic, chronic fear of abandonment in relation-

ships," Twitter, January 22, 2023, 9:23 p.m., https://twitter.com/Theholisticpsyc/status/1617347376502702080?lang=en.

61. Allen Frances (@AllenFrancesMD), "Complex PTSD was roundly rejected by DSM-IV & DSM-5 bec: 1) Symptom pattern so broad it overlaps w most disorders 2) Traumas so common covers most patients 3) Poor research support 4) People pushing it not respected 5) Too easily sold as explain-all to gullible therapists/patients," Twitter, August 7, 2021, 2:13 p.m., https://twitter.com/allenfrancesmd/status/1424116458007580672?lang=en.

62. See, for example, Nicole LePera (@Theholisticpysc), "Let's talk about nice guy syndrome. We have a generation of men struggling to understand their anger who act out in dysfunctional ways: Many men are conditioned to be 'nice guys' form a young age. They're raised to have a sense of over-responsibility and to caretake the emotions of their parent figures. This can look like—being the 'little man' of the house—comforting their parents through conflict—repressing their emotions to appear strong—showing a 'brave face'—not looking for emotional comfort—not talking about emotions," Twitter, December 29, 2022, 10:08 a.m., https://twitter.com/Theholisticpsyc/status/1608525480499769345.

63. Nicole LePera (@Theholisticpysc), "Do you feel numb, shut down, disconnected from yourself, and get stuck procrastinating? You're not lazy. You're not unmotivated. This is a trauma or stress response." Twitter, December 31, 2022, 9:26 a.m., https://twitter.com/Theholisticpsyc/status/1609239511787245568. See also Nicole LePera (@Theholisticpysc), "If you were called 'mature for your age' you might have been parentified. Parentification is when a child is made to fill an adult role. This is an 'invisible' trauma that has life long impact. Here's why," Twitter, March 25, 2023, 12:36 p.m., https://twitter.com/Theholisticpsyc/status/1639712962641539073.

64. Nicole LePera (@Theholisticpysc), "If you procrastinate, it's not because you're lazy. It's because your body is in a threat state," Twitter, March 4, 2023, 5:34 a.m., https://twitter.com/Theholisticpsyc/status/1632011612973576192.

Chapter 7: Hunting, Fishing, Mining: Mental Health Survey Mischief

1. "Elementary School Climate Student Survey," Colorado SAFE Communities Elementary Schools, Center for the Study and Prevention of Violence, University of Colorado, January 7, 2020, questions 74–90.

2. National Association of School Psychologists, *Guidance for Measuring and Using School Climate Data* (Bethesda, MD: National Association of School Psychologists, 2019), 1.

3. For "passive consent," see "The Protection Of Pupil Rights Amendment (PPRA)," US Department Of Education, accessed September 16, 2023, www.research.uky.edu/uploads/ori-d600000-us-dept-educationprotection-pupil-rights

-amendment-ppra-pdf. I've also talked to parents who specifically opted out, only to discover that their children had been presented the surveys and taken them. See also Sanzi, Erika, "Make Intrusive School Surveys 'Opt-In' Rather Than 'Opt-Out,'" American Enterprise Institute, March 2022, www.aei.org/wp-content/uploads /2022/03/Make-Intrusive-School-Surveys-%E2%80%9COpt-In%E2%80%9D -Rather-Than-%E2%80%9COpt-Out%E2%80%9D.pdf?x91208.

4. "What Is the Protection of Pupil Rights Amendment (PPRA)?," US Department of Education, accessed September 16, 2023, https://studentprivacy.ed.gov/faq/what -protection-pupil-rights-amendment-ppra#:~:text=The%20Protection%20of %20Pupil%20Rights%20Amendment%20(PPRA)%20applies%20to %20the,the%20U.S.%20Department%20of%20Education.

5. *C.N. v. Ridgewood* (3rd Cir. 2005), https://casetext.com/case/cn-v-ridgewood -board-of-education-4#8894046b-0124-4d54-b778-86907c2af476-fn4. ("A voluntary, anonymous and confidential student survey without individually identifiable results that was administered only after fair notice to parents does not amount to a constitutional privacy violation.")

6. "2021 Middle School Youth Risk Behavior Survey," Centers for Disease Control and Prevention, 2021, question 33, www.cdc.gov/healthyyouth/data/yrbs/pdf /2021/2021-YRBS-Standard-MS-Questionnaire.pdf. See also "2023 Middle School Youth Risk Behavior Survey," Centers for Disease Control and Prevention, www .cdc.gov/healthyyouth'/data/yrbs/pdf/2023/2023_YRBS_Standard_MS _Questionnaire.pdf.

7. "Florida High School Youth Risk Behavior Survey," 2021, question 14. "Florida's Education Commissioner Manny Diaz called the federal survey 'inflammatory' and 'sexualized.' In letters to school districts, he all but ordered them to stop participating in the CDC's youth survey." LaGrone, Katie, "Guns, Dating Violence, Sexual Violence All Eliminated from New Florida Youth Survey," WPTV 2, June 2023, https://www.wptv.com/news/local-news/investigations/florida-rejected-federal -youth-health-survey-for-being-too-sexual-so-it-came-up-with-its-own.

8. "2022 Illinois Youth Survey, 8th Grade Form," University of Illinois, School of Social Work; Illinois Department of Human Services, questions P4 and P6.

9. "Georgia Student Health Survey (Grades 6–12)," revised September 28, 2021, question 18, www.gadoe.org/wholechild/Documents/GSHS%20questions_FY22 .pdf?csf=1&e=ghjAIm.

10. "Florida High School Youth Risk Behavior Survey" (on file with Parents Defending Education). See also "Florida High School Youth Risk Behaviors" (state-level data), 2021, www.flhealthcharts.gov/ChartsDashboards/rdPage.aspx?rdReport=Survey Data.YRBS.HSReport&tabid=HSYRBS.

11. "Florida Middle School Youth Risk Behavior Survey," questions 61–64.

12. See also Georgia Department of Education, "Georgia Student Health Survey

(Grades 6–12)," revised September 28, 2021, question 37, www.gadoe.org/whole child/Documents/GSHS%20questions_FY22.pdf?csf=1&e=ghjAIm.

13. "Florida High School Youth Risk Behavior Survey," questions 61–64.

14. Westfall, Austin, "Suicide Prevention Lifeline Will Be Printed on Student ID Cards in Several States," *New York Post*, August 12, 2021, https://nypost.com/2021/08 /12/suicide-prevention-lifeline-will-be-printed-on-student-id-cards-in-several -states.

15. "2022 Illinois Youth Survey, 8th Grade Form."

16. "Healthy Youth Survey Form B: Grades 8, 10 and 12," Washington State Healthy Youth Survey, 2021, www.askhys.net/Docs/HYS%202021%20Form%20A%20e -survey_Final.pdf.

17. "Wisconsin Dane County Youth Assessment" (Middle School and High School versions) (on file with Parents Defending Education).

18. "Arizona Youth Survey," 2022, questions 82–101, www.azcjc.gov/Portals/0/Docu ments/pubs/AYSReports/2022/2022_AYS_Scantron_Survey.pdf.

19. "Arizona Youth Survey," questions 102–103.

20. "7th–12th Grade Questionnaire," Indiana Youth Survey, https://inys.indiana.edu /docs/survey/INYS_questionnaire.pdf.

21. "2022 Illinois Youth Survey, 8th Grade Form."

22. "Missouri Student Survey Questionnaire 2020," Missouri Department of Mental Health, https://dmh.mo.gov/media/pdf/missouri-student-survey-questionnaire -2020.

23. These breaches absolutely occur. See, for example, Cook, Sam, "US Schools Leaked 28.6 Million Records in 1851 Data Breaches Since 2005," Comparitech, December 15, 2021, www.comparitech.com/blog/vpn-privacy/us-schools-data-breaches.

24. "Florida High School Youth Risk Behavior Survey."

25. "2023 State and Local Youth Risk Behavior Survey."

26. "2021 Delaware Middle School Youth Risk Behavior Survey," University of Delaware Center for Drug and Health Studies, https://bpb-us-w2.wpmucdn.com/sites .udel.edu/dist/9/12983/files/2022/08/YRBS-MS-2021.pdf.

27. Gould, Madelyn, et al., "Evaluating Iatrogenic Risk of Youth Suicide Screening Programs: A Randomized Controlled Trial," *JAMA* 293, no. 13 (April 6, 2005): 1635–43, https://pubmed.ncbi.nlm.nih.gov/15811983.

28. See, for example, Mota, Natalie, and Christine Henriksen, "For Years, We Worried '13 Reasons Why' Could Provoke Suicidal Behaviors. Now We Have the Evidence," CBC News, September 3, 2019, www.cbc.ca/news/opinion/13-reasons-why -1.5267786#:~:text=Opinion-,For%20years%2C%20we%20worried%2013 %20Reasons%20Why%20could%20provoke%20suicidal,of%20the%20show's %20first%20season.

29. See Hawton, Keith, and Kathryn Williams, "Influences of the Media on Suicide,"

BMJ 325, no. 7377 (December 14, 2002): 1374–375, https://doi.org/10.1136 /bmj.325.7377.1374. See also Gould, Madelyn, "Suicide and the Media," *Annals of the New York Academy of Sciences* 932, no. 1 (January 25, 2006): 200–224, https:// doi.org/10.1111/j.1749-6632.2001.tb05807.x. ("In summary, the existence of the suicide contagion no longer needs to be questioned. We should refocus our research efforts on identifying which particular story components promote contagion under which circumstances and which components are useful for preventive program- ming.")

30. Sonneck, G., et al., "Imitative Suicide on the Viennese Subway," *Social Science and Medicine* 38, no. 3 (1982): 453–57, https://doi.org/10.1016/0277-9536(94)90 447-2.

31. Stack, S., Suicide Contagion and the Reporting of Suicide: Recommendations from a National Workshop," *Morbidity and Mortality Weekly Report* 54, no. 2 (April 1994): 9–17, www.cdc.gov/mmwr/preview/mmwrhtml/00031539.htm.

32. "2021 Delaware Youth Risk Behavior Survey Middle School Youth Risk Behavior Survey," *cf.* "2023 State and Local Youth Risk Behavior Survey."

33. "Florida Middle School Youth Survey 2021," questions 61–64.

34. Lopez, German, "Why Anti-Drug Campaigns Like DARE Fail," *Vox*, September 1, 2014, www.vox.com/2014/9/1/5998571/why-anti-drug-campaigns-like-dare-fail.

35. "Neuroticism is an index of your baseline sensitivity to negative emotion," Peterson reminded me, referring to one of the "Big 5 traits" psychologists believe form a sta- tistically valid measure of personality. Which words and phrases indicate someone high in neuroticism? Peterson asks me, before answering his own question: "Any- thing associated with self-conscious apprehension."

36. In fact, there is some evidence that "behavioral activation" therapy—a version of cognitive behavioral therapy that treats depressed patients by focusing not on changing thoughts but on changing behaviors (getting patients to *do* things they enjoy—errands, hobbies, anything that gives a sense of purpose and completion) may help alleviate depression. Hellerstein, David J., "Case Study: Finding His Wings. Drugs Lifted Frank's Depression, but He Had to Find Meaningful Activity to Relaunch His Life," *Scientific American,* July 1, 2016, www.scientificamerican .com/article/case-study-finding-his-wings.

Chapter 8: Full of Empathy and Mean as Hell

1. She is identified only as "D.P." in court filings since she was a minor at the time of the incident. Out of respect for the family, I have continued to shield her identity.

2. *Parker v. Trustees of the Spence School*, Sup. Ct. NY (June 2019) (complaint).

3. "Diversity and Equality," The Spence School, accessed August 14, 2023, https:// www.spenceschool.org/about-spence/diversity-and-equity.

4. "Diversity and Equality."

5. CASEL, the nation's leading social-emotional learning organization, defines SEL as the "process through which all young people and adults" acquire and apply the knowledge, skills and attitudes to develop healthy identities, manage emotions . . . [and] feel and show empathy for others." "What Is the CASEL Framework?," CASEL, accessed August 6, 2023, https://casel.org/fundamentals-of-sel/what-is-the-casel-framework.

6. Woolf, Nick, "CASEL Releases New Definition of SEL: What You Need to Know," Panorama Education, www.panoramaed.com/blog/casel-new-definition-of-sel-what-you-need-to-know.

7. "What Is the CASEL Framework?"

8. Paul Bloom, *Against Empathy* (New York: Ecco, 2016), 33.

9. Remember that the Nazis felt intense sympathy toward Germans who had suffered economically as a result of Versailles. Bloom points out that Nazi leader and head of the Luftwaffe, Hermann Goring, was so concerned about animal cruelty, he imposed rules restricting hunting and the boiling of lobsters and crabs—and sent those who violated these rules to concentration camps. Such empathy for animals entirely coexisted with monstrous cruelty to Jews. Bloom, *Against Empathy*, 196.

10. Doherty, William J., and Steven M. Harris, "Relationship-Undermining Statements by Psychotherapists with Clients Who Present with Marriage or Couple Problems," *Family Process* 61, no. 3 (September 2022): 1195–1207, https://doi.org/10.1111/famp.12774. ("That is, many individual therapists, when presented with a client's marital or relationship problem, tend to portray an absent spouse in highly unfavorable ways.")

11. Bloom, *Against Empathy,* 200–201.

12. Heym, Nadja, "The Dark Empathy: Characterizing Dark Traits in the Presence of Empathy," *Personality and Individual Differences* 169 (February 1, 2021): 9, https://doi.org/10.1016/j.paid.2020.110172.

13. Levin, Dan, "Colleges Rescinding Admissions Offers as Racist Social Media Posts Emerge," *New York Times*, July 2, 2020, www.nytimes.com/2020/07/02/us/racism-social-media-college-admissions.html. See also Levin, Dan, "A Racial Slur, a Viral Video, and a Reckoning," *New York Times*, December 26, 2020, www.nytimes.com/2020/12/26/us/mimi-groves-jimmy-galligan-racial-slurs.html; Brooks, David, "Harvard's False Path to Wisdom," *New York Times*, June 17, 2019, www.nytimes.com/2019/06/17/opinion/harvard-admission-kyle-kashuv.html.

Chapter 9: The Road Paved by Gentle Parents

1. The divorce rate in the United States peaked in both 1979 and 1981. See "Highlights of a New Report from the National Center for Health Statistics (NCHS): Advance Report of Final Divorce Statistics, 1989 and 1900," Centers for Disease

Control and Prevention, April 18, 1995, https://www.cdc.gov/nchs/pressroom/95facts/fs_439s.htm.

2. According to the American Psychological Association, 26 percent of Gen Xers received therapy or other mental health treatments in 2018 alone. "Stress in America™: Generation Z," American Psychological Association, October 2018, www.apa.org/news/press/releases/stress/2018/stress-gen-z.pdf.

3. "Parenting in America," Pew Research Center, December 17, 2015, www.pewresearch.org/social-trends/2015/12/17/parenting-in-america.

4. "Only 55% of Gen Z and millennials plan to have children. One in four of those surveyed, aged between 18 and 34, has ruled out parenthood entirely, with the most common reason cited being 'wanting time for themselves.'" See India, Freya, "Why Doesn't Gen Z Want Children," *UnHerd*, July 29, 2023, https://www.freyaindia.co.uk/p/why-doesnt-gen-z-want-children.

5. Shrier, Abigail, "'Knock It Off' and 'Shake It Off': The Case for Dad-Style Parenting," *The Wall Street Journal*, March 13, 2018, A15.

6. An earlier version of this observation appeared in my piece in the *Wall Street Journal*. Shrier, "'Knock It Off' and 'Shake It Off.'"

7. As a *New Yorker* article recently explained, "The gently parented child, the theory goes, learns to recognize and control her emotions because a caregiver is consistently affirming those emotions as real and important." Winter, Jessica, "The Harsh Realm of 'Gentle Parenting,'" *The New Yorker*, March 23, 2022, www.newyorker.com/books/under-review/the-harsh-realm-of-gentle-parenting.

8. Kilgannon, Corey, "A 425-Pound Tiger Living in a Harlem Apartment? Yes, It Happened," *New York Times*, April 18, 2020, www.nytimes.com/2020/04/18/nyregion/ming-tiger-harlem-nyc.html.

9. Maté, Gabor, *The Myth of Normal* (New York: Avery, 2022), chapter 9.

10. Joe Rogan and Gabor Maté, "#1869—Dr. Gabor Maté," September 13, 2022, in *The Joe Rogan Experience*, podcast, 2:24:11, https://podtail.com/en/podcast/the-joe-rogan-experience/-1869-dr-gabor-mate.

11. Gessen, Keith, *Raising Raffi: The First Five Years* (New York: Viking, 2022), 99.

12. Gessen, *Raising Raffi*, 87.

13. Gessen, *Raising Raffi*, 51.

14. Siegel, Daniel J., and Tina Payne Bryson, *The Whole-Brain Child: 12 Revolutionary Strategies to Nurture Your Child's Developing Mind* (New York: Bantam Books, 2011), 3.

15. Siegel and Bryson, *Whole-Brain Child*, 3.

16. Baumrind, Diana, "Effects of Authoritative Parental Control on Child Behavior," *Child Development* 37, no. 4 (December 1966): 887–907, https://www.jstor.org/stable/1126611.

17. Baumrind, "Effects of Authoritative Parental Control on Child Behavior," 889.

18. Baumrind, "Effects of Authoritative Parental Control on Child Behavior," 890.
19. Baumrind, "Effects of Authoritative Parental Control on Child Behavior," 891.
20. See, for example, Baumrind, "Effects of Authoritative Parental Control on Child Behavior."
21. Doucleff, Michaeleen, *Hunt, Gather, Parent* (New York: Avid Reader, 2021), 2.
22. *See* Doucleff on the *Honestly Podcast, Bari Weiss and Michaeleen Doucleff*, "What's the Best Way to Raise Good People? A Debate," May 18, 2022, podcast, 55:20–57:14, https://podcasts.apple.com/us/podcast/whats-the-best-way-to-raise-good-people-a-debate/id1570872415?i=1000562261922. ("[Spanking] is universal at some level," outside of the West, Doucleff notes. "A small spanking is universal.")
23. Faber, Adele, and Elaine Mazlish, *How to Talk So Kids Will Listen and Listen So Kids Will Talk* (New York: Scribner, 1980), 94.
24. Baumrind, "Effects of Authoritative Parental Control on Child Behavior," 897.
25. See "Spanking Study Gets Big Play in the Media," American Psychological Association, December 2001, www.apa.org/monitor/dec01/spanking. (Notes that Baumrind's study showing "occasional, mild spanking does not harm a child's social and emotional development," but makes clear that she "did not advocate spanking and warning that regular and intense spanking could cause great mental strain in children.")
26. Ferguson, Christopher J., and Robert E. Larzelere, "Improving Causal Inferences in Meta-Analyses of Longitudinal Studies: Spanking as an Illustration," *Child Development* 89, no. 6 (November 2018): 2038–050, https://doi.org/10.1111/cdev.13097, www.christopherjferguson.com/Larzelere%20et%20al.,%20CD.pdf.
27. Baumrind, "Effects of Authoritative Parental Control on Child Behavior," 889.
28. Pollak, Joel B., *Rhoda: A Biography* (Johannesburg: University of Johannesburg Press, 2022).
29. See, for example, Klein, Melissa, "Wealthy NYC Woman Busted in BLM Rampage," *New York Post*, September 5, 2020, https://nypost.com/2020/09/05/wealthy-nyc-woman-busted-in-blm-rampage.
30. Decter, Midge, *Liberal Parents, Radical Children* (New York: Coward, McCann & Geoghegan, 1975), 36.
31. Decter, *Liberal Parents, Radical Children*, 36–37.

Chapter 10: Spare the Rod, Drug the Child

1. Ophir, Yaakov, *ADHD Is Not an Illness And Ritalin Is Not a Cure: A Comprehensive Rebuttal of the (Alleged) Scientific Consensus* (Singapore: World Scientific Publishing Company, 2023), vii.
2. Visser, Susanna N., et al., "Trends in the Parent-Report of Health Care Provider-Diagnosed and Medicated Attention-Deficit/Hyperactivity Disorder: United

States 2003–2011," *Journal of the American Academy of Child & Adolescent Psychiatry* 53, no. 1 (2014): 34–46.e2, https://doi.org/10.1016/j.jaac.2013.09.

3. Schwarz, Alan, *ADHD Nation: Children, Doctors, Big Pharma, and the Making of an American Epidemic* (New York: Simon & Schuster, 2016), 197–99.

4. Ophir, Yaakov, "Are We Medicating Millions of ADHD Children without Scientific Justification?," Brownstone Institute, March 1, 2023, https://brownstone.org /articles/are-we-medicating-millions-of-adhd-children-without-scientific -justification. ("In 2020, thousands of real-life medical records from Israel suggested that over 20 percent of all children and young adults (5–20 years) received a formal diagnosis of ADHD.") See also Satel, Sally, "The Ritalin Generation: The Blame Lies with Overzealous Physicians; Nervous Parents; Schools Looking to Rein in Troublemakers; and Pushy Drug Companies," *Wall Street Journal*, September 11, 2016, https://www.wsj.com/articles/the-ritalin-generation-1473630453.

5. Segal, Michael, "The Military Needs Recruits with ADHD," *Wall Street Journal,* January 19, 2023, www.wsj.com/articles/the-military-needs-recruits-with-adhd -overstimulation-standards-learship-advantage-join-symptoms-11674056740.

6. See, for example, Morton, W. Alexander, "Methylphenidate Abuse and Psychiatric Side Effects," *Primary Care Companion to the Journal of Clinical Psychiatry* 2, no. 5 (October 2000): 159–64, https://doi.org/10.4088/pcc.v02n0502. See also Schwartz, Casey, "Generation Adderall," *New York Times*, October 12, 2016, https://www .nytimes.com/2016/10/16/magazine/generation-adderall-addiction .html.

7. Armstrong, Thomas, *The Myth of the ADHD Child* (New York: Penguin Random House, 1995).

8. Nesse, Randolph M., "Proximate and Evolutionary Studies of Anxiety, Stress and Depression: Synergy at the Interface," *Neuroscience and Biobehavioral Reviews* 23, no. 7 (November 1999): 895–903, https://doi.org/10.1016/s0149-7634(99)00 023-8.

9. See Nesse, Randolph M., *Good Reasons for Bad Feelings: Insights from the Frontier of Evolutionary Psychiatry* (New York: Dutton, 2019), 89–94. (Discusses the evolutionary benefits of depression in helping us to withdraw from competition when we're overmatched and cope with failure or problems requiring a major life change.)

10. MacMillan, Amanda, "Why People with Anxiety May Have Better Memories," *Time*, February 27, 2018, https://time.com/5176445/anxiety-improves-memory.

11. Lehrer, Jonah, "Depression's Upside," *New York Times*, February 25, 2010, www .nytimes.com/2010/02/28/magazine/28depression-t.html.

12. Andrews, Paul W., and J. Anderson Thomson, "The Bright Side of Being Blue: Depression as an Adaptation for Analyzing Complex Problems," *Psychological Review* 116, no. 3 (2009): 620–54, https://doi.org/10.1037/a0016242.

13. The mental health industry used the analogy of a "chemical imbalance" in the brain to explain depression to the public for years. It has since been discredited, but much

of the public still buys into it. See, for example, Cosgrove, Lisa et al., "Why Psychiatry Needs an Honest Dose of Gentle Medicine," *Frontiers in Psychiatry* 21 (April 2023): 1167910, doi:10.3389/fpsyt.2023.

14. Richtel, Matt, "This Teen Was Prescribed 10 Psychiatric Drugs. She's Not Alone," *New York Times,* August 27, 2022, www.nytimes.com/2022/08/27/health/teens-psychiatric-drugs.html.

15. I often think about the fact that less than a century ago, the pioneer of the frontal lobotomy received medicine's Nobel Prize. See Tan, Siang Yong, and Angela Yip, "Antonio Egas Moniz (1874–1955): Lobotomy Pioneer and Nobel Laureate," *Singapore Medical Journal* 55 no. 4 (April 2014): 175–76, https://doi.org/10.11622/smedj.2014048.

Chapter 11: This Will Be Our Final Session

1. He asked not to be quoted or credited on the grounds that he is leery of commenting outside of his official area of expertise. If only our mental health experts operated with the humility of research-based academics.

2. Hayden, Robert, "Those Winter Sundays," accessed September 17, 2023, https://poets.org/poem/those-winter-sundays.

3. Kennair, Leif, et al., "Risky Play and Growing Up: How to Understand the Overprotection of the Next Generation," in Allison B. Kaufman and James C. Kaufman, eds., *Pseudoscience: The Conspiracy Against Science* (Cambridge: MIT Press, 2018), 175.

4. The great Lebanese American thinker and essayist Nassim Nicholas Taleb introduced me to this idea in his essential work, *Antifragile.* As in so much of life, often "we know what is wrong with more clarity than what is right, and that knowledge grows by subtraction." This is the principle he associates with the ancient concept of "Via Negativa." Taleb, Nassim Nicholas, *Antifragile: Things That Gain from Disorder* (New York: Random House, 2012), 303–08.

5. McFillin well understands that self-injury, in certain contexts, can be a serious behavior that requires professional help. But, in the current state of our mental health system, a single instance of cutting (irrespective of context) is often enough to involuntarily hospitalize a teen and get her on a regimen of powerful psychiatric drugs. Turning a teen's "vulnerable time into chronic disability" is a perfect description of therapeutic iatrogenesis and is precisely what McFillin is committed to avoiding.

6. Gray, Peter, et al., "Decline in Independent Activity as a Cause of Decline in Children's Mental Well-Being: Summary of the Evidence," *Journal of Pediatrics* 260 (September 2023): 13352, https://doi.org/10.1016/j.jpeds.2023.02.004.

7. Gray, et al., "Decline in Independent Activity."

8. Gray, et al., "Decline in Independent Activity."

9. Gray, et al., "Decline in Independent Activity."

10. Korbey, Holly, "Young Adults Are Struggling with Their Mental Health. Is More Childhood Independence the Answer?," *Mind/Shift*, December 20, 2022, www .kqed.org/mindshift/60624/young-adults-are-struggling-with-their-mental -health-is-more-childhood-independence-the-answer.

11. Korbey, "Young Adults Are Struggling."

12. Ortiz, Camilo, "Treating Childhood Anxiety with a Mega-Dose of Independence," *Profectus*, March 14, 2023, https://profectusmag.com/treating-childhood-anxiety -with-a-mega-dose-of-independence.

13. Elsharouny, Mary, "Let Go and Let Grow: An Assessment of a School and Community-Based Intervention Encouraging Independence in Children" (PhD diss, Long Island University, July 2012), https://digitalcommons.liu.edu/post_ful text_dis/43.

14. This is one of the best-known findings of twentieth-century psychology, known as the Yerkes-Dodson law. See "Yerkes–Dodson Law," Wikipedia, accessed September 17, 2023, https://en.wikipedia.org/wiki/Yerkes%E2%80%93Dodson_law.

15. The Yerkes-Dodson Curve shows that added stress can result in better perfor-mance, until a point, and then it becomes counterproductive. See Pietrangelo, Ann, "What the Yerkes-Dodson Law Says About Stress and Performance," Healthline, October 22, 2020, www.healthline.com/health/yerkes-dodson-law#stress-perfor mance-bell-curve.

16. Deighton, Katie, "More Chicken, Lighter Beer, Pink Drinks: Companies Craft New Products for Gen Z Tastes," *Wall Street Journal,* July 3, 2023, https://www.wsj .com/articles/more-chicken-lighter-beer-pink-drinks-companies-craft-new -products-for-gen-z-tastes-88d96c7a.

17. Elder, Glen, *Children of the Great Depression* (New York: Routledge, 1999).

18. Elder, *Children of the Great Depression*, 281.

19. Elder, *Children of the Great Depression*, 277–79.

20. Frankl, Viktor E., *Man's Search for Meaning* (Boston: Beacon Press, 2006), 105.

21. Frankl, *Man's Search for Meaning,* 43.

22. Hernandez, Cindy M., et al., "The Hispanic Paradox: A Moderated Mediation Analysis of Health Conditions, Self-Rated Health, and Mental Health among Mex-icans and Mexican-Americans," *Health, Psychology, and Behavioral Medicine* 10, no. 1 (February 2022): 180–98, https://doi.org/10.1080/21642850.2022.2032714.

23. See Barber, Charles, "What a Decades-Long Harvard Study Tells Us about Mental Health," *The Wilson Quarterly*, Winter 2013, https://www.wilsonquarterly.com /quarterly/_/what-can-decades-long-harvard-study-tell-us-about-mental-health. I became aware of the study from a tweet that summarized its findings elegantly and succinctly. Kevin Bass (@kevinnbass), "In the Harvard Grant Study, the world's longest running and most comprehensive psychological study, the five most ma-ture, health defense mechanisms associated with higher life satisfaction were: 1.

Altruism: focusing on others' wellbeing 2. Humor: making light of difficult or stressful events or experiences 3. Sublimation: turning anger or frustration into productive energy 4. Anticipation: maintain a realistic view of the future and its difficulties 5. Suppression: consciously suppressing unproductive and distressing thoughts," Twitter, June 24, 2023, 8:02 a.m., https://twitter.com/kevinnbass/status/1672621150583640064?s=51&t=6zNf58uKGIhK1SyexwAIpw.

Chapter 12: Spoons Out

1. Twenge, Jean, "Teens Have Less Face Time with Their Friends—and Are Lonelier Than Ever," The Conversation, March 20, 2019, https://theconversation.com/teens-have-less-face-time-with-their-friends-and-are-lonelier-than-ever-113240.

2. See, for example, Twenge, Jean M., et al., "Decreases in Self-Reported Sleep Duration among U.S. Adolescents 2009–2015 and Association with New Media Screen Time," *Sleep Medicine* 39 (2017): 47–53, https://doi.org/10.1016/j.sleep.2017.08.013. ("The number of adolescents getting insufficient sleep abruptly increased after 2011–2013. By 2015, more than 40% of adolescents did not get 7 or more hours of sleep on most nights across both data sets.") See also Twenge, Jean M., et al., "Associations Between Screen Time and Sleep Duration Are Primarily Driven by Portable Electronic Devices: Evidence From a Population-Based Study of U.S. Children Ages 0–17," *Sleep Medicine* 56 (2019): 211–18, https://doi.org/10.1016/j.sleep.2018.11.009.

3. Haidt, Jonathan, "Get Phones Out of Schools Now: They Impede Learning, Stunt Relationships, and Lessen Belonging. They Should Be Banned," *The Atlantic*, June 6, 2023, www.theatlantic.com/ideas/archive/2023/06/ban-smartphones-phone-free-schools-social-media/674304.

4. See Haidt, Jonathan, "Social Media Is a Major Cause of the Mental Illness Epidemic in Teen Girls. Here's the Evidence," February 22, 2023, https://jonathanhaidt.substack.com/p/social-media-mental-illness-epidemic.

5. Indeed, the first major call by any psychologist to ban smartphones from schools did not arrive until 2023, and then, from Jonathan Haidt (not any psychological association). See Haidt, "Get Phones Out of Schools Now."

6. Richtel, Matt, "This Teen Was Prescribed 10 Psychiatric Drugs. She's Not Alone," *New York Times*, August 27, 2022, www.nytimes.com/2022/08/27/health/teens-psychiatric-drugs.html.

7. It may have even been older.

8. See, for example, Grose, Jessica, "Early Motherhood Has Always Been Miserable," *New York Times*, November 9, 2019, www.nytimes.com/2019/11/09/opinion/sunday/babies-mothers-anxiety.html.

Select Bibliography

American Psychiatric Association. *Diagnostic and Statistical Manual of Mental Disorders, Fifth Edition*, text revision, American Psychiatric Association Publishing, 2022.

Barsky, Arthur. *Worried Sick: Our Troubled Quest for Wellness*. New York: Little, Brown, 1988.

Bloom, Paul. *Against Empathy: The Case for Rational Compassion*. New York: Harper Collins, 2016.

Bonnano, George A. *The End of Trauma: How the New Science of Resilience Is Changing How We Think About PTSD*. New York: Basic Books, 2021.

Coleman, Joshua. *Rules of Estrangement: Why Adult Children Cut Ties & How to Heal the Conflict*. New York: Harmony Books, 2021.

Dawes, Robyn M. *House of Cards: Psychology and Psychotherapy Built on a Myth*. New York: Simon & Schuster, 1994.

Decter, Midge. *Liberal Parents, Radical Children*. New York: CM&G, 1975.

Diller, Lawrence H. *The Last Normal Child: Essays on the Intersection of Kids, Culture, and Psychiatric Drugs*. Westport, CT: Praeger, 2006.

Doucleff, Michaeleen. *Hunt, Gather, Parent: What Ancient Cultures Can Teach Us About the Lost Art of Raising Happy, Helpful Little Humans*. New York: Simon & Schuster, 2021.

Ecclestone, Kathryn, and Dennis Hayes. *The Dangerous Rise of Therapeutic Education*. New York: Routledge, 2009.

Elder, Glen H. *Children of the Great Depression: Social Change in Life Experience*. New York: Routledge, 1999.

Faber, Adele, and Elaine Mazlish. *How to Talk So Kids Will Listen and Listen So Kids Will Talk*. New York: Scribner, 1980.

Frances, Allen. *Saving Normal: An Insider's Revolt Against Out-of-Control Psychiatric Diagnosis, DSM-5, Big Pharma, and the Medicalization of Ordinary Life*. New York: Harper Collins, 2013.

Frankl, Victor. *Man's Search for Meaning*. Boston: Beacon Press, 1959.

Furedi, Frank. *Paranoid Parenting: Why Ignoring the Experts May Be Best for Your Child*. Chicago: Chicago Review Press, 2002.

———. *Therapy Culture: Cultivating Vulnerability in an Uncertain Age*. New York: Routledge, 2004.

Gessen, Keith. *Raising Raffi: The First Five Years*. New York: Viking, 2022.

Gibson, Lindsay C. *Adult Children of Emotionally Immature Parents: How to Heal from Distant, Rejecting, Self-Involved Parents*. Oakland: New Harbinger, 2015.

Gottlieb, Lori. *Maybe You Should Talk to Someone: A Therapist, HER Therapist, and Our Lives Revealed* New York: Houghton Mifflin Harcourt, 2019.

Illouz, Eva. *Saving the Modern Soul: Therapy, Emotions and the Culture of Self-Help*. Berkeley: University of California Press, 2008.

Kurcinka, Mary Sheedy. *Raising Your Spirited Child*. New York: William Morrow, 2015 (first published: 1992).

Lasch, Christopher. *The Culture of Narcissism: American Life in an Age of Diminishing Expectations*. New York: W. W. Norton, 1979.

Liau, Alex, and Jed Baker. *School Shadow Guidelines*. Arlington, TX: Future Horizons, 2013.

Lukianoff, Greg, and Jonathan Haidt. *The Coddling of the American Mind: How Good Intentions and Bad Ideas Are Setting Up a Generation for Failure*. New York: Penguin Press, 2018.

Maté, Gabor. *The Myth of Normal: Trauma, Illness & Healing in a Toxic Culture*. New York: Avery, 2022.

McNally, Richard, *Remembering Trauma*. Belknap Press, 2003.

Moskowitz, Eva S. *In Therapy We Trust: America's Obsession with Self Fulfillment*. Baltimore: Johns Hopkins University Press, 2001.

Nesse, Randolph M. *Good Reasons for Bad Feelings: Insights from the Frontier of Evolutionary Psychiatry*. New York: Dutton, 2019.

Ophir, Yaakov. *ADHD Is Not an Illness and Ritalin Is Not a Cure*. New Jersey: World Scientific, 2022.

Pendergrast, Mark. *The Memory Warp: How the Myth of Repressed Memory Arose and Refuses to Die*. Hinesburg, VT: Upper Access Books, 2017.

———. *The Repressed Memory Epidemic: How It Happened and What We Need to Learn From It.* Colchester: Springer, 2017.

Pope, Harrison. *Psychology Astray.* Boca Raton: Upton, 1997.

Romero, Victoria E., Ricky Roberson, and Amber Warner. *Building Resilience in Students Impacted by Adverse Childhood Experiences: A Whole-Staff Approach.* Thousand Oaks, CA: Corwin, 2018.

Sax, Leonard. *The Collapse of Parenting: How We Hurt Our Kids When We Treat Them Like Grown-Ups.* New York: Basic Books, 2016.

Siegel, Daniel J., and Tina Payne Bryson. *The Whole-Brain Child: 12 Revolutionary Strategies to Nuruture Your Child's Developing Mind.* New York: Bantam Books, 2011.

Skenazy, Lenore. *Free Range Kids: Giving Our Children the Freedom We Had Without Going Nuts with Worry.* New York: Jossey-Bass, 2010.

Sommers, Christina Hoff, and Sally Satel. *One Nation Under Therapy: How the Helping Culture Is Eroding Self-Reliance.* New York: St. Martin's Press, 2005.

Taleb, Nassim Nicholas. *Antifragile: Things That Gain from Disorder.* New York: Random House, 2012.

Twenge, Jean. *iGen: Why Today's Super-Connected Kids Are Growing Up Less Rebellious, More Tolerant, Less Happy—and Completely Unprepared for Adulthood—and What That Means for the Rest of Us.* New York: Atria, 2017.

———. *Generations.* New York: Atria, 2023.

Van der Kolk, Bessel. *The Body Keeps the Score: Brain, Mind, and Body in the Healing of Trauma.* New York: Viking, 2014.

Vermeulen, Karla. *Generation Disaster: Coming of Age Post-9/11.* Oxford: Oxford University Press, 2021.

Whitaker, Robert. *Anatomy of an Epidemic: Magic Bullets, Psychiatric Drugs, and the Astonishing Rise of Mental Illness in America.* New York: Broadway Paperbacks, 2010.